P9-BZP-073

ADDITIONAL PRAISE FOR

Charlie Chan: The Untold Story of the Honorable Detective and His Rendezvous with American History

"*Charlie Chan* is a unique and fascinating book. Not only is it superbly researched, but it is written with both verve and poignance, interweaving the substantial biographies of both Chang Apana (the real Honolulu detective) and E. D. Biggers together with touches of personal memoir that are revelatory and liberating. The book defines a kind of international postmodernity—urbane, compassionate, questing, and dedicated to the unmasking of the story of genuine travail and accomplishment behind the racist travesty that has been perpetuated in literature and film." —Garrett Hongo, author of *Volcano: A Memoir of Hawai'i*

"Charlie Chan, much like the classic geisha dolls on bookcase shelves, has survived for generations as little more than a paper-thin stereotype. Now, in this impressive and highly original work, Yunte Huang has brought this fictional character out of the dusty shadows into three-dimensional life, offering us not only a picture of a little-known swath of American history but the surprising story of this Chinese detective's American creator, and the real-life figure who inspired him." —Arthur Golden, author of *Memoirs of a Geisha*

"Witty and erudite, *Charlie Chan* intrigues and surprises as it unravels the three guises of this American original—a real-life, Hawaiian-born Chinese detective; a literary creation; and a movie character. Racist stereotypes, we come to see in this exemplary work, can convey monstrous fictions as well as complex, multifaceted truths."

—Gary Y. Okihiro, author of *Pineapple Culture: A History of the Tropical and Temperate Zones*

"Yunte Huang restores our pleasure in Charlie Chan, and deepens it. Reading Huang, American fans of Chan novels and movies will feel relief from the automatic guilt we have learned to identify with the pleasure of enjoying a racially marked character. Huang knows his hybrid hero as well as he knows his own hybrid self, linked by a love of ironies. Chan's misplaced expressions and the pleasantly unsettling effects of getting English delightfully, and intentionally, wrong sometimes show up standard usage as unremarkable, not to say boring. Chan's superior intelligence, like Huang's, plays on the expectations of 'native' responses in order to outdo them. So enjoy the chuckles; in Huang's hands we recognize ourselves to be the butt of the Chinaman's humor and the beneficiaries of his wisdom."

—Doris Sommer, author of *Bilingual Aesthetics: A New Sentimental Education*

CHARLIE CHAN

ALSO BY YUNTE HUANG

Transpacific Imaginations: History, Literature, Counterpoetics (2008)

CRIBS (2005)

Transpacific Displacement:
Ethnography, Translation, and Intertextual Travel in Twentieth-Century American Literature (2002)

Shi: A Radical Reading of Chinese Poetry (1997)

CHARLIE CHAN

THE UNTOLD STORY OF THE HONORABLE DETECTIVE AND HIS RENDEZVOUS WITH AMERICAN HISTORY

Yunte Huang

W. W. NORTON & COMPANY

NEW YORK • LONDON

Frontispiece: Warner Oland in *Charlie Chan on Broadway*, 1937
(Courtesy of Everett Collection)

Printed in the United States of America
First Edition

Manufacturing by Courier Westford
Book design by Chris Welch Design
Production manager: Julia Druskin

Library of Congress Cataloging-in-Publication Data

Huang, Yunte.
Charlie Chan : the untold story of the honorable detective and his rendezvous with American history / Yunte Huang. — 1st ed.
p. cm.
Includes bibliographical references and index.
ISBN 978-0-393-06962-4 (hardcover)
1. Apana, Chang, 1871-1933. 2. Chan, Charlie (Fictitious character)
3. Detectives—Hawaii—Biography. I. Title.
HV7571.H3H83 2010
363.25092—dc22
[B]
2010016653

W. W. Norton & Company, Inc.
500 Fifth Avenue, New York, N.Y. 10110
www.wwnorton.com

W. W. Norton & Company Ltd.
Castle House, 75/76 Wells Street, London W1T 3QT

1 2 3 4 5 6 7 8 9 0

FOR ISABELLE AND IRA, AS ALWAYS;

AND FOR GLENN MOTT, A FRIEND COMING FROM AFAR,
AS CONFUCIUS SAYS

Contents

List of Illustrations xi
Introduction xv
Prologue 1

PART ONE THE "REAL" CHARLIE CHAN

1 Sandalwood Mountains 7
2 Canton 22
3 *Paniolo,* the Hawaiian Cowboy 28
4 The Wilders of Waikiki 37
5 "Book 'em, Danno!" 44
6 Chinatown 54
7 The See Yup Man 61
8 Desperadoes 68
9 Double Murder 73

PART TWO CHARLIE CHAN'S POP

10 The Other Canton 83
11 Lampoon 96
12 The Raconteur 102
13 The House Without a Key 108

PART THREE CHARLIE CHAN, THE CHINAMAN

14 The Heathen Chinee 117
15 Fu Manchu 136
16 Charlie Chan, the Chinaman 146
17 Kaimuki 161
18 Pasadena 171
19 A Meeting of East and West 181

PART FOUR CHARLIE CHAN AT THE MOVIES

20 Hollywood's Chinoiserie 189
21 Yellowface 198
22 Between the Real and the Reel 205
23 Rape in Paradise 211
24 The Black Camel 230
25 Racial Parables 238

PART FIVE CHARLIE CHAN CARRIES ON

26 Charlie Chan in China 247
27 Charlie Chan Soldiers On 259
28 The Fu Manchurian Candidate 268
29 Will the Real Charlie Chan Please Stand Up? 278
Epilogue 289

Appendix I: A List of Charlie Chanisms 299
Appendix II: A List of Charlie Chan Films 302
Acknowledgments 305
Notes 307
Selected Bibliography 329
Index 337

List of Illustrations

xiii *Map of the Hawaiian Islands*

1 *Chang Apana's bullwhip*

5 *Chang Apana, circa 1917*

7 *Diamond Head, 1870s*

22 *Canton, China, late 1890s*

28 *Chinatown, Honolulu, late 1890s*

37 *A Chinese store in Chinatown, Honolulu, late 1890s*

44 *Hawaiian Humane Society Seal*

54 *Map of Chinatown, Honolulu, circa 1900*

57 *Chinatown after the 1900 fire*

61 *A See Yup Man*

68 *During the 1900 Chinatown fire, residents were evacuated under police direction*

73 *Honolulu Police Detective Division, on the steps of the old downtown station, August 6, 1911*

81 *Earl Derr Biggers at his Pasadena, California, house, late 1920s*

83 *The Saxton House, Canton, Ohio*

96 *The Signet House, Cambridge, Massachusetts*

102 *Earl Derr Biggers, circa 1907*

108 *J. A. Gilman residence, Honolulu, 1908*

115 *Cover design for E. D. Bigger's* Behind the Curtain, *1928*

117 *Bret Harte, "The Heathen Chinee," 1870*

136 *Boris Karloff in* The Mask of Fu Manchu, *1932*
146 *Cover design for E. D. Biggers's* The House Without a Key, *1925*
161 *Chang Apana's house, Kaimuki, Hawaii*
171 *Earl Derr Biggers's house, Pasadena, California*
181 *Earl Derr Biggers with a stand-in Charlie Chan, July 1928*
186 *Earl Derr Biggers and Chang Apana, July 5, 1928*
187 *Kamiyama Sojin as Charlie Chan in* The Chinese Parrot, *1927*
189 *Grauman's Chinese Theatre, Hollywood*
198 *Warner Oland and Anna May Wong on the set of* Old San Francisco, *1927*
205 *Chang Apana and Warner Oland, Honolulu, 1931*
210 *Wo Fat Restaurant, Chinatown, Honolulu*
211 *Chang Apana, circa 1932*
230 *Chang Apana and Chief Charles Weeber, 1932*
238 *Warner Oland and Stepin Fetchit in* Charlie Chan in Egypt, *1935*
245 *Charlie Chan's Bar, Sydney, Australia*
247 *Chinese movie poster for* Charlie Chan in Shanghai, *1936*
257 *Movie poster for* Charlie Chan Smashes an Evil Plot, *1941*
259 *Sidney Toler, circa 1910*
268 *Warner Oland in* The Mysterious Dr. Fu-Manchu, *1929*
278 *Warner Oland and his stand-in on the set, early 1930s*
289 *Chang Apana's grave at the Chinese Cemetery, Manoa, Hawaii*
295 *The gravestone of Chang Apana*

Map of the Hawaiian Islands *(Courtesy of Hawaiian State Archives)*

Introduction

IN THE SPRING of 2002, I was scheduled to give a talk on my new book, *Transpacific Displacement,* followed by that rite of passage most authors come both to anticipate and to dread, the book signing. Without my knowledge, an amiable secretary in the English Department at Harvard, where I was then teaching, made a flyer for the event at the Harvard Book Store in Cambridge. Her concoction was—how shall we say it—an intriguing collage. My name and the book title were highlighted in bold, with a map of the Pacific Rim fading out in the background. A silhouette of the Swedish actor Warner Oland, playing Charlie Chan, stood atop the sprawling, vast Asian continent and peered menacingly in the direction of North America. The secretary told me that she, a Caucasian woman in her late fifties, had grown up watching Charlie Chan movies. My inveterate wisecracking—which I was not shy to dispense around the department—had reminded her of her favorite, aphorism-spouting Chinese detective. Given my affection for her and my own sense of civility, I did not dare question her creative enterprise, informing her that this image of a bellicose Chan would be offensive to most Asian Americans. I did not initiate that conversation because I knew it would take a book's worth of pages to explain the tortured legacy of Charlie Chan in America, even to myself. Instead, I thanked her in my polite Chinese manner for her sprightly design. And now I have written this book about Charlie Chan, in part to carry on my imaginary dialogue with this well-meaning lady.

So, who is Charlie Chan?

To most Caucasian Americans, he is a funny, beloved, albeit somewhat inscrutable—that last adjective already a bit loaded—character who talks wisely and acts even more wisely. But to many Asian Americans, he remains a pernicious example of a racist stereotype, a Yellow Uncle Tom, if you will; the type of Chinaman, passive and unsavory, who conveys himself in broken English. In this book, however, I would like to propose a more complicated view. As a ubiquitous cultural icon, whose influence on the twentieth century remains virtually unexamined, Charlie Chan does not yield easily to ideological reduction. "Truth," to quote our honorable detective, "like football—receive many kicks before reaching goal."

To write about Charlie Chan is to write about the undulations of the American cultural experience. Like a blackface minstrel, Charlie Chan carries both the stigma of racial parody and the stimulus of creative imitation. It is no coincidence that Stepin Fetchit, the most celebrated black comic actor in the 1930s, and one of the most reviled since the civil rights movement, had also starred in Charlie Chan movies. Fetchit played a lazy, inarticulate, and easily frightened Negro. And so did Mantan Moreland, another popular black comedian, who brought to the Chan movies his extraordinary vaudeville talent. Charlie Chan's racial ventriloquism in the hands of such white actors as Warner Oland, Sidney Toler, and Roland Winters finds strong historical parallels with Aunt Jemima, Uncle Tom, and Nigger Jim. Before jumping to any ideologically reductive conclusion, we should pause and think: What would American culture be without minstrelsy, jazz, haiku, Zen, karate, the blues, or anime—without, in other words, the incessant transfusion (and co-opting) of diverse cultural traditions and creative energies?

A glance at Charlie Chan's fictional biography reveals just how far his nimble steps have taken him into the American psyche. Most Americans don't realize that he is based on a real person: Chang

Apana, a legendary Honolulu police officer, whose biography will make up a large part of this book. Like Apana, Charlie Chan came of age in colonial Hawaii, riven by endemic racial tension. As a young man, he worked as a houseboy for a rich white family in Honolulu. As a detective, he traveled extensively in the islands, the American West, Asia, and Europe. He stood witness to the plights and sufferings of his fellow Chinese as indentured laborers on sugarcane plantations, as gold miners bullied by their white competitors, as railroad builders taking on the most dangerous jobs, and as laundrymen toiling away with steam and starch, supposedly muttering, "No tickee, no washee." Some of these ethnic experiences and stereotypes are so deeply ingrained in American culture that even as late as the 1990s, a Republican senator would use the infamous phrase, "Not a Chinaman's chance," when addressing the loss of manufacturing jobs to China at a congressional hearing. Abercrombie & Fitch would sell T-shirts that read, "Wong Brothers Laundry Service. Two Wongs Can Make It White." In many ways, Charlie Chan is a distillation of the collective experience of Asian Americans, his résumé a history of the Chinese in America.

Although Charlie Chan embodies some stereotypical traits, his fictional creator, the early twentieth-century novelist Earl Derr Biggers, succeeded in minting a unique and appealing image. As a Chinaman, Charlie Chan is like a multilayered Chinese box or a Russian doll. He may have slanted eyes, a chubby and inscrutable face, and a dark goatee, but he prefers Western suits to his native garments and wears a Panama hat in the tropical sun. He is no fan of tea; he prefers to drink sarsaparilla. Moreover, unlike a timid, inarticulate Chinaman, Chan is voluble and enjoys spouting fortune-cookie witticisms that are alternately befuddling and enlightening. This is the strength of his character: his beguiling Oriental charm, his Confucian analects turned into singsong Chinatown blues.

When Chan debuted on the silver screen in 1926, anti-Chinese hysteria had already quieted down on the West Coast and in Hawaii. A series of anti-Chinese laws in place since 1882 had effectively limited immigration from China. America was ready for an image of a Chinaman more benign than the chimera of a decade earlier, Dr. Fu Manchu, a Mongol Satan who plotted to take over the West. Chan's Hollywood career took off. The film series had a grand run of more than two decades, and Chan became one of America's most beloved movie characters.

Being the country's first beloved Chinaman is not, however, the only legacy of Charlie Chan. In the decades after World War II, his influence reached into the hard-boiled world of film noir, where characters with Chinese names and Charlie Chan mustaches loom ominously in the dark background. Terms such as *Shanghai*, *Manchurian*, and *opium den* ricochet around like eerie echoes from a stylized underworld. Chinatown becomes synonymous with all that is rotten in the sordid urban space of midcentury America, standing in abject contrast to the clean, white, suburban sprawls of *Leave It to Beaver* and *Father Knows Best.* In the hackneyed symbolism of Chinatown and the clichéd notion of Chinese inscrutability, Charlie Chan has maintained a haunting presence.

Given the perpetuation of this insidious brand of Orientalism, it was hardly surprising that Asian American activists and writers, pioneers such as Frank Chin and Jessica Hagedorn, began a campaign in the 1980s to heighten the public's awareness of these negative racial tropes and deeply trenched stereotypes. Given this climate of silence that had stilled debate or scrutiny for decades, one can hardly blame Hagedorn for pronouncing, "Charlie Chan is dead." Carrying the historical weight of the Asian American experience, Hagedorn's shocking rhetoric was necessary to create a new consciousness, to make all Americans aware of how Charlie Chan had been used in the past to reinforce negative cultural symbols. But, contrary to Hagedorn's dramatic pronouncement, rumors of Chan's death may have been exaggerated. Newly restored versions of the old movies are being released on DVD every year to enthusiastic response, Web sites extol his mystique, and spoofs and sequels are produced constantly. We can no longer explain Chan's longevity by referring simply to the persistence of racism. There is a deeper American story we need to retrieve and properly frame.

As a detective, Charlie Chan should take his place in film history alongside sagacious gentlemen like Sam Spade, Philip Marlowe, Hercule Poirot, and Lieutenant Columbo, yet his ethnic identity marks him as different. Charlie Chan is far from the emasculated Chinaman his critics have claimed he is. Anyone with a passing knowledge of the movies and novels would know that Chan can be as mentally brazen and combative as Bruce Lee or Jackie Chan. His courage matches that of his real-life original, Chang Apana, who, despite his diminutive height, walked dangerous beats carrying a coiled bullwhip and caught dozens of criminals singlehandedly without firing a shot.

But the core strength of Chan's character lies in his pseudo-Confucian, aphoristic wisdom. Unlike the Kung Fu movies, which showcase a Chinese penchant for ass-kicking and sword-brandishing, Chan reveals the Chinaman as a sage: a wise, calm, responsible, and commonsensical man who also happens to be a hilarious wisecracker. These depictions prepared television audiences of the 1970s for *Kung Fu*, featuring David Carradine as a Shaolin master wandering the American West and fighting for justice in a constant sea of flashbacks. There is even a good deal of Charlie Chan's wit in the torqued physicality of Jackie Chan's slapstick.

For me, a real Chinaman, who didn't grow up in this country but hasn't been shielded from the arrows of American racism, it is fascinating that Charlie Chan is an American original, "made in the U.S.A." Make no mistake: Charlie Chan is an American stereotype of the Chinaman. Anyone who believes that Chan is Chinese would probably also believe that the fortune cookie is a Chinese invention. Charlie Chan is as American as Jack Kerouac, that stalwart of the American hipster who was born French Canadian and spoke the dialect of *joual* as his first language. Call it the melting pot or the pu pu platter, but Brahmin Boston is where the chop suey of Charlie Chan was first stir-fried by the Harvard-educated Biggers, only to be recast later by wisecracking screenwriters and directors in bronzed and lacquered Hollywood. What Stanley Crouch calls cultural miscegenation as the catalyst of the American experience has found another exemplar in Charlie Chan. Simply put, Charlie Chan's Chinatown beat, like jazz, is a distinctly American brand, not a Chinese import.

My goal in writing this book, then, is to demonstrate that Charlie Chan, America's most identifiable Chinaman, epitomizes both the racist heritage and the creative genius of this nation's culture. To my chagrin, because I am a big fan of the genre, this book is no high-speed detective fiction with gun molls and badinage. The mystery of Charlie Chan is as deep as any "Confucius say." I have had to unravel it by tracing several dry streams to the source of long dormant wells. It wasn't hard to get them roiling again, like an old and faithful geyser in the American psyche that dependably gives insult. The clues I found in these backwaters would not always converge, but I have come to see this as the true nature of American legends: they need something foreign to make them live again. Hollywood has always known this, with such directors as Billy Wilder and Ang Lee producing scalding interpretations of the most American of stories. But I must confess that I am not in the packaging business. The legends that Hollywood perpetuates can never be entirely circumscribed, wrapped up with string. Instead, in my far-flung research and peripatetic travels, I found not one but four unique stories of Charlie Chan.

The first story, of course, is the man himself, beginning with Chang Apana, the bullwhip-toting Cantonese detective in Honolulu. Then there is Earl Biggers's story, unwinding from the cornfields of small-town Ohio to the old-boy parlors of Harvard Yard, followed by Chan's reinvention on the silver screen, a legend annealed in Hollywood and America's racial tensions. And, finally, there is Chan's haunting presence during the era of postmodern politics and ethnic pride in contemporary America. Each of these streams is a story in itself, a slice of bona fide Americana. Together, they form the biography of Charlie Chan, the honorable detective whose labyrinthine matrix we have only now begun to fathom.

Prologue

Chang Apana's bullwhip, on display at the Honolulu Police Department Museum *(Photo by author)*

On a balmy July night in 1904, a wiry wraith of a man sauntered alone through the dim alleys of Honolulu's Chinatown. A mere five feet tall, with intense shoulders and a ramrod-straight back, the man was wearing a Canton-crêpe blouse, threadbare trousers, and a Panama hat. A pair of dark glasses obscured the scar above his eye. His upper lip, blackened by burnt cork, gave the impression that he needed a shave. From a distance, he was unmistakably Chinese, barely distinguishable as he walked among the shuffling throng of his countrymen.

The hot, southerly Kona weather, which had piled the breakers high along the coast and sapped the spirit out of every living being, had departed the island by sundown. A gentle trade wind blowing in from the northeast had brought renewed energy to the city. A local boy was plucking soft tunes on his ukulele, perhaps down on the moonlit beach not far below the street, fringed with coconut palms and licked by the lazy surf. When the serenade paused, a cock mynah gave out a clear-throated cry, ruffling its plumage beneath the canopy of a perfumed night.

Under the sickle moon, the Chinaman reached the corner of Smith Street in the heart of Chinatown. He slowed his pace on the darkened street, where shops and restaurants displayed clapboard signs scrawled in his native language. They had shut their doors much earlier, except for one nondescript building where he saw a glint of light escaping through an upstairs window. A faint smile flickered at the corners of his mouth. He drew a deep breath; the night air was a strange mélange of odors that lingered from the oil of woks and the salty tang of the Pacific wind.

Through the unlit front gate he stepped cautiously inside the building and passed by the doorman undetected. He did the same at the next three doors, each guarded by someone, each leading him deeper into what seemed like a maze of Chinese boxes.

Climbing up the rickety stairs to the second floor, he turned and faced a room packed with gamblers, all Chinese, huddling over games of fan-tan, pai gau, craps, and mah-jongg. The air was a mix of smut and smoke, the den ringing with curses, jeers, and the sound of clicking dice and mah-jongg tiles.

He observed the ballyhoo through his dark lenses. Someone at the mah-jongg table looked up and immediately recognized the face of the infamous cop, whose name elicited shudders from the spines of Honolulu criminals.

"*Chailow!*"

Before the Cantonese cry for "cop" dropped to the ground, a five-foot bullwhip had uncoiled like a hissing rattlesnake from the detective's waist. One crisp snap of the whip and the entire room froze like a gambling-hall diorama under glass. Only clouds of cigarette smoke still wavered, the afterthoughts of exploded firecrackers, not sure where to settle in the deafening silence.

Many there had already heard of, and some had even tasted, the might of this unusual weapon wielded by the former rough-riding *paniolo* (cowboy). Resisting arrest would be futile, even though they knew he had, as usual, brought no backup. His whip had spoken, louder than any law or gun.

Telling them the jig was up, the Chinaman, known to the locals as "Kana Pung," lined up the gamblers, forty in all, and marched them out of the room and down to the police station on Bethel Street. Not a single shot was fired.[1]

Kana Pung's real name was Chang Apana. An officer of the Honolulu Police Department, he would later acquire a more fascinating moniker: Charlie Chan. His colorful exploits, like the bravado on this July night, would one day draw the attention of mainland novelist Earl Derr Biggers. From 1925 onward, a total of six novels and forty-seven films, in addition to radio programs, newspaper comics, and countless faux-fortune-cookie witticisms, would make Charlie Chan, Apana's fictional double, one of the most enduring cultural icons of twentieth-century America.

PART ONE

THE "REAL" CHARLIE CHAN

CHANG APANA, CIRCA 1917 *(Photo by On Char, courtesy of Bishop Museum)*

1

Sandalwood Mountains

DIAMOND HEAD, 1870S *(Courtesy of Hawaii State Archives)*

The loveliest fleet of islands that lies anchored in any ocean.
—Mark Twain

A BOY NAMED Ah Pung was born sometime around 1871 in a thatched hut by a muddy creek in Waipio, a tiny village tucked away in the rolling sugarcane fields to the east of Honolulu. His father, Chang Jong Tong, was a Chinese coolie laborer from southern China, and his mother, Chun Shee, had been born in Hawaii of Chinese parents.[1] Ah Pung was their second son. The proud father took the day off from fieldwork and started dyeing eggs, according to Chinese custom. Later he would go around the small, tight-knit plantation community carrying not only a basket of boiled red eggs but also the good tidings of his newborn. An illiterate man from a humble peasant family, Chang had no idea that the baby snuggling comfortably next to his mother inside their shabby hut would one day turn out to be a legend.

As with other Hawaiian coolie families of the nineteenth century, crucial records of Ah Pung's birth are murky and unreliable. The *Delayed Birth Records* issued in 1909 by the Department of Health lists December 26, 1871, as his birth date, as does his official employment record at the Honolulu Police Department. But the 1930 census lists his age as sixty-one, which means he must have been born around 1869, a date confirmed by the obituaries published upon his death in 1933, as well as by his death certificate. Gilbert Martines, who did pioneering research on Apana for his thesis at the University of Hawaii in the late 1980s, believes that Apana was in fact born December 26, 1864.[2] But Apana's gravestone, which still stands in the verdant Upper Manoa Valley, states "1870," in Chinese characters, as his year of birth.

"Tombstones," says Charlie Chan, "often engraved with words of wisdom." But in this case, words at Apana's resting place are not at all reliable, as his tombstone also records 1934 as the year of his death—in this case, a factual error.

At the time of Ah Pung's birth, Honolulu was a bustling seaport town of about 15,000 souls. Isabella Lucy Bird, a British traveler who spent six months in the islands in 1873, described Honolulu as a place that "looks like a large village, or rather like an aggregate of villages."[3] With shadowy huts and houses made of straw, wood, adobe, or coral that perched on streets as straight as a line or as crooked as a corkscrew, the town was a distant cry from what it is today.[4] Waikiki, nowadays a jungle of high-rises inundated with two million tourists each year, was then only a stretch of white sand running from Diamond Head to the harbor. Here and there, a few grass shacks straggled along swamps and ponds. A stream ran from Manoa Valley down to the sea.[5] Under the ten-year reign (1863–72) of King Kamehameha V—a benevolent monarch who dressed plainly and enjoyed poking around town on his old horse—tourism as an industry had just begun to grow. The first hotel in town, reincarnated in 1927 as the palatial pink Royal Hawaiian, did not even have its cornerstone laid until 1871, just around the time of Ah Pung's birth.

To better know this man's true story, we need to take a detour and look at some snapshots of early Hawaiian history, at the events that would impact directly—or at times more obliquely—the life of our future Charlie Chan. As the honorable detective says, compared to the grandeur of history a man is merely "one minute grain of sand on seashore of eternity."

The Hawaiian Islands, also known as the Sandwich Islands, only emerged as an economic center a hundred years after Captain James Cook's arrival in 1778. After Cook's death at Kealakekua Bay, where his body was butchered and devoured by the natives on the beach, the missionaries soon came in waves—British, American, French—bringing the Word of God and trying to convert the "cannibals" who had barely finished digesting the roasted flesh of the man once regarded as their god Lono. And after the missionaries inevitably came the businessmen, fortune-seekers, and scavengers of the Pacific, bringing, in the parlance of the Kanakas (natives), the word of Rum.

Koolau the Leper, a colorful character in one of Jack London's infamous leprosy stories, summarizes the early colonial history of Hawaii in a few poetic sentences full of pain and resentment:

> They came like lambs, speaking softly. Well might they speak softly, for we were many and strong, and all the islands were ours. As I say, they spoke softly. They were of two kinds. The one kind asked our permission, our gracious permission, to preach to us the word of God. The other kind asked our permission, our gracious permission, to trade with us. That was the beginning. Today all the islands are theirs, all the land, all the cattle—everything is theirs.[6]

For the United States, the islands possessed a lure far beyond their natural beauty or their strategic location for maritime travel. In some ways, the islands, indeed the whole Pacific basin, perpetuated the notion of Manifest Destiny, holding the key to the future of the young republic as it grappled for international respect.

On February 22, 1784, shortly after the Revolutionary War, the merchant ship *Empress of China*, used as a privateer during the war and still fitted with guns, sailed from New York for China with a supercargo of ginseng, furs, raw cotton, and lead. The transpacific trade was in large measure an attempt to rescue the battered economy of a nation suffocating under a war debt of more than $50 million. To make matters worse, markets accustomed to American raw products were now limited or closed. Refusing to open its home ports on an equal basis to American shipping, Great Britain also closed its West Indies colonies to Yankee suppliers. France also restricted American trade with its West Indies colonies, and Spain continued its exclusionary mercantilist policies toward the United States. As a result, Americans had to turn to the Pacific in order to overcome their nation's economic setback, and in Hawaii they were in luck.

The *Empress*, the first American ship to dock at a Far East port, returned from Canton in 1785, making a 20 percent profit on invested capital. In the following years, China trade expanded rapidly. By 1800, the number of American ships that cleared Canton in one year had swelled to one hundred. In trade volume, America now ranked second only to Great Britain.

The boom in trading, however, was buttressed more by the natural products that merchants collected from the Pacific, especially in the Hawaiian isles, than by the native products of the American continent. Although the *Empress* voyage was a success, the Chinese soon discovered that the ginseng they bought from the Americans was not the same as the Korean herb that had been used for centuries in traditional Chinese medicine. Consequently, it became increasingly difficult for American traders to sell products brought from their native land. They had to look for alternatives, soon finding that the Pacific abounded with natural products that would cater to the demands of East Asian as well as American markets. Fortune-seekers moved into the Pacific to scavenge for furs, whales, bêche-de-mer (sea cucumbers), tortoiseshell, pearls, shark fins, birds' nests, grain, fish, salt, coal, sandalwood, lumber, copra, cowhide, tallow, arrowroot, vanilla, spices, guano, human heads, and even human beings. These commodities gave currency to the nineteenth-century term *curio,* famously adopted by Herman Melville in *Moby-Dick* (1851): The New England innkeeper, Peter Coffin, told Ishmael that the Pacific savage Queequeg had "a lot of 'balmed New Zealand heads (great curios, you know)." The *Oxford English Dictionary,* in fact, cites Melville's sentence as the earliest recorded use of the word.[7]

Among the Pacific curios, two were uniquely abundant in Hawaii: sandalwood and sugar. Called *'iliahi* in Hawaiian, sandalwood is a parasite that attaches itself to the root of another tree. As it grows, it becomes a hard, fragrant wood. Hawaiians used sandalwood sticks to make bows for their traditional musical instrument, the ukeke. They also ground the wood into a powder and sprinkled it on *kappa* (bark cloth) garments as a perfume.[8] For centuries, China, Japan, and other Asian countries had also been using sandalwood for "incense, fuel for funeral rites, temple carvings, handmade boxes, medicine, and as a basic ingredient in perfume."[9] Ornate cabinets and chests made of sandalwood were considered rarities, gracing houses much as antique vases and authentic artworks do today.

The beginning of the Hawaiian sandalwood trade, as historian Michael Dougherty tells us, can be traced to John Kendrick, the captain of the American clipper *Lady Washington.* Born about 1740 in Harwich, Massachusetts, Kendrick came from a long line of seamen. A true patriot, he participated in the Boston Tea Party and fought bravely in the Revolutionary War, where he was captured by the British navy and later released on a prisoner swap. After the war, he became commander of the first American ships of discovery, setting out to explore the Pacific Northwest.[10]

Sponsored by a Boston merchant, Kendrick's expedition set sail on October 1, 1787. After clearing the Falkland Islands and Cape

Horn, Kendrick sailed up the coast of Vancouver Island in June of 1788. He traded for furs with the Haida and other tribes and then sailed for Macao to unload the cargo. His ship stopped by the Sandwich (Hawaiian) Islands to restock food, water, and firewood. While stir-frying his popular chop suey for the Western sailors, the Chinese cook on board realized to his amazement that the logs and sticks burning under his sizzling wok gave out a distinctive fragrance.[11]

Up to this point, China had been importing white sandalwood from India and the East Indies, but the supply had become insufficient to meet market demand. The cook's discovery of red sandalwood, though of a quality inferior to the white species, made Kendrick recognize a potential new trade item for the Canton market. He immediately sent men ashore with instructions to collect the wood. Kendrick, however, did not live long enough to reap the full benefits of their fragrant discovery, for he was accidentally killed by a cannon shot from a British warship saluting his return to Honolulu Harbor in December 1794.[12] Still, the era of the sandalwood trade had begun. The islands emerged as a major source for the wood supply to China, and the archipelago soon became known in China as *Tan Heung Shan,* Sandalwood Mountains.

The transpacific trade had profound and tragic effects on the natural environment of the islands. Kamehameha I (also known as Kamehameha the Great), perhaps the most powerful monarch in the history of Hawaii, who by 1810 had unified all the main islands, maintained a monopoly over the export of sandalwood. In 1812, three shrewd Bostonians, Jonathan and Nathan Winship and William Davis, persuaded Kamehameha to sign a ten-year agreement for the sale of sandalwood. According to the agreement, the king would "have the sandalwood gathered and waiting" for the American merchants; the latter would "sail it to Chinese ports, sell it, and, upon return, give Kamehameha one quarter of the net profits."[13]

Greed quickly took hold of the king and local chiefs, who would command thousands of commoners to trudge up the steep slopes of valleys to harvest and transport the prized logs. The work was dangerous and gruesome. Historians have given sobering accounts of the misery that the wood trade inflicted on the native people:

> Slavery replaced freedom to the people. Natives were treated like cattle. Up and down the treacherous mountain trails they toiled, logs and sandalwood strapped to their sweating shoulders. Men and women actually became deformed due to the tremendous weight of the logs on their backs. The forced laborers in the sandalwood forests had no time to farm—food grew scarce and famine came.[14]

By 1819, intensive harvesting had stripped almost all of the Hawaiian sandalwood forests. It also caused market oversaturation and led to a precipitous price decline from the highest average of $13 per picul (133 1/3 pounds) to merely $1.50 per picul.[15]

Within just three decades, the dramatic rise and fall of the sandalwood trade left the Hawaiian economy in shambles. For years, the island kings and chiefs "had been buying all sorts of luxury goods and contracting to pay in sandalwood." Now, the wood was disappearing but the debts remained. In 1826, when the first two American warships, USS *Dolphin* and USS *Peacock*, arrived in Honolulu, the king and the chiefs were forced to acknowledge debts to American traders in an amount close to $160,000.[16]

But fortune smiled on the islands once again. Following the demise of the sandalwood trade, sugar miraculously emerged as the one product that would restore the economy. From the Hawaiian perspective, however, new contacts with the outside world brought new hazards, be they germs, viruses, or vices—the so-called gifts of civilization.

A type of giant perennial grass, sugarcane had originated in India but was brought to Hawaii by the Polynesians as they migrated outward from the South Pacific sometime during the first millennium. The plant was growing plentifully in the islands at the time of European discovery. In his travelogue, Captain Cook noted the abundance of sugarcane in the islands. On his third and last voyage, Cook wrote, "Having procured a quantity of sugarcane and finding a strong decoction of it produced a very palatable beer, I ordered some more to be brewed for our general use."[17] The natives, however, had made no use of it beyond that of food until its commercial value was recognized in the nineteenth century. It was again a Chinese who was credited with the first attempt to manufacture sugar from the native Hawaiian canes in 1802.

Chinese had begun to settle in Hawaii soon after Cook arrived. Most of them were skilled workers hired as carpenters and cooks on European and American vessels. In 1788, some forty-five Chinese carpenters, under the direction of Captain John Meares of the *Felice*, were taken to Nootka Sound on Vancouver Island to build a forty-ton schooner, the *North West America*. Upon the completion of the project, and on the Chinese team's homebound journey via Hawaii the next year, Kamehameha I asked for some of the workmen to stay and build him a ship just like *North West America*. But the request was denied by Captain Meares, though one Chinese carpenter did build "a small platform for a swivel gun on one of Kamehameha's canoes." There has been speculation that some of these Chinese might have "jumped ship and remained in Hawaii."[18] But the more probable first Chinese settlement was in 1789, when an American trader, Captain Simon Metcalf, sailed from Macao for the northwestern United States on the *Eleanora* and made a stop in Hawaii—the first of the American vessels in the China trade to stop over in the islands—to give the crew of forty-five Chinese and ten Americans some rest. It is likely that one or more Chinese remained in the islands, as the Chinese community celebrated the 150th anniversary of the first Chinese arrival in Hawaii in 1939.

The first recorded sighting of a Chinese living in Hawaii was documented by Edward Bell, who in 1794 wrote that the foreigners seen standing with Kamehameha I at Kealakekua Bay when the ships arrived were "John Young, Isaac Davis, Mr. Boid, 1 Chinaman, and 7 other whites."[19] In the absence of reliable historical documents, it is impossible for us to ascertain who that "1 Chinaman" was, and what business he had standing there with the most powerful king in Hawaii's history. It is said that Kamehameha relished, perhaps more than anything else, haggling with ships' captains over supplies and cargoes. "Wherever he was," writes historian Gavan Daws,

> Kamehameha immersed himself in trading, and with great gusto. A visiting ship would anchor and wait for clearance from the king's harbor masters. For merchant vessels and naval ships alike the royal guards fired their cannon in salute, and then Kamehameha came out on his platformed canoe, sometimes wearing only a loin cloth and alone except for an interpreter and a few attendants, sometimes dressed in European magnificence, seated on a gun chest with his hand on a silver sword, and surrounded by feather-cloaked chiefs and courtiers, but always with his tooth-edged calabash spittoon beside him.[20]

In either setting, whether in a team of white compradors such as John Young and Isaac Davis or among the Hawaiian chiefs and courtiers, a long-queued Chinese would certainly stand out to an observant Western explorer. Most likely the Chinese seen by Bell was a merchant participating in the king's haggling on the dock.

The man credited with the first attempt at making sugar out of Hawaiian canes was Wong Tze-chun. Not much is known about this Chinese man except that he arrived in Hawaii on a sandalwood trading ship in 1802. He was obviously a *tong see* (sugar master) in South China, where for centuries sugarcane had been cultivated and manufactured into sugar. In rural areas in southern China, as Bob Dye describes in his book *Merchant Prince of the Sandalwood Mountains,*

> itinerant *tong see* went by boat to the creek villages with their pots, rollers, and drying mats. Villagers brought them freshly

> cut cane that they fed between two huge stones, kept in motion by men or beasts, which ground and crushed the cane to express the crude juice. This liquid was boiled in kettles and then boiled again while being furiously whisked. The hot syrup was then spread in thin layers on mats to cool. Later the brittle sheets were cut into small squares, which were stored in jars.[21]

We do not know if this was Master Wong's first overseas adventure, but he had at least come into contact with other Chinese who had visited Hawaii and recognized the sugar plant. Like thousands of Chinese who jumped aboard the minute they heard about gold in America, Master Wong must have had a "sweet" dream when he heard of the abundance of cane lying wasted in the Sandalwood Mountains. On this trip, Wong carried with him a vertical stone mill, boilers, and other tools of his trade. Upon arrival, he set up his apparatus on the small island of Lanai, ground off a small crop, and started making sugar. But Lanai was the least hospitable island for growing sugarcane, and Master Wong, true to the spirit of itinerancy, folded his mat and returned to China the next year.[22]

In 1811, other Chinese began making small quantities of sugar and molasses at a mill owned by the king. Next came John Wilkinson, an Englishman who, having had experience with sugarcane in the West Indies, established a plantation in Manoa Valley. But Wilkinson's establishment was abandoned after his death in 1827, and the South China sugar manufacturers soon filled the gap with the founding of the Hungtai Sugar Works at Wailuku, Maui, in 1828. Induced by the decline of the sandalwood trade, William French, an American China trader, undertook sugar cultivation and production in Waimea, Kauai, in 1835. French hired Chinese workmen and recruited four *tong see* from China. The latter brought with them "a mill, a simple apparatus—granite cylinders turned by wooden cogs and operated by human muscle power." Later that year, French advertised that he had ten tons of sugar and a thousand gallons of "Sandwich Island Molasses" for sale.[23] Clearly, the great era of the Hawaiian sugar industry was underway. It was an industry that fundamentally changed the course of Hawaiian history and reshaped the destiny of millions in the Pacific Rim, including little Ah Pung, born in the cane fields of Waipio.

Though no record has been found to verify the date of arrival of Ah Pung's father, Chang Jong Tong, we know that he was among the early waves of Chinese coolies brought to Hawaii to work in the sugarcane plantations, so we can speculate on the basis of the few facts we do have about him.

Unlike on the U.S. mainland, where the clamor of "The Chinese must go!" was a clarion call for almost all parties in the mid-nineteenth century (more on this point later), the general sentiment in Hawaii was "The Chinese must come!" Economy, as they say, is the king, and several economic factors joined forces to create increasing demands for labor in Hawaii; among them were whaling, the nascent sugar industry, and the ripple effects of the California gold rush.

Nearly three decades before the discovery of gold at John Sutter's mill, whaling ships were docking at Hawaiian ports. More than a hundred whaling ships stopped at these ports in 1824, and more than 170 in 1829. During the next twenty years, Pacific whaling expanded rapidly, with the fleet doubling in size and then nearly doubling again. As the industry moved northward from the equatorial hunting grounds to the Sea of Japan—a geographical shift noted in Melville's *Moby-Dick*—and finally to the Arctic, the Hawaiian Islands became a vital entrepôt of a booming trade. For eight years—before the 1859 discovery of petroleum in Pennsylvania sounded the death knell for the whaling industry—the annual ship arrivals at Hawaiian ports totaled more than five hundred. In the record year of 1846, almost six hundred ships crowded the islands. These vessels spent much time in island waters and took on vast supplies of fresh provisions. As Daws puts it, sailors on shore leave meant business for everyone—not just for Hawaiian women.[24]

The California gold rush, started in 1848, also created a new market for Hawaiian produce. The whaling season of 1847–48 was particularly dismal, and many stores on the islands were badly overstocked. But with gold fever hitting thousands of men, including hundreds of natives, the stores were soon "stripped of everything that might be useful in the goldfields, from pickaxes, shovels, and lamps to Bibles and playing cards." In San Francisco, prices of food and durables skyrocketed: a 500 percent rise in the price of beef and a fourfold increase in the price of flour; a single droplet of laudanum (an opium tincture used as an analgesic) would go for as much as $40.[25] All this created an unparalleled opportunity for Hawaii, where potatoes, corn, wheat, coffee, squash, turnips, and other vegetables could grow plentifully because of the islands' superior climate and fertile soil. Potato patches on Maui even acquired an epithet, "Nu Kaleponi" (New California), because potatoes, "snapped up by the shipload and sent to San Francisco," were as good as the gold being dug out of the ground.[26] Once again, plantation owners were crying out for workers as the native population dwindled precipitously, as a result of either epidemics or emigration to California's goldfields.[27]

The gold rush and the subsequent trade opportunities for Hawaii did not, however, last long. By the end of 1851, as Daws tells us, "surface gold in California was mined out. The West Coast market collapsed . . . and Hawaii found itself in the midst of depression."[28] The quick boom-and-bust of whaling and the gold rush taught local businessmen a lesson: they needed to rely on the soil and not the sea. Sugar emerged as the obvious choice to be the staple of the islands' economy. With the subsequent rising export of sugar and molasses, the white plantation owners yearned for cheap and reliable labor. They looked and found the Chinese.

On January 3, 1852, 175 Chinese field laborers and twenty-three houseboys arrived in Honolulu Harbor after a rough fifty-five-day voyage, with a loss of five men, on Captain John Cass's *Thetis*. The laborers had agreed to work for five years, at $3 per month as field hands or $2 per month as houseboys, in addition to receiving passage money, clothing, room and board.[29] Thus began the Chinese contract-labor migration, the infamous "pig trade." Visiting the islands in 1866, a fledgling American writer—who had adopted the pseudonym "Mark Twain" shortly before the trip—provided colorful descriptions of the labor-recruitment system, for which he would become an avid advocate:

> The sugar product is rapidly augmenting every year, and day by day the Kanaka race is passing away. Cheap labor had to be procured by some means or other, and so the Government [of Hawaii] sends to China for coolies and farms them out to the planters at $5 a month each for five years, the planter to feed them and furnish them with clothing. The Hawaiian agent fell into the hands of Chinese sharpers, who showed him some superb coolie samples and then loaded his ships with the scurviest lot of pirates that ever went unhung. Some of them were cripples, some were lunatics, some afflicted with incurable diseases, and nearly all were intractable, full of fight, and animated by the spirit of the very devil. However, the planters managed to tone them down and now they like them very well. Their former trade of cutting throats on the China seas has made them uncommonly handy at cutting cane. They are steady, industrious workers when properly watched.[30]

Mark Twain was commissioned that year by the *Sacramento Union*, a leading newspaper in the West that was often called "the Miners' Bible," to spend a month in the islands as a traveling correspondent. With the newly inaugurated steamer *Ajax* running between San Francisco and Hawaii, the paper saw an opportunity to serve readers who might soon visit the islands. The publisher hired Twain, who had only recently lost his newspaper job in Nevada due to his sympathy for Chinese miners, to assess the lay of the land in Hawaii.

The twenty-five picturesque letters Twain would write from the islands in the next six months served the paper's purpose quite well. He documented in great detail the islands' scenery and climate, politics, social conditions, history, and legends, but he conveniently forgot to mention the prevalence of leprosy, for fear that it might frighten off the businessmen who would be reading his letters with an eye toward possible trade opportunities.

What particularly impressed Twain, besides the flamboyant tales of Captain Cook's demise and the indigenous cannibalism, was the sugar-industry boom supported by shrewd local planters' use of Chinese coolie labor. The master ironist did a little math: with more than 250 sugar plantations in Louisiana and Mississippi, the aggregate yield was only twenty-five million pounds in 1866. By contrast, Hawaii's mere twenty-nine small plantations yielded a total of twenty-seven million pounds that year. The secret, Twain concluded, lay not just in the fertile soil or advantageous weather but also "in their cheap Chinese labor." When one company paid only $5 a month for labor that another company had to hire for $80 and $100, there was no question which business would fare better.[31]

Twain's testimony to its benefits partly explains the continuation of the Chinese coolie trade until 1898, when Hawaii was annexed by the United States, which by then had effectively stopped Chinese immigration with 1882's Chinese Exclusion Act. What Twain considered to be the secret to Hawaii's success, "cheap Chinese labor," was regarded as a disaster for the white labor force on the mainland. Only four years after Twain penned these letters, his close friend and collaborator, Bret Harte, would publish "The Heathen Chinee," one of the most popular poems about Chinese to rear its racist head in the nineteenth century. In the poem, white miners lamented, "We are ruined by Chinese cheap labor." But for decades, before becoming a U.S. territory, Hawaii hugely benefited from the steady supply of cheap Chinese labor. From 1852 to 1898, an estimated 46,500 Chinese laborers flowed into the islands.[32]

Many of these indentured laborers, realizing that a coolie's life was certainly not what they had bargained for, chose to return to China upon the expiration of their five-year contract. Others moved to expanding towns such as Honolulu and looked for other forms of livelihood. Ah Pung's parents, with two children and a third on the way, homesick for their native land, decided to move the growing family back to China. Thus, at the age of three, Ah Pung took his first and only journey to his ancestral hometown in southern China. His stay would form an indelible impression on the young boy, but it would not prove permanent.

2

Canton

CANTON, CHINA, LATE 1890S *(Courtesy of the Second Historical Archives of China)*

China, like the purse of a generous man, has endured much.
—Charlie Chan

IT IS HARD to imagine how shocking the scene of rural Canton might have appeared to Ah Pung's parents when they arrived back in their hometown. The two punishing Opium Wars (1839–42 and 1856–60), combined with the brutal Taiping Rebellion (1851–64), had ravaged the countryside in the Pearl River Delta, which sprawled out to the South China Sea. With endemic poverty that was decimating the population, hardscrabble peasants were living lives that were, to use a Chinese expression, *niuma buru*—worse than those of cattle and horses.

Little Ah Pung's ancestral hometown, Oo Sack, a small village in Hsiangshan District, south of Canton on the western bank of the Pearl River, was no stranger to this devastation. Later, the district would change its name to Chungshan, in honor of its best-known native son, the founding father of the Republic of China, Sun Yat-sen, who, like Ah Pung, would come of age in Honolulu.

There is, sadly, no record of Ah Pung's life in Oo Sack. But one of his contemporaries, Chung Kun Ai, provides in his memoir, *My Seventy Nine Years in Hawaii*, a description of this pattern of dreary subsistence in rural Canton in the 1870s. Chung, better known as C. K. Ai, was born in 1865, a few years before Ah Pung, in Sai-San, a short distance northwest of Oo Sack. Despite the difference in spelling (thanks mostly to the crude imagination of U.S. customs officers, who baptized millions of immigrants by assigning last names they had acoustically approximated from Chinese, Yiddish, and Polish alike), "Chang" and "Chung" are transliterations of the same Chinese character. Chang Apana and Chung Kun Ai, in other words, share a family name, even though there is no record to indicate they are immediately related. Later, orbiting in the same microcosm of Honolulu's Chinatown, with Apana as famous cop and Ai as leading businessman, it is possible that their paths might have crossed again.

Poverty, as Ai recalls, plagued the shabby villages scattered around the delta south of Canton. Bombed by British battleships during the Opium Wars and scorched in what historians have characterized as "the most destructive civil war in the history of humanity,"[1] this area suffered from famines, bandits, and epidemics. Adding to the miseries were the constant fights between the *Punti* (local people) and the *Hakkas* (guest people) over land possession. Feuds between clans could turn bloody. A Chinese immigrant recalled the bitter memory of being forced to flee from the violence and turmoil:

> In a bloody feud between the Chang family and the Oo Shak [i.e., Oo Sack] village we lost our two steady workmen. Eighteen villagers were hired by Oo Shak to fight against the huge Chang family, and in the battle two men lost their lives protecting our pine forests. Our village, Wong Jook Long, had a few resident Changs. After the bloodshed, we were called for our men's lives, and the greedy, impoverished villagers grabbed fields, forest, food and everything, including newborn pigs, for payment. We were left with nothing, and in disillusion we went to Hong Kong to sell ourselves as contract laborers.[2]

Cantonese from this area, out of economic necessity, were among the first to sell themselves into the dreaded coolie system. Like Irish peasants after the potato famine, they were the most active in venturing overseas during the second half of the nineteenth century. A government report of the time noted: "Ever since the disturbances caused by the [bandits], dealings with foreigners have increased greatly. The able-bodied go abroad. The fields are clogged with weeds."[3]

In Ai's plain language, we sense the dearth of materials and supplies in the life of these villagers left behind:

> Ours was such a small village that we had no stores or restaurants. A small local shop supplied such often used items as sauce and bean-curds, but for the other household and kitchen items that we needed we must wait for the market days to come around.[4]

On so-called market days, vendors convened at a particular village; the markets rotated among adjacent villages. There was simply not enough commerce to justify maintaining a regular store in one location and keeping it open daily. Market days were the few occasions when children like Ai and Ah Pung could, if allowed by their family budget, purchase a taste of life outside of its impoverished norm.

Ai, coming from a well-to-do family of country gentry, did manage to experience such temporary relief. Writing his memoir in his eighties, when he had retired comfortably to Hong Kong, the Hawaiian business tycoon remembered with almost boyish delight the bowls of soup he had gulped down with such eagerness in the early years of his life:

> As Yung Mark was but a mile and a half from our village, I would visit Yung Mark on market days and spend money on a bowl of rice-soup of fish, pork, or chicken. The cheapest was fish rice-soup, at sixteen cash a bowl. After I have had my fill of rice-soup, I would return home.[5]

Ah Pung, however, had no chance for even as simple a treat as a bowl of fish- or meat-flavored soup. His family was poor, as evidenced by his lack of schooling—any family that could afford it would have been obliged to send their kids to school at that time, or in almost any other period of Chinese history. Ah Pung, in fact, never learned to read in either Chinese or English, even though later in life he taught himself to read Hawaiian. Toys were rare in a family like his.

It is worth noting that even a full century later, little had changed. When I was growing up, for example, in a small village in the waning days of Mao's China, my "toys" were mud-pies, tadpoles, ants, fireflies, grasshoppers, and whatever luckless insects fell into my hands. Occasionally I could catch a fledgling sparrow learning to fly if I suddenly clapped my hands and yelled loudly. The frightened young bird would fall to the ground and make a good, hapless pet—but only for a few days, since caged sparrows have a fiery, rebellious temperament and do not survive for long.

Such were the simple, rustic delights of childhood in rural China, both for Ah Pung and for me.

There would be endless chores that even a three-year-old such as Ah Pung would have to share: gathering fallen tree leaves and twigs for kitchen fuels, collecting animal droppings for fertilizer, keeping birds and animals away from grain drying on the ground, and so on. The slightly older kids would have to babysit their siblings, wash dishes, do laundry, herd water buffalo, or simply work in the fields like adults.

In such a harsh environment, a child prone to accidents and disease would be lucky to grow to maturity. Child kidnapping was a common, daily fear in Ah Pung's day. Occasionally, when a famine broke out, cannibalism might become the last resort for families on the brink of starving to death; they were forced by necessity to make exchanges with other equally desperate families so they could at least avoid eating their own children or siblings.

The decade of the 1870s, as Ah Pung's parents would come to realize, was a particularly dire time for China. Teetering in the wake of the crushing wars, the Manchu regime could no longer maintain the imperial façade of the Middle Kingdom. Still four decades from its collapse but already in decline, the Ching dynasty understood that more troubles loomed on the horizon. Among them were fears that the repeated military and economic invasions by the Western powers would make the empire, increasingly carved up through territorial concessions, resemble nothing more than a juicy melon. Regional and nationwide rebellions accompanied this imperial plunder as well. The entire situation was exacerbated by the scourge of opium, which the British had imposed on the Chinese, resulting in an addiction problem for millions.[6] Not surprisingly, the Chinese carried this addiction to Hawaii, where Chang Apana, as a cop, would be charged with eradicating this vice.

Hoping for a better future for their offspring, Ah Pung's parents decided to send him out of the country. Even though they themselves had not had any luck in Hawaii, the islands were an unquestionable improvement over rural Canton in a country on the verge of political and moral collapse. Ah Pung's uncle, later known in Hawaii as

C. K. Aiona, had signed aboard a ship to try his luck in the Sandalwood Mountains. So, at the age of about ten, in 1881, Ah Pung accompanied his uncle and sailed for his birthplace.

The young boy had little clue about what lay ahead. Having left Hawaii at three, he might possibly have had faint memories of the soaring cliffs, verdant valleys, and kaleidoscopic flora and fauna. But more than that? Not likely. As the ship departed from Whampoa Harbor and drifted down the Pearl River, Ah Pung watched the wretched countryside float by. Straw huts—not unlike the one in which he had been born ten years earlier in Hawaii—dotted rural Canton's bleak landscape, like bird nests perched on barren trees in the dead of winter. Here and there, a skinny water buffalo would be toiling in rice paddies at a languid pace. Rent from his parents at this impressionable age, Ah Pung would never see China again.

3

Paniolo, the Hawaiian Cowboy

CHINATOWN, HONOLULU, LATE 1890S *(Courtesy of Hawaii State Archives)*

You gaze at this cattle ranch from high on the misty heights of Hawaii's Mauna Kea, and from the volcano's sloping shoulder you see 227,000 acres, a breathtaking vista spread out on the highlands of this great mountain. A soothing wind drifts from the mountain and cools the lava wastes. Seemingly limitless, the area includes forests, valleys, seashores, plateaus, meadows, hills, streams, and canyons. This is the sprawling, mysterious, majestic Parker Ranch, with the largest Hereford herd in the world.

—Joseph Brennan, The Parker Ranch of Hawaii, *1974*

THE GLIMPSE OF the island of Oahu at the end of a forty-day sea voyage provided a stark contrast to Ah Pung's last view of China. As the boat neared the harbor, epic peaks soared into towering clouds and expansive azure. In deep clefts of lush green, waterfalls streaked down like the long, silvery hairs of a mermaid. Under the tropical sun, the Diamond Head promontory humped like the gnarled back of a giant whale, softened only by the wavy line of palms stretched out along the white beaches of Waikiki. The amphitheater of Punchbowl, the future, fictional home of Detective Charlie Chan, stood majestically at the center of the butterfly-shaped island, beckoning the new arrivals.

Almost all travel writers worth their salt have spoken of the romance of arriving in Hawaii. They often evoke a timeless scene. Bands play aloha music, native girls in grass skirts dance hula, and matronly women in colorful *holokus* hang leis around the necks of visitors. But for the Chinese coolie laborers who had been packed in the crowded steerage with no privacy or comfort for weeks, this moment of landing was one of utter confusion, anxiety, and humiliation.

Trudging down the gangplank in a stream of blue cotton, they were greeted not by sirens chanting but by immigration officials shouting incomprehensible commands and questions at them. In frustration, the laborers, coached by their booking agents, shouted back the names of their intended plantations. These were the only two or three English/Hawaiian words they knew or would ever need to know: "Puunene Maui!" "Waialua Sugar Company!" "Naalehu Hawaii!"

After they had been identified by the plantation representatives, a *bango*—a numbered metal tag on a chain, hardly a welcome lei—was placed around each of their necks. Then, like cattle heading to market, they were piled into the waiting wagons and taken to their ultimate destinations.[1]

Ah Pung, along with his uncle and other laborers, was sent to a plantation in Waipio, his birthplace. The already-sketchy paper trail that follows Ah Pung's early life unfortunately stops here, at his return around 1881. When he emerges again in our story with any certainty—in 1891, to be exact—Ah Pung, having adopted his official name of Chang Apana, would already be a young man. Despite the absence of reliable information, there exist personal recollections and circumstantial accounts that enable us to piece together a plausible picture of Apana's life during this time.

In these ten or so formative years, we are certain that Apana did at least two things: first, he learned to handle horses, and second, he became a stableman for the wealthy Wilder family in Honolulu. There are accounts of Apana winning the title of the best horseman among the Chinese in Hawaii.[2] Later, as a policeman, he would always wear a cowboy hat and carry a bullwhip, reminders of those tough riding days. In his funeral procession in 1933, thronged by hundreds in Honolulu, a handler led a white horse without a rider. This was said to be the mount used by Apana while on active duty in the Honolulu Police Department.[3]

Horses, then, apparently played an integral role in Apana's illustrious career, so, to know the true color of our future "supersleuth," one needs some familiarity with the hardscrabble life of those dashing, devil-may-care *paniolos*, the Hawaiian cowboys.

NOT UNTIL 1803 did the first horse arrive in Hawaii, aboard the China trader *Lelia Bird*. Captain Richard J. Cleveland brought a stallion and two mares from Baja California as gifts for Kamehameha the Great. They caused quite a stir among the natives, who crowded the ship's decks to see these bizarre equine creatures. Noticing their quizzical looks, a sailor jumped on the back of one of the horses and did a demonstration of galloping. The king, however, failed to show any interest. He took a careless look at the horses and made a remark that greatly disappointed Cleveland. He could not, the king said, perceive that the ability to transport a person from one place to another, in less time than he could run, would be adequate compensation for the food the animal would consume and the care it would require.[4]

The king, however, was alone in his nonchalance. Other groups, like the Native Americans a few centuries earlier, had quickly adopted these continental imports as their daily companions. In the words of a catalogue distributed by the Hawaiian Humane Society, "From the day the first mare awed Kona residents in 1803, native Hawaiians were hooked on horses." Half a century later, as the *Pacific Commercial Advertiser* reported in 1864, "The passion of the Kanaka, male or female, for horses is the most marked trait in their character."[5]

The horse, however, is only one of the two animals essential to the life of a cowboy, the cow of course being its plodding companion. Cattle had first arrived in Hawaii a decade earlier than horses. In 1793, Captain George Vancouver, the famous English circumnavigator, brought five cows as gifts to Kamehameha the Great at Kealakekua Bay on the Big Island. Vancouver had originally loaded nine cattle—two bulls and seven cows—aboard the *Discovery* in Monterey, but the animals fared poorly on the long voyage from California. A bull and a cow died en route, and the remaining bull expired soon after landing. It was a glancing blow to Vancouver's hope to establish a breed of cattle in the islands.

Learning from his blunder, Vancouver brought three bulls and two more cows the following year, this time in good condition. He convinced the king to declare a *kapu* (taboo) upon all the cattle for ten years and to punish by death anyone who might injure or kill any of his animals. Thus, protected by royal decree, the bovines grazed freely on the grassy upland range of Waimea. With the aid of natural feed and friendly climes, the animals multiplied, perhaps even more rapidly than the king had anticipated. By 1813, only twenty years after their introduction, thousands of maverick cattle were roaming the plains, valleys, and forests of northern Hawaii.[6]

The wild beasts became a nuisance to the natives, munching crops of potatoes, ravishing taro patches, and trampling forest growth. The natives were forced to build stone fences to ward off the invading hordes. In some regions, branches of koa trees were cut and twisted into crude fences. The cattle were also a menace to local residents, who had to avoid thicketed areas where wild bulls reigned supreme and were prone to attack human intruders.[7]

The problem with these roving herds created a golden opportunity in 1815 for a keen-eyed young New Englander, John Palmer Parker, who, as Hawaii's first cowboy, would build the largest cattle dynasty west of Texas. Born on May 1, 1790, near the Charles River in Newton, Massachusetts, Parker seemed destined to sail the high seas—his father had inherited the family whaling-ship business, while his mother was a descendant of shipyard owners and operators.[8] Arriving in Hawaii aboard a sandalwood trader in 1809, Parker was smitten by the beauty of the tropical isles and decided, like Herman Melville in the Marquesas twenty years later, to jump ship.

With the help of friendly natives, Parker built a small *hale* (house) and tilled an area around the hut to plant seeds. He learned the Polynesian language and acquainted himself with the king. Kamehameha gave the young haole (white man) a job tending the royal fishponds.[9] Soon the seafaring itch set in again, and in 1811, when a New England merchant ship passed through Hawaii, Parker signed on for a voyage to China. Unfortunately, the ship, sidelined by a British blockade, was stuck in Canton during the War of 1812.

Finally returning to Hawaii in 1815, Parker realized that even though wandering the high seas was his calling by birth, he would prefer a more secure life. With the longhorns running wild on the island, Parker recognized an opportunity where others only saw nuisance and hazard. He made a business proposal to Kamehameha, asking the king to allow him to shoot cattle. Deep in debt due to his ill-managed sandalwood trade, Kamehameha was willing to give a second chance to the haole who had played hooky from the fishpond job. He hired Parker as his *konohiki* (agent) for the supplies of "garden vegetables, taro, meats, and hides for local and foreign consumption," making him the only person for whom the twenty-two-year-old *kapu* on cattle was lifted.[10] Armed with a musket, the tall, rawboned Parker became, if you will, a pre-Hollywood John Wayne. He spent long days riding into forests and valleys and shooting the king's cattle. It was hard and dangerous work, for the animals were wild and vicious and would often, like Ahab's Moby Dick, hunt the hunter.

In this gruesome slaughter business, Parker was fortunate to have a partner, Jack Purdy, who was easily Parker's match in sturdiness and courage. Purdy had come to Hawaii aboard a whaling vessel and had, like Parker himself, jumped ship at Kawaihae, on the Big Island. He had also married a Hawaiian woman and had children who all became *paniolos*. Mary Low, one of Parker's great-granddaughters who grew up at the ranch, later recalled stories she had heard about tough Jack Purdy. One tale concerned an Englishman named Brenchley, a man of fortune and a great traveler of Herculean strength. When in Hawaii, Brenchley took Purdy as his guide and claimed that he could do anything or go anywhere that the guide could. One day Purdy proposed that they go out with only their guns and blankets. They rode toward Mauna Loa and subsisted only on geese, ducks, and plovers. Finally they ran out of gunpowder, which worried Brenchley. Purdy took him to a swamp and told him to get in; Brenchley sank to his knees. Telling him to stay there, Purdy disappeared into thick brush near the swamp. Soon, from the brush came a wild bull with an eye of fire and a tail erect. The animal charged toward Brenchley, plunged into the swamp, and stuck fast. "There's our dinner!" yelled Purdy. He gathered some twigs and tied them into two bundles. He put one bundle on the mud and stepped on it. "Then he cast the other bundle ahead and stepped on that, picking up the first bundle and casting it before him. In this way, he reached the bull and, drawing his knife, cut the animal's throat and soon sliced off some pieces of beef. Returning to firm ground in the same manner as he had gone to the bull, he kindled a fire and in a short time invited Brenchley to dinner."[11] After this, Brenchley had to concede that he had finally met a man who surpassed him in daring.

As a team, Parker and Purdy would trek into the ruggedest regions to obtain beef. Each time they shot a bull or cow, they would "cut away the meat from the carcass and haul it to where [they] could salt it and pack it in barrels." Faced with the generous bounty of nature, many would have succumbed to greed and engaged in mindless killing and reaping of bonanzas, as has occurred with the near-extinction of the whales in the Pacific, buffalo on the American plains, and elephants in Africa. But Parker was no Captain Ahab, no Mr. Kurtz. He was a wise man with a shrewd business sense. As the king's agent, he took his salary in the form of selected live cattle, which enabled him to choose the best breed for domestication. Very soon he had tamed and fenced in enough herds to start a ranch of his own.[12]

The primary market for beef was not the Hawaiian natives, whose traditional diet had been confined to fish, pig, and poi (taro paste). The best customers were the whaling fleets that made island calls to winter the crew and replenish their supplies. As the hunt for the ocean's leviathans intensified at a maddening pace, the demand for Parker's beef increased, soon surpassing what his small team could procure from the great wilderness or from his growing ranch. More help was needed.

Still strapped for cash because of his expensive purchases of luxury items on credit, Kamehameha agreed to Parker's request and sent for help from California. Help came in the form of a team of colorful Spanish *vaqueros*, who one day arrived on the pier clad in woolen ponchos, slashed leggings, brightly colored sashes and bandannas, and floppy sombreros. These artisans from the mainland taught the Hawaiian natives everything they needed to know about horses and cattle, and every skill of ranching: how to capture wild horses and break them to saddle, how to lasso raging bulls, how to tan leather with tree bark, how to braid rawhide quirts and lariats, and how to build saddles. Not only were the natives eager to learn the arts of the cowboy, they also were quick to emulate the exotic costumes and the lifestyle that came with the profession. After calling the *vaqueros* "the Españols," they referred to themselves as "*paniolos*," a variation of the former word.[13]

In short order, the Parker Ranch grew rapidly, and so did the number of *paniolos*, who would soon include Hawaiians, Caucasians, Asians, and other mixed-race men. After John Parker died in 1868, the vicissitudes of the ranch rose and fell, as do all dynasties in history, throughout the remaining decades of the nineteenth century and into the twentieth. But the ranch has always remained under the control of the Parker family, making it even today the second-largest family-run ranch in the United States.

IT WAS AT the Parker Ranch in Waimea that young Chang Apana learned and honed his cowboy skills. Although no verifying record has been found, at least two reliable sources place Apana at the ranch. Chester A. Doyle, a court interpreter who had worked closely with the Honolulu Police Department, described in a 1935 letter a dinner meeting he had once hosted for Earl Derr Biggers. According to this letter, addressed to the editor of the *Honolulu Star-Bulletin*, Biggers had arrived on the island to scout for materials for his next book, and Doyle threw a dinner party at his home in honor of the famous Charlie Chan novelist. Among the twenty or so guests was Apana, who, according to Doyle, spoke about his days at the Parker Ranch.[14]

Doyle's letter was full of factual errors, many of which were disputed by Helen K. Wilder in a letter subsequently published in the same newspaper a month later. Wilder differed with Doyle on many points except for one, that Apana did work at the ranch in Waimea.[15]

The Parker Ranch, when Apana spent time there in the late 1880s and early 1890s, was plagued by poor management. After John Parker's death, ownership of the ranch passed down to his descendants. Troubles loomed when the cattle dynasty reached Samuel Parker of the third generation, who preferred the leisurely life of a playboy to the hard work of a rancher. A close friend of King Kalakaua, who was dubbed "the Merry Monarch" for his love of life's pleasures, Samuel Parker spent more time hobnobbing in the royal court than running the ranch. Not surprisingly, the business suffered.

Nonetheless, work went on for the hundred or so hired *paniolos.* Joining this most colorful group, young Apana certainly acquired a great knowledge of ranching. The 227,000-acre ranch, lying in the northwest of the Big Island, high up on Mauna Kea's bare volcanic slopes, had breathtaking vistas of natural beauty as well as rough terrain unsuitable for the faint of heart. From sunrise to sunset, Apana joined other *paniolos* in herding, cutting, holding, roping, throwing, branding, castrating, inoculating, ear-clipping, medicating, sorting, loading, and shipping.[16] Even after sundown, there would still be plenty of odd jobs to do: tending to the horses, caring for the saddle and tack, repairing the lassos, chopping wood, and more.[17]

A cowboy's life demanded courage and built character. The experience would have a lasting effect on Apana, and for the rest of his life he was known as a top-rider and hunter—fearless, dashing, devil-may-care. From dress to talk, from weapon to walk, the future "supercop" would maintain a *paniolo*'s way of life. He would always wear a cowboy hat and carry a bullwhip that he had fashioned himself, just as a *paniolo* handcrafts his own lasso and saddle. Dark and sinewy like a bull, he walked straight and fast, with an energetic gait. According to his daughters, Apana could "tell time down to the minute by observing the shadows that the sun cast." And he kept the same schedule of getting up and going to bed every day, like a clock. In his "high shrill voice," he spoke fluent Hawaiian, the crisp syllables popping like firecrackers.[18]

By the time Helen Wilder hired him, in 1897, as the first officer for the newly founded Hawaiian chapter of the Humane Society, Apana the *paniolo* was ready for the proverbial wide, wild world.

4

The Wilders of Waikiki

A Chinese store in Chinatown, Honolulu, late 1890s

(Courtesy of Hawaii State Archives)

In my youth, I am house-boy in the Phillimore Mansion.

—Charlie Chan

In the hierarchical world of late nineteenth-century Hawaii, where the racial pyramid put white plantation owners and missionaries on top, even above the indigenous chiefs and queens, an uneducated yellow man like Chang Apana would not have stood a "Chinaman's chance" without luck or help.

Unlike earlier times, when hospitable Hawaiians would extend alohas and leis to people of all races arriving on their shores, racism became more visible as the haoles became more established in the islands. Steadily and persistently, an elite group of American businessmen and missionaries and their descendants had begun, since the midcentury, to consolidate power. The Provisional Government under their control, while severely corroding the role of the native monarchy, had passed laws and implemented policies that all too often became carbon copies of what existed on the racist mainland.

Apana's luck was a result of his relationship with the Wilders, the affluent and influential family who, like the Parkers, dominated Hawaii's economy and politics for generations. The first Wilder to come to the islands was Samuel Gardner Wilder, born in Leominster, Massachusetts, in 1831. He had grown up in Geneva, Illinois, and left school at the age of nine in order to work and contribute income to his family of five siblings and a widowed father, all eking out a living on a farm mortgaged to the hilt. At eighteen, he hopped on a "prairie schooner" (a covered wagon) and lit out for the West to try his luck in the California goldfields. Failing to strike it rich, he supported himself with odd jobs in San Francisco, where he met Elizabeth Kinau Judd, daughter of Dr. Gerrit P. Judd. A pioneer of American missions to Hawaii, Judd had arrived in the islands on the third missionary ship from Boston in 1828 and became a close friend and adviser of several Hawaiian monarchs. Elizabeth, his eldest daughter, was said to be the first white girl born in Honolulu, with her middle name chosen in honor of the sister of the then-reigning monarch, Kamehameha III.[1]

Samuel Wilder and Elizabeth Judd were married at her father's

Honolulu house in 1866. It became a historic occasion, with Edgar Allan Poe's brother as one of the witnesses and distinguished guests who included Mark Twain, King Kamehameha V, and Queen Emma. Wilder's conjugal tie to the prominent Judd family enabled him to get a foothold in Hawaii. He started off by trading in guano—droppings of seabirds mined from uninhabited Jarvis Island, near the equator, and sold to the U.S. mainland as fertilizer and as a gunpowder ingredient. Soon he bought his own steamships and built up an empire, the Wilder Steamship Company. He also owned sugarcane plantations in Hawaii.

Among his various business adventures, Wilder's one-shot involvement in the coolie trade was generally regarded as his worst and most embarrassing failure. In 1870, as the agent for the Hawaii Planters' Society, Wilder sailed for China with plans to recruit 541 coolie laborers. In Hong Kong he ran into snags with local laws banning contract-labor emigration. After some secret maneuvering and loophole jumping, Wilder gathered about four hundred Chinese men to go to Hawaii. He gave each of them clothing and $10 cash advances. Just as the ship was about to set sail, someone spread the rumor that they were sailing to South America rather than Hawaii. The whole ship burst into an uproar, and most of the recruits went overboard, without returning the advances. "The result of Mr. S. G. Wilder's mission to China," an article in the *Pacific Commercial Advertiser* reported after Wilder's return, "is before us in the 168 Chinese coolies which were brought in the ship *Solo* from Hong Kong. The enterprise is looked upon as a failure, and Mr. Wilder has been soundly berated upon the street by some of those who were most anxious that he should be sent."[2]

In contrast to this disaster, Wilder's finest business deal was his purchase, again against opinions on the street, of the wrecked *Eskbank*. One day, a merchant ship ran aground off Diamond Head. Aroused from his morning nap by his children, Wilder looked through the spyglass and saw it was *Eskbank*, a vessel with a valuable cargo. He told his wife, "I am going to buy the *Eskbank* and what I make out of it I will build you a house with." As the weather worsened, the raging waves completely destroyed the bark, and the vessel was sold at auction for $1,100. Wilder, who made the winning bid, once again became the butt of jokes on the street, for people thought he was throwing money away. But Wilder hired divers, sent out steamers, and salvaged a staggering $175,000 worth of goods from the ship. All the skeptics—or, rather, the whole island—got drunk and made merry for days with the bottles of gin and port that washed ashore.[3]

True to his word, Wilder built his wife a big house by using part of the profits from the wrecked *Eskbank*. He named the house after the ship. It was a saga so fascinating that it inspired Robert Louis Stevenson, the adopted son of the South Seas, to write *The Wrecker*, a Pacific mystery about the rogue cargo of the wrecked *Flying Scud*:

> "There is something in wrecks, too," said Havens. "Look at that man in Honolulu, and the ship that went ashore on Waikiki Reef; it was blowing a kona, hard; and she began to break up as soon as she touched. Lloyd's agent had her sold inside an hour; and before dark, when she went to pieces in earnest, the man that bought her had feathered his nest. Three more hours of daylight, and he might have retired from business. As it was, he built a house on Beretania Street, and called it for the ship."[4]

"That man in Honolulu" is unmistakably Samuel Wilder. And in the spirit of fiction, Stevenson also changed the name of the street where the house was built, from the original Judd to Beretania Street.

Later in her memoir, Elizabeth remembered fondly the redwood house built on the street named after her father. "Eskbank," she said, "was a beautiful house, well adapted for entertaining, having large, airy rooms and wide verandas." It boasted a banquet hall, salon, library, billiards room, cupola, and a large stable.[5] An extant photo of the house shows a two-story wood building with a lanai going all around, capped by a prominent widow's walk on the roof—reminiscent of the couple's New England roots—and surrounded by royal palms, banana trees, ribbon-leafed lauhala, and flaming hibiscus.

AS A SEASONED *paniolo* skilled with horse and rope, Apana was hired by the Wilders in 1891 to take care of their stable at Eskbank. He lived in the servants' quarters in the barn behind the big mansion.[6] It is conceivable that he shared other chores at the house as well. Later in life, Apana was remembered as an excellent cook. According to Gilbert Martines, when the Prince of Wales visited the islands in 1920, Apana was the chef in charge of the big celebratory luau. When interviewed in the 1980s, Apana's daughters spoke fondly of their father's daily cooking and freshly baked cookies.[7] There was a regular cook at Eskbank as well as a Chinese housemaid, a former slave girl named Sibilo, whom Wilder had bought for $50 at a Canton marketplace during his infamous 1870 trip.[8] But the Wilders were raising a family of five children; a good hostler at such an establishment had to have been a jack-of-all-trades, ready to step up wherever and whenever his service was needed.

While *The Chinese Parrot* (1926), the second Charlie Chan novel but the first featuring Chan as the central character, is fictional, there is a striking resemblance between the early life of Chang Apana and the fictional Charlie Chan. In the novel, the honorable detective recalls his early days of serving the wealthy Phillimore family: "In my youth, I am house-boy in the Phillimore Mansion. Still in my heart like old-time garden bloom memories of kindness never to be repaid. . . . Life would be dreary waste, if there was no thing called loyalty."[9] In the book, Chan is taking what he calls "a postman's happy walk on holiday," a leave of absence from the Honolulu Police Department, and performing a personal service: to protect and deliver a precious piece of pearl jewelry for Sally Phillimore, his former employer. Chan's résumé, as described in this novel, closely resembles Apana's career. "Detective-Sergeant Chan, of the Honolulu police," is the way Sally Phillimore introduces him to her friends in San Francisco. "Long ago, in the big house on the beach, he was our number-one boy. . . . Charlie left us to join the police force, and he's made a fine record there."[10] Later in the story, Chan disguises himself as Ah Kim, a cook and houseboy at financial tycoon P. J. Madden's desert ranch, in order to solve the mysterious case of the Chinese parrot. The skills he acquires earlier in life as a hostler certainly come in handy to assist his sleuthing.

Race and class differences notwithstanding, the master and the servant often build a bond longer lasting and more reciprocal than what exists between the employer and the employee in a capitalist enterprise. More than a nexus defined solely by naked self-interest and callous cash payment, the feudal relation, both patriarchal and idyllic, often presumes a lifetime obligation. The same was true with Apana and the Wilders. When he lay dying at the Queen's Hospital in Honolulu in 1933, Apana requested that a member of the Wilder family be present at his deathbed. Not only had he, in the words of Helen Wilder, "looked upon our family as his own," but, more important, he obviously had not forgotten that it was the Wilders, especially daughter Helen, who had set the stage for his debut in white-dominated Honolulu society. The feisty and compassionate Helen gave Apana, a humble coolie's son and an illiterate Chinaman who spoke broken English, a chance to show what he was truly made of.[10]

Helen Kinau Wilder, born in 1869, was the youngest child of Samuel and Elizabeth Wilder. Like her maternal grandfather, Helen was a champion of social reform throughout her life. Her most significant historical legacy is the founding of the Hawaiian chapter of the Humane Society in 1894. Originally called the American Society for the Prevention of Cruelty to Animals, the Humane Society had been formed by Henry Bergh in New York in 1866. After the New York State legislature passed the first law in the United States against animal cruelty, Bergh successfully lobbied many other states to follow suit, and new chapters of the society sprouted like bamboo shoots after a spring rain.

In the early 1890s, Helen Wilder used her family influence and wealth to launch a personal campaign in Honolulu to save what many considered to be dumb animals from ill-treatment. Her initial efforts proved unsuccessful, and the society she founded soon disintegrated. But her luck changed one day in 1896. It was a Sunday morning, and folks were on their way to church on their horses, in buggies, or on foot, all traversing Honolulu's dusty, unpaved streets. Helen was late, and when she got to her church, the sermon had already started. Tethering her mount to the hitching post and hurrying inside, she noticed that something was wrong with the minister's horse: the tongue of the horse was tied to the post! Obviously the animal had a bad habit of jerking its head up, and the minister was trying to teach it a lesson. But now its tongue was nearly cut off by the rope.

Storming inside, the apparently indomitable twenty-six-year-old denounced the minister to the entire congregation before he could finish his prayer. The poor minister slipped out of the church in a hurry and was gone for good. The people at the scene were so impressed that they began to chip in for Helen's cause. Their support ignited a new movement, and the Humane Society was relaunched, this time successfully.[12]

On February 27, 1897, Helen was deputized by the Marshal of the Republic of Hawaii to enforce animal cruelty laws. She now had the legal authority to stop horse owners from beating their animals. Her organization came to the aid of neglected cattle, and it rescued cats and dogs abused by their owners. Helen served without pay, but she and her friends pooled their resources to hire an animal case investigator.[13] That new job went to Chang Apana, the charismatic stableman of Helen's parental home, a former *paniolo* versatile in roping and riding. Thus, the future "Charlie Chan" debuted before the public as the first humane officer in Honolulu.

5

"Book 'em, Danno!"

Hawaiian Humane Society Seal *(Courtesy of Hawaiian Humane Society)*

The undersigned, sensible of the cruelties inflicted upon dumb animals by thoughtless and inhuman persons, and desirous of suppressing same—alike from considerations affecting the well-being of society as well as mercy to the brute creation—consent to become patrons of a Society having in view the realization of these objects.

—Henry Bergh, drafting the first charter for the American Society for the Prevention of Cruelty to Animals

Fans of *Hawaii Five-O*, the longest-running crime show on American television before *Law & Order*, will not forget the signature punch line of Jack Lord's tough character. Like a thunderclap, Steve McGarrett's catch phrase, "Book 'em, Danno!" tolls the death knell for hapless criminals.

Chang Apana's daily routine as a humane officer in the twilight years of the nineteenth century might not have been as colorful and dramatic as that of McGarrett's fast-paced special unit, but his work was full of challenges. These were the early days of animal-rights protection. The newly passed law had yet to reach the hearts and minds of Honolulu's rough-and-tumble public. Stories were legion about early crusaders for animal rights running into stubborn owners who were incredulous that there was a law forbidding them to beat their animals into subordination. The apparently relentless Helen Wilder once stopped Sanford Dole, president of the Republic of Hawaii, on the street to point out a large sore under his horse's collar, and she ended up incurring no small degree of his wrath. On another occasion, "when [she] arrested a Honolulu Rapid Transit driver who had run over a dog with his mule-drawn tram, he sued her for $50,000." She was lucky that time to have both the law and a friendly jury on her side. On her acquittal at the trial, she received a bottle of champagne with a card reading, "From your friends, the Jurymen."[1]

Apana, a *paniolo*-turned-officer, a Chinaman with no standing in the higher echelons of Honolulu society, certainly had his work cut out for him. He might have grown a tough hide as a cowboy, but the general conditions for pets and especially working animals in Honolulu were far from ideal. C. K. Ai, whose memoir provided a glimpse into Apana's childhood life in rural Canton, reflected on the maltreatment of animals in Honolulu at the time:

> The Hawaiians traveled about on horseback. Those who owned horses along the waterfront usually did not pay enough attention to the feeding of their animals, especially with Manini hay costing fifty cents the bundle. During the day they let their horses out to foray for grass; at night, they stabled their horses in a small corral on Maunakea Street. The horses were therefore thin and completely at the mercy of their masters.[2]

Cruelty was by far the norm rather than the exception. Ailing, even cachectic horses were forced to work, overburdened with oppressive loads. Cattle were routinely abandoned in the streets, while dogs and cats were brutalized and sometimes even consigned to cooking pots. So appalling were the conditions for the new urban immigrants that vicious cockfights could hardly seem cruel.

Patrolling the dusty streets of Honolulu, Apana ran into another problem. As a Chinese, he came from a culture that even today believes in the reincarnation of souls. Under the influence of Buddhism, many Chinese believe that a soul after the death of a person will inhabit another body, but there is—and this is the tricky part—no guarantee that the latter will be a human body. If you have done something evil in this life, then in the next life your soul will inhabit the body of a dog, pig, horse, or any animal that belongs to a lower rung on the ladder of species. So, to a Chinese eye, the unenviable life of a working mule is punishment for the bad deeds committed in the last life by the soul currently occupying the body of the mule. This does not mean that the Chinese do not love their animals or pets—just that they would be even less willing to accord rights to animals than an ordinary person walking on the streets of Honolulu. Apana himself might have outgrown such a Chinese belief. As a former *paniolo* and stableman, he obviously loved his horses. Even a run-of-the-mill cowboy would have harbored affection for the steed that was his daily companion. But for Apana to enforce the animal-rights law in Honolulu would put him at odds with the beliefs of the Chinese community.

In *The Chinese Parrot*, Charlie Chan is confronted by his cousin, Chan Kee Lim, and accused of being in cahoots with the "foreign devils," the Americans. "You come in the garb of a foreign devil, and knock on my door with the knuckles, as rude foreign devils do," Lim says, trying hard to conceal his disapproval. "It is too much to say that I do not approve, but I do not quite understand. The foreign devil police—what has a Chinese in common with them?" There is no evidence to suggest that before he wrote the first three Chan novels, including *The Chinese Parrot*, Earl Biggers had known much about Apana's life. The two would not meet until 1928, but Biggers seemed to have an uncanny ability to imagine the complexity of being a Chinese law enforcer in a multiracial society like Honolulu around the turn of the century. In the novel, or, rather, in Biggers's imagination, Chan is made to concur politely with Lim, "There are times, honorable cousin, when I do not understand myself."[3]

In reality, Apana was much less circumspect about toeing the line of "foreign devils." He was as adaptable as his fictional double. By this time, he had acquired the nickname of "Kana Pung," short for "Kanaka Pung," because he looked more Hawaiian than Chinese. Not only was he dark-skinned and always wearing a coat and tie, he had also lost the key marker that defined a Chinaman in the nineteenth century: the queue. Under the Manchu rule, every Chinese man had to grow a queue and let it swing like a pigtail or wrap it around his head like a turban. The punishment for a violator was beheading. No queue, no head. Even though the Chinese immigrants were already beyond the reach of the laws of their native land, most of them had kept the queues like a birthmark for the Celestials.

"I was the only one without my queue in the 80's and 90's," Apana reminisced during an interview in 1932.[4] We do not know when he decided to stop wearing one, but we do get the picture that the humane officer who rode on top of a strong horse and kept a sharp eye out for any sign of abused animals on the streets of Honolulu did not look quintessentially Chinese, nor *was* he an ordinary Chinese. And he meant business.

His meteoric success as an animal-cruelty-prevention officer reveals at once his abilities. In his best month, Apana reported 140 cases: 11 arrests, 8 convictions, 129 "remedied without prosecution," 5 "horses humanely killed," 21 "cases of horses found unfit for work and ordered out of harness," 12 "cases of beating or whipping," 7 "overloading," 18 "driven when lame and galled," 7 "animals abandoned to die." The fines amounted to $84.[5]

Years later, Apana's nephew, Walter Chang, fondly recalled the days when Apana patrolled the streets trying to protect animals as well as children, whose rights and well-being by then also fell under the jurisdiction of the Humane Society: "When you see the horse 'cock-cock-cock' coming, oh those kids they run. 'Apana coming.' You think we can play on the sidewalk like this? You cannot. He get after you, he use whip. The kids, when they hear Apana coming, but he no whip them, he chase them go school."[6]

Walter's recollection, transcribed in the late 1980s, depicts a strict but warmhearted man, an officer who would do more than his share to keep neighborhoods safe and sound, a person well respected by his community:

> The whole public, every time they see Apana, "hey, comes Apana." You see. Baseball game, football game he always down the park. "All right, you know, stand back." You see, everybody like him. He's a very strict man, but not a cruel man. When he use a whip on somebody over there, he tell you "go back, go back—stay back behind the line," you see.[7]

So successful was Apana's work with animals that he drew the notice of the Marshal of the Republic of Hawaii. In August 1898, only days after the islands became a U.S. territory, Apana was officially deputized and joined the Honolulu Police Department.

THE ANNEXATION OF Hawaii by the United States had been long in coming. In the words of President William McKinley, who had been elected to office in 1896, annexation was no new scheme but "a consummation" of a relationship steadfastly maintained for three-quarters of a century. The *Hawaiian Star* concurred with the annexationist president: "Hawaii may be regarded as a bride whose marriage day is not yet definitely fixed, but who is prepared to go through the ceremony whenever the signal is given."[8] In 1898, the signal was, as they say, loud and clear.

Ever since the 1891 death of King Kalakaua—an adamant nationalist who despised the United States—American elements on the islands had been working steadily to usurp Queen Liliuokalani's power. Aided by troops from the USS *Boston* and backed by U.S. Minister to Hawaii John L. Stevens, a coup d'état was staged to force the queen to abdicate in January 1893. Blue-jacketed marines surrounded the Royal Palace while the local armed militia took over the police station and the government building. The queen yielded her authority under protest, expecting that she would be reinstated once the U.S. government learned the facts and undid the action of its representatives. But her hopes were in vain.[9] On July 4, 1894, a date charged with American symbolism, the Republic of Hawaii was inaugurated, ending the indigenous monarchy that had ruled the islands for centuries and bringing Hawaii one step closer to becoming part of the United States.

In the ensuing years, there were heated debates in the American media and the chambers of Congress over the pros and cons of annexation. The stakes were high because the Hawaii question symbolically reflected the United States's position in the world, its role as a rising empire. At a conference held during the World's Columbian Exposition in Chicago, only a year before the founding of the republic, a young Harvard history professor named Frederick Jackson Turner proposed a now-famous Frontier Thesis. Drawing on John O'Sullivan's 1839 idea of "Manifest Destiny," Turner contended, in bold strokes, that the spirit and success of the United States was directly tied to the country's westward expansion. Standing at the juncture between the civilization of settlement and the savagery of wilderness, the frontier was a crucible for the forging of a "unique and rugged American identity," by breaking the bond of custom, offering new experiences, and creating new institutions.[10]

Now that this expansion had reached its continental limit and a new frontier loomed in the Pacific Ocean, would America be ready to take the risk and the responsibility as well as the rewards? Annexing a "noncontiguous territory" like Hawaii would either fulfill or pervert America's Manifest Destiny. Both sides seemed to agree on the economic and strategic advantages of annexation: American shipping and commerce would benefit, and Japan, which was winning its war against Russia at the time and had begun to flex its muscles in the Pacific, could be curbed. But the moral, political, and especially racial pictures were far more complex. The Constitution of the United States had no provisions that legitimated the annexation of territory. Hawaii's people were not only different from those of the United States, they also were considered by the anti-annexationists "unfit to be incorporated" into the great democracy. "Bad blood and bad customs," as one politician put it, "will drive out good." When Congress was debating the resolution on annexation in June 1898, Missouri Congressman James Beauchamp Clark expressed concerns over the indefatigable "jingo bacillus." He warned that the insatiable imperial appetite for a territory swarming with "a rabble of brown men and yellow men" would be ruinous to the Union. What if Hawaii one day became a state? "How can we endure our shame," he asked, "when a Chinese Senator from Hawaii, with his pigtail hanging down his back, with his pagan joss in his hand, shall rise from his curule chair and in pidgin English proceed to chop logic with George Frisbie Hoar or Henry Cabot Lodge?"[11]*

The annexationists eventually won the debate when the United States went to war against Spain in 1898. As the American warships, under the command of Commodore George Dewey, sank a Spanish fleet in the harbor of Manila, America's Manifest Destiny in the Pacific became as clear as the broth of wonton soup. While the 1588 defeat of the Spanish Armada had presaged the rise of the British

* Clark's hypothetical nightmare did, in fact, come true: When Hawaii became the fiftieth state in 1959, "a rabble" of predominantly brown and yellow voters in the islands sent the nation's first Chinese senator, Hiram Fong, to Washington. A self-made millionaire and son of a Chinese immigrant, Senator Fong would take his seat in the congressional chamber across from Strom Thurmond and James Eastland, two staunch segregationist Dixiecrats. The more astonishing fact—that a boy born in Honolulu to a white Kansan mother and a black African father would one day be elected president of the United States—would be simply beyond the pale of Clark's wildest imaginings.

Empire in the Atlantic, the Battle of Manila three centuries later portended the emergence of a new empire in the Pacific. This empire would fulfill the old typology that the center of the world has moved throughout history from the Mediterranean to the Atlantic and then to the Pacific. And if the United States was going to occupy the Philippines, it would make no sense at all to oppose the annexation of Hawaii, which could serve as a base for military maneuvers in the Pacific. After Congress passed the joint resolution by a vote of 209 to 91, President McKinley swiftly signed the bill.

On August 12, 1898, a ceremony for transferring sovereignty was held at Iolani Palace. Marines from two U.S. warships stood by the Hawaii National Guard. On a platform decorated in red, white, and blue bunting, U.S. Minister to Hawaii Harold M. Sewall read the annexation resolution, and white-bearded Sanford Dole, president of the Republic of Hawaii, responded with a short speech, declaring: "I now, in the interest of the Hawaiian body politic and with full confidence in the honor, justice and friendship of the American people, yield up to you as the representative of the Government of the United States, the sovereignty and public property of the Hawaiian Islands." After Sewall accepted the sovereignty, the band played a dirgelike rendition of "Hawaii Ponoi" for the last time as the anthem of an independent nation, and the Hawaiian flag was lowered, "like the fluttering of a wounded bird," as one bystander observed.[12] From then on, the Stars and Stripes would fly in the sky over the flower-bedecked golden statue of Kamehameha the Great. The long spear clutched in his hand, once wielding such mighty power over his kingdom, could no longer protect his land and people from the white haoles.

If for some it was a day of exuberant toasts and libations, for many others it was at best a mixed blessing, a moment marked by sadness and shame, a day filled with fervent prayers. For Chinese immigrants, in particular, annexation meant that America's racist laws and policies would now be fully implemented in the territory, including the 1882 Chinese Exclusion Act as well as the federal law denying their citizenship eligibility. Born in Hawaii, Apana was at least by law a U.S. citizen. His deputization as a police officer was a further boost to his status in Hawaii's hierarchical world.

The police department that Apana joined in 1898 had a unique history inseparable from the islands' tribal past. The institution of Hawaiian law enforcement dates back to the pre-Cook era, under what was called the *kapu* system. In service to the king and senior chiefs, a team of warriors called the *ilamuku* worked as enforcers of law and order. When justice needed to be served, the *ilamuku* would visit the taboo-breaker at night to kill or otherwise punish the person. The *mu* in *ilamuku* means "body snatcher."

The arrival of Christian missionaries in 1820 disrupted the century-old oral-based *kapu* system. With the adoption of writing, the first formal criminal code was published by Kamehameha III on December 8, 1827. Clearly showing missionary influence, the code prohibited murder, theft, gambling, sales of liquor, fornication, prostitution, and drunkenness. On October 8, 1840, the same king published the first Constitution of the Kingdom of Hawaii, in which chapter V provided for the creation of a police force. Under this chapter, the governor of each island was authorized to appoint police officers and constables for the protection of the people and villages. The constitution also provided for a means of identification for the law enforcers: "a stick made round at one end with the name of the king on it." But these constables were still a loose cluster of lawmen. They received no wages; instead, "they were given a percentage of the fine assessed any offender whom they arrested and who was convicted in court." During the boom whaling years, the native constables made so much money by catching fun-seeking sailors committing small indiscretions on shore that the Honolulu police fort was dubbed "The Mint."[13]

A better system of supervision and organization was established, with the creation of the post of Marshal of the Republic of Hawaii in 1847. Under a new law passed in the previous year, the marshal was to choose sheriffs of each island, and the sheriffs were to select their own deputies.[14] This system ran smoothly for more than fifty years and still existed when Apana became a deputy.

The man who handpicked Apana for the police force was himself a local legend. Arthur Morgan Brown had been born and raised in Honolulu. His father, Jacob Brown, a sea captain from New Bedford, Massachusetts, had once been shipwrecked on the rough coast of Siberia with his wife and infant daughter. They spent four months in inhospitable Siberian snows until rescued by a whaling ship and brought to Hawaii. Arthur Brown had received his early education at Punahou, then and now Hawaii's best preparatory school, before graduating from Boston University Law School. In 1893, at the age of twenty-six, Brown had become Marshal of Hawaii. He remained marshal until the position was changed to High Sheriff of the Territory in 1900; he held the latter office until 1906, when he went into private legal practice.[15] An influential man in Honolulu, Brown befriended many illustrious visitors from the mainland, including Jack London and his second wife, Charmian Kittredge London, who often stayed at Brown's house on their many lengthy visits to the islands.

As Helen Wilder's right-hand man at the Humane Society, Apana soon caught the attention of her friend Marshal Brown. Anticipating a raft of changes after annexation and incorporation of Honolulu, law-enforcement officials knew that they would require more manpower. Headed by Brown, the police organization on the island of Oahu in 1898 comprised one sheriff, 23 deputy sheriffs, 172 police officers, and 24 mounted patrols.[16] As the only Chinese, Apana stood out like a tropical bird among the predominantly native Hawaiian officers and the predominantly haole chiefs. But his service was a bonanza to the department, because Honolulu's Chinatown had already become a breeding warren for crime, and the police needed someone who could make inroads into that labyrinthine underworld.

Apana turned out to be a godsend.

6

Chinatown

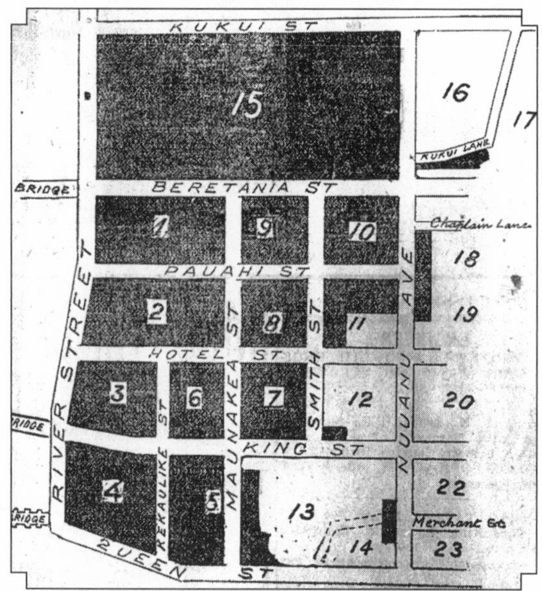

Map of Chinatown, Honolulu, with darkened blocks indicating areas burned in the 1900 fire *(Courtesy of Hawaii State Archives)*

Aromatically and mysteriously and defiantly different from all the rest of [the city].
—Simon Winchester, referring to Chinatown[1]

To call the architecture of Honolulu's Chinatown eclectic in the waning days of the nineteenth century would be a misnomer; in fact, it was filled with "wretched jumbles," as one observer remarked.[2] A warren of structures circumscribed in four directions by River Street, Nu'uanu Avenue, Queen Street, and Beretania Street, Chinatown sprawled over a dozen blocks like an overbuilt checkerboard on the verge of tilting into the harbor. Evolving from just a few waterfront stores in the mid-1850s, it eventually occupied thirty-seven acres, with claptrap restaurants, grocery stores, laundries, bakeries, pharmacies, slaughterhouses, warehouses, whorehouses, gambling parlors, and opium dens in littered, claustrophobically congested streets. When Chang Apana started walking that beat, Chinatown was already a golden phoenix, albeit a sodden and soiled one, having fully sprung from the 1886 conflagration that had, temporarily, eradicated its filth in the eyes of authorities.

The fire of April 18, 1886, was said to have started in a back room located over a Chinese restaurant in a two-story wooden building. Investigators claimed that "about twenty Chinese men were gambling in the room when an argument broke out and in the ensuing scuffle a stove was knocked over and its fire ignited the building."[3] Whether or not this single incident was the true spark of the fire, the allegation jibed well with anti-immigrant sentiments on the island as well as the mainland. The Great Chicago fire of 1871, for instance, had also been blamed on an immigrant: infamous Irishwoman Catherine O'Leary, whose milk cow had allegedly knocked over an oil lamp, starting the inferno that destroyed much of the city. In a popular 1881 comic poem, "The City That a Cow Kicked Over," satirist Anna Matson identified the poor working woman, or the cow (the pun in the title unlikely lost on the readers), as "a sinister and little known 'other' that might in fact bring down the entire city."[4] As the poem runs,

These are the Ruins—sad to tell!
Towards which those Gifts were poured pell-mell,
By rail and river and ocean's swell,
For the beggared people—Lawk-a-deary!
Who had left their homes so bright and cheery,
Wrapped in flames from that Hovel dreary,

That sheltered the famous Mrs. O'Leary,
That milked the Cow forlorn and weary,
That kicked the Lamp, that started the
Fire that burned the City.

Likewise, haole-controlled Hawaiian newspapers invariably linked the 1886 Chinatown fire to what they called "the pernicious gambling habits of the Chinese." The fire caused $1,750,000 in damage to property and left more than 7,000 Chinese and 350 native Hawaiians homeless. The next day, King Kalakaua, who had personally directed the efforts to put out the fire and had even caught a nasty cold in the process, convened a Privy Council meeting to set up a relief fund and make plans for rebuilding. Although the fire was a nightmare for the predominantly Chinese residents, it was, in the words of one historian, "a city planner's dream: some thirty acres of nothing, on which to exercise imagination, artistry, and the financial muscle of the taxpayer." Hawaiian newspapers also embraced the tragedy as an opportunity. "Sweet and Clean," ran a headline, referring to what remained of Chinatown. An editorial in the *Pacific Commercial Advertiser* urged the city to "turn a natural disaster into an ultimate blessing."[5] Despite the overt racism expressed in these reactions, Honolulu, still under the rule of a benevolent monarchy, was far more tolerant than mainland American cities, which often took advantage of disasters like this to further segregate immigrants. After its 1906 earthquake and fire, for instance, San Francisco rezoned the city blocks in an attempt to drive Chinatown to the outskirts or beyond.

According to the rebuilding plan, Honolulu was to survey burned districts, make improvements, widen and straighten streets, regulate construction, and enforce sanitation rules.[6] But bureaucracy and corruption inevitably got in the way of city planning, and the new Chinatown that emerged after reconstruction, as far as fire safety was concerned, was another disaster waiting to happen.

Disaster was not long in coming. In January 1900, less than a month into the new century, the bubonic plague broke out in Chinatown.

With victims marked by swollen lymph nodes in the armpit, groin, and neck, the bubonic plague was considered the same infamous Black Death that had devastated the urban populations of Europe in the mid-fourteenth century. Hawaii's Board of Health embraced the counsel of doctors who claimed that Hong Kong had prevented the plague's spread by burning all buildings in the infected areas, thereby killing plague-carrying rats.

Accordingly, on January 20, the Board of Health brought in fire engines and started burning condemned buildings within infected, quarantined areas. The fire was supposed to be controlled, but it soon got out of hand. By midmorning, the wind changed direction and whipped up gusts, which sent sparks flying everywhere. Adjacent buildings, all constructed of wood save for one church, went up in flames. By two o'clock that afternoon, all of Chinatown had become a doomsday inferno. It was many days before the embers cooled, and the whole area was transformed into a wasteland.[7]

The great conflagration left 4,000 people homeless, with a finan-

CHINATOWN AFTER THE 1900 FIRE *(Courtesy of Hawaii State Archives)*

cial loss in excess of $3 million. The destroyed area, which comprised more than a dozen blocks, was enclosed with a high board fence to prevent the spread of the plague. For months, the formerly bustling thoroughfares and teeming markets stood as quiet as a graveyard. It was forbidden turf. Not even a rat or an animal could be seen moving there.[8]

Rebuilding did not commence until May 17, when the soil was finally pronounced clear of plague bacilli. It took another year or so for Chinatown to regenerate, with improved building structures, sanitation systems, water supplies, and road plans. Regaining its charm and vitality after two calamities, Chinatown was finally ready for the new century—one in which the dominating social issue would be, in the words of W. E. B. Du Bois, "the problem of the color-line."

It is a common assumption that Chinatowns in major U.S. cities around the turn of the twentieth century were breeding grounds for crime and squalor. The mere mention of "Chinatown" immediately calls up images of pestilential slums, opium dens, filthy brothels, and gambling parlors, all crowded by Chinamen with their long, plaited queues and baggy pantaloons. But most people do not know that Chinatowns were also hotbeds for the early twentieth century's Chinese revolution. Honolulu's Chinatown in particular played a crucial role in the birth of modern China. It was here that Sun Yat-sen, founding father of the Republic of China, came of age and struck the first spark of revolution, which would put an end to four thousand years of monarchical rule in China.

Sun Yat-sen was, as noted in chapter 2, born in Hsiangshan District, in the village of Choy Hang, about twenty miles north of Chang Apana's ancestral village, Oo Sack, on November 12, 1866. In 1879, at the age of thirteen, Sun left for Hawaii to live with his elder brother, Sun Mei, who had established himself as a successful businessman. After clerking in his brother's store for a few months, Sun attended the prestigious Iolani School in Oahu. Though he did not know a word of English, he was a fast and diligent learner. When he graduated from Iolani three years later, Sun was second in grammar and received a prize from King Kalakaua. He then studied for a year at Oahu College (later renamed Punahou School), where he learned about Christianity. Shocked that his younger brother might betray Chinese culture for a "foreign" religion, Sun Mei sent him back to China. But the exposure to Western culture and ideas had already left an indelible mark on Sun Yat-sen's mind. As soon as he returned to Choy Hang, he created a scandal by vandalizing the wooden statues of the protective deities at the village temple. Within two years, he would be baptized by an American Congregational missionary, Dr. Charles Hager, in Hong Kong.[9] In his later recollection, Sun would claim Hawaii, not the provincial Choy Hang, as his spiritual hometown. "This is my Hawaii," he said, "Here I was brought up and educated; and it was here that I came to know what modern, civilized governments are like and what they mean."[10] After his first extended stay in Hawaii, Sun would make five more trips to the islands during his lifetime, chiefly to develop political organizations, raise funds, and recruit volunteers to participate in uprisings in China.

On a dark, moonless night in November 1894, a meeting was held at a quiet bungalow on Emma Lane, within a stone's throw of Chinatown. Led by Sun, about twenty Chinese, including C. K. Ai, lined up for an initiation ceremony. One by one, they placed their hands on the Bible and asked God to witness their oath to "drive away the Tartars, recover China for the Chinese, and establish a republic."[11]

This clandestine meeting was a milestone in Chinese history. *Hsing Chung Hui* (Revive China Society), the small organization born on that occasion, would later develop into a strong political party called *Tung Meng Hui* (Alliance Society). In 1911, Tung Meng Hui led a successful uprising, overthrew the Manchu regime (which had ruled China since 1644), and founded the Republic of China. Tung Meng Hui would later change its name to *Kuomintang* (Nationalist Party) and control China for three decades, until 1949. If, as Sun said, "Hua Qiao [overseas Chinese] are the mother of revolution," Honolulu's Chinatown certainly deserves to be called the cradle of modern China.

Sun and his comrades had to keep secret the 1894 meeting, and many others like it, because the Manchu regime had put a price on Sun's head, and Chinese consuls in Hawaii maintained a close watch on his activities. There is no record to indicate that Chang Apana ever crossed paths with Sun, although the fact that Apana had cut off his queue might have sat well with the anti-Manchu revolutionary. But Apana received medals from two visiting Manchu princes in 1910, literally on the eve of the Ching dynasty's collapse, suggesting that Apana probably had stayed above the fray of ideology. When the so-called hatchet wars broke out between Manchu royalists and the Hsing Chung Hui members in Chinatown, Hawaiian newspapers invariably branded these hatchet-wielding, knife-slashing street battles as "tong wars." But no matter whose turf it was, Apana had to walk the most dangerous beat in Honolulu. He was a cop, pure and simple.

7

The See Yup Man

A SEE YUP MAN *(Courtesy of Hawaii State Archives)*

In appearance he looked like any other Chinaman, wore the ordinary blue cotton blouse and white drawers of the Sampan coolie, and, in spite of the apparent cleanliness and freshness of these garments, always exhaled that singular medicated odor—half opium, half ginger—which we recognized as the common "Chinese smell."

—Bret Harte, "See Yup"[1]

CHANG APANA DID not incur any direct loss in the 1900 fire. He was living on Morris Lane, outside of the burn zone. But Chinatown was the epicenter of activity for the roughly 25,000 Chinese living in Hawaii at the time. Apana also knew the neighborhood as a family man, not just as a cop. He enjoyed grocery shopping and going home to cook supper every night after work. The big Chinatown market on Bethel Street was only a few blocks from the police station, and a daily stop for him. Most weekends Apana could be found at Oo Sack Kee Loo, the social club for men from Oo Sack, which was located nearby on Kamakila Lane. It was here that Apana would hold forth, trading stories with other men in the Hsiangshan dialect. Like Charlie Chan, Apana was a teetotaler. But he loved tobacco, Chesterfield being his preferred brand. Blowing smoke rings and sipping a cup of tea, he would listen as others read newspapers to him, catching up on the news from China. After the Chinatown fire, such places were no more. Rebuilding their foundations took far more than timber and brick. Another year would pass before the social life and the network of associations for the immigrants could be revived.[2]

Apana's first marriage was to a Chinese woman, a union that produced a daughter. Both the wife and the daughter, who have remained anonymous in the broken trail of records, went back to China at some point and would never return. According to friends and relatives, Apana would continue to send them money as long as he lived.[3]

Several years later, he married again, this time to one of the sisters of the half-Chinese, half-Hawaiian Lee Kwai family. Since 1882, the exclusionary immigration policies in the United States had created a predominantly bachelor society of Chinese Americans. The ratio of Chinese men to women in 1900 was a lopsided 36 to 1.[4] That same year in Hawaii, only 10 percent of the 18,595 Chinese men had wives living with them, while 20 percent had wives in China, who were not allowed to emigrate.[5] Faced with such a reality, some Chinese men resorted to polygamy, taking common-law wives in China and in the United States, as did Apana.

Apana and his second wife had three daughters: Helen, Victoria, and Cecilia. But his wife died soon after Cecilia's birth, leaving Apana devastated. Though not a particularly handsome man, Apana had undeniable charisma, and his plight garnered the sympathy of the younger Lee Kwai sister, Annie. Apana's marriage to Annie would last until his death.

At the Honolulu Police Department, Apana was secretly known to his colleagues as "the See Yup Man," the cover he used for sting operations. His small physical stature and unassuming looks were an asset that allowed him to blend in. But it was his skill at disguise and his insider's knowledge of Chinatown that made him indispensable during the department's drive to clean up criminal activity bred in newly built neighborhoods and beyond.

Under the leadership of High Sheriff Arthur Brown, Apana worked closely with Deputy High Sheriff Charles Chillingworth, an old-time haole born and raised in Hawaii, and Arthur McDuffie, who was later promoted to chief of detectives. One of the major vices that the police were charged with stamping out was gambling, which happened to be a favorite pastime of many Chinese. It is not an exaggeration to say that even today we Chinese will place a bet on anything. From lottery tickets to card games, anything that involves probability and luck ties into the deep-seated connection between the Chinese psyche and numeracy. Apana's fellow Chinese would even loiter around a fruit hawker's stand and wager on the number of pips in a mandarin orange.[6] The loser would have to pay for the fruit to be shared and devoured, to the winner's satisfaction and the peddler's delight. The peddler might even have a side bet with the shill.

In Chinatown, gambling parlors were as ubiquitous as flies around an outhouse, and proprietors of these rabbit warrens had ingenious ways of foiling police raids. Gamblers at a King Street joint, for instance, had repeatedly eluded capture. Every time the police stormed into this three-story tenement building, they found the gambling room on the top floor as empty as last year's bird nest. On the night of May 20, 1904, the police finally received a tip from an informer and prepared to bust the secret den. This time, the raiding squad split in two, with some men remaining on the first floor and the others heading upstairs. As usual, they found the upstairs room deserted, except for a couple of Chinese sitting calmly, grinning like josses in a temple. One of them even tossed the raiders a Cantonese-accented taunt: "Ya alight, boss?" Their glee was short-lived. A commotion erupted from downstairs. The police on the first floor got full bags as the gamblers slid down a chute through a secret trap door, right into the arms of the officers.[7]

Not always were the police so successful; they needed insider knowledge of all the tricks and stunts that gamblers might pull. This was how Apana became one of the HPD's first undercover cops. Posing as a "See Yup Man" was his favorite disguise. In an 1898 story titled "See Yup," the novelist Bret Harte, who had made a career out of caricaturing the Chinese, speculated on the etymology of the singsong name of his protagonist:

> I don't suppose that his progenitor ever gave him that name, or, indeed, that it was a *name* at all; but it was currently believed that—as pronounced "See *Up*"—it meant that lifting of the outer angle of the eye common to the Mongolian. On the other hand, I had been told that there was an old Chinese custom of affixing some motto or legend—or even a sentence from Confucius—as a sign above their shops, and that two or more words, which might be merely equivalent to "Virtue is its own reward," or "Riches are deceitful," were believed by the simple Californian miner to be the name of the occupant himself. Howbeit, "See Yup" accepted it with the smiling patience of his race, and never went by any other.[8]

Harte's explanation, though colorful, is as believable as a three-dollar bill.

The moniker actually originated from Cantonese. The Hawaiian Chinese generally came from a few districts of Canton Province, including the four often lumped together under the name "See Yup" (meaning, literally, "four districts"): Tai Shan, Xin Hui, En Ping, and Kai Ping. Around the turn of the century, See Yup Men made up more than half the arrivals in Hawaii, and they engaged in professions as diverse as tradesmen, contract labor, laundrymen, and restaurant workers.[9] What stood out in the public's eye, however, was the unique image of the See Yup Man as a street peddler who dangles two baskets of goodies on either end of his shoulder pole. Hawking such wares as fruits, candies, fish, and household items, a See Yup Man was essentially an itinerant merchant who enjoyed the flexibility of a movable kiosk but had to walk long miles and shoulder the weight of his goods. The more he sold, the lighter his burden and the merrier his heart. Coming from a neighboring district but speaking a slightly different dialect, Apana loved to impersonate a See Yup Man in order to uncover the secrets in Chinatown's nefarious underworld.

As described in the prologue, Apana's bravado was displayed on the night of July 12, 1904, when he singlehandedly arrested forty gamblers in one such sting operation. He had reportedly cased the joint for days by dressing as a See Yup Man, circling the blocks and pretending to hawk his wares. On that particular night, he had to walk through four doors and pass four watchmen before reaching the upstairs room. "Apana, like other members of the raiding force at the police station," read the newspaper article about his exploits, "is now so well known that it is impossible for him to go anywhere, at night, in Chinatown undisguised without Chinese missing the cry of 'cop.' The Chinese have posted various men, whose business is to know by sight every known police officer and informer, to watch the entrance to gambling resorts and on the approach of the police raise the alarm in time."[10]

To the crime bosses in Honolulu, bullwhip-toting Chang Apana was a veritable thorn in their side. They slept restlessly, plagued by the need to get rid of this wiry, tenacious Chinaman. As George Kelai, a former HPD officer who had once worked with Apana, recalled in a later interview, "They threaten his life. They wanna kill him because he was spoiling lotta business."[11] Apana once climbed up walls like a pre–Spider-Man sleuth and slipped into an opium dive in the rear of a tenement building on Pauahi Street. The dark room was overcrowded with Chinese dopers. Some, lying in double bunks with their heads and shoulders propped up on pillows, were busy inhaling the bubbling dope's blue fumes through bamboo pipes. Others were sleeping off their debauches, dreaming of Elysium. In corners, on the matted floors, or even under the bunks, these poppy-soaked figures, emaciated and ragged, filled every inch of the room, reeking of stink and squalor.[12]

Apana's surprise entrance did not disturb any of the euphoric dopers, but it did catch the attention of the dive's proprietor and his hired guards. Among the latter was a notorious character named Pak Chew, aka "the man with a rubber stomach." Well trained in martial arts, Chew was said to be able to poke his forefinger through a half-inch board and to crack open a coconut with his bare fist. His biggest stunt was to let anyone make a punching bag out of his stomach; even the most determined puncher would fail to make him blink. On this day, Chew and other hatchetmen were ready for Apana. Using the darkness as cover, four of them snuck up on Apana from behind. The ensuing scuffle woke the dopers and sent them running for the door. A table went over and dark opium wads flew out of a tray, scattering like ping-pong balls on the floor. Apana tried to fight off the stranglehold of Chew's claws while dodging the punches raining down from the other assailants. He finally freed one hand and reached for the bullwhip coiled around his waist. When his opponents saw the dreaded weapon, they fought desperately to subdue him. Together they grabbed Apana, who weighed only 130 pounds, lifted him up, and hurled him out the second-floor window. Miraculously, Apana landed on his feet and walked away like the proverbial cat.[13]

A few days later, a scene unfolded on the dock just after sunset. A few swimmers still dallied in the water that minutes before had shone with the last rays of a golden dusk. A slice of moon now hovered in the corner of the sky. A See Yup Man, seemingly reluctant to call it a day, hung around the pier, dangling two baskets of coconuts on a bamboo shoulder pole. With an oversize straw hat covering most of his face, he wore a sweat-stained blue shirt and a pair of soiled trousers, a man indistinguishable from Chang Apana undercover. A cargo ship had just arrived from Hong Kong, and the HPD had received a tip that there was contraband aboard.

A team of stevedores were coming down the planks, carrying heavy boxes on their backs. Throwing off his disguise, Apana walked toward the stacked boxes. Out of the corner of his eye, he glimpsed a horse and buggy charging at him. It came too fast to dodge, and he was knocked to the ground. As the wheels caught him underneath the carriage, he lost consciousness. The police squad arrived just in time to seize the contraband and arrest the smugglers who had made the attempt on Apana's life. And the See Yup Man survived, with broken ribs and legs, to fight another day.

8

Desperadoes

DURING THE 1900 CHINATOWN FIRE, RESIDENTS WERE EVACUATED UNDER POLICE DIRECTION *(Courtesy of Hawaii State Archives)*

When he goes there, he's going to pick up those fellas, and he never miss.
—HPD Officer George Kelai, referring to Chang Apana[1]

A MASTER OF DISGUISE, Chang Apana shared with his fictional double, Charlie Chan, the exceptional ability to outwit opponents. Like his cinematic twin, he also showed a steely determination to hunt down the guilty. The comparison, however, cannot stretch too far. Unlike the portly detective whose body severely impedes his mobility, Apana had a physical side to his modus operandi. His thin and wiry body was the frame of a rough-and-tumble *paniolo.* His were the early days of law enforcement in Hawaii, when brute physical strength was more critical than fast-flying bullets.

During one raid on a Japanese gambling ring, an expert Japanese wrestler—as if out of a comic—threw Apana and another officer over his shoulder and onto the ground. Weeks later, Sheriff Chillingworth, a tall and muscular man who knew a thing or two about wrestling, tangled with another gambler who turned out to be an even more daunting opponent. According to a *Pacific Commercial Advertiser* article, Chillingworth tackled the Japanese, who was about as tall as he was. "The fellow at once showed that he was skilled in the art of wrestling, for the instant Chillingworth extended his hand to grasp him, the Japanese caught his wrist and turning his back toward him, made as if to throw him over his shoulder." The article continues:

> Chillingworth knows several of the tricks of the profession, and luckily escaped the throw, with the result that both went to the ground together, where each attempted to be the upper man. They struggled, both applying every muscle. Both finally got to their feet, and the scientific battle went on again. Now it was Chillingworth, now it was the Japanese. The deputy attempted to catch the bullet head of the Jap between his hand and elbow and bend it over almost to the breaking point, but so surely as Chillingworth made the attempt he was balked by a counter move at his wrist.

When Chillingworth finally subdued his opponent with an expert throw, he was immediately grabbed by a fellow officer who mistook him for the Japanese, for by this time, Chillingworth's coat had become totally soiled in the hands-on combat.[2]

Apana had his fair share of physical fights. As described in the previous chapter, he was no stranger to being hurled from an upstairs window or run over by a buggy; his encounters with danger and death were hardly infrequent. According to the *Pacific Commercial Advertiser*, Apana had a confrontation in March 1905 with a Chinese named Lee Leon, who subsequently sued Apana "for $2,000 damages on account of assault and battery with fists, hands, and feet." The plaintiff claimed that the officer had beaten him up so badly that he "was laid up for a month and incurred a doctor's bill of $100, besides detention from business."[3] The cause of that fight remains unknown, but Apana's other confrontations, often with criminal desperadoes, are well documented.

Chillingworth once assigned Apana to capture two fugitive lepers. Apprehending lepers was, in the words of John Jardine, a veteran HPD detective, "one of the most controversial duties ever given the police in Hawaii."[4] As Apana later recalled, his knees did quake a little when he got the assignment.[5] Leprosy, one of the oldest known human diseases—in fact, older than the Bible—had long been the unspoken dark secret of Hawaii. Jack London incurred no small fury and animosity from the islanders in 1909 after he published stories about Hawaiian lepers. Leprosy first appeared in the islands as early as 1830. The natives called it *mai pake* (Chinese sickness), because they believed that a Chinese had brought the malady to Hawaii. By 1865, leprosy had become so serious a threat that the Hawaiian legislature passed an act to prevent its spread. In 1866, the year of Mark Twain's visit, the government schooner *Warwick* began transporting lepers to a newly created lazaretto on an isolated peninsula on the island of Molokai. The dreaded journey was Hawaii's Bridge of Sighs, a hopeless one-way trip. Even after Norwegian scientist Armauer Hansen identified the bacillus *Mycobacterium leprae* in 1868, there was still no cure for leprosy and very little knowledge of how the disease was transmitted. By the end of the 1860s, more than a thousand lepers had been sent to Molokai, where they would wait helplessly while the cursed disease slowly ate away their bodies—peeling off their skin, disfiguring their faces, and extinguishing their vision. They would die in agony, forgotten by the world.[6]

Dreading such a horrible fate, some lepers tried to put up resistance or evade capture by the police. The most infamous among these fugitives was a *paniolo* named Koolau. In 1893, immediately following the overthrow of Queen Liliuokalani, the thirty-one-year-old Koolau was helping the haole government round up known lepers on the island of Kauai. When he discovered that he had contracted the disease, he agreed to go to Molokai under the condition that his healthy wife, Piilani, could live with him on the leper colony. But at the last minute, she was held back by government officials, and Koolau leaped overboard and swam back to shore. He then fled with his wife, their young son, and a small band of lepers into the almost-inaccessible Kalalau Valley. For three years, they hid in the valley and resisted capture. Armed with a single rifle, Koolau held off the sheriff's posses and killed several deputies. Then his child succumbed to leprosy, and the grieving couple buried him there. Two months later, Koolau died and was buried in a grave dug by his wife with a small knife. Jack London, whose 1909 story, "Koolau the Leper," has immortalized the character, heard the tale from Bert Stolz, a young crewman working on the deck of his yacht, the *Snark*. Bert's father, Louis H. Stolz, was one of the deputy sheriffs shot by Koolau on the perilous ridges of Kalalau.[7]

The two Japanese lepers Apana had to capture were almost as dangerous as Koolau. The Kokuma couple, who had successfully evaded the police and had put out the word that any attempt to take them would mean a fight to the death, were hiding out on Dillingham Ranch, at upland Kawaihapai.

The posse consisted of Captain Robert Parker Waipa, Apana, and two other officers. They arrived at the foot of the high slopes of Kawaihapai in the early morning. Through a thin layer of fog, they could see, about a mile up, a rambling plantation house. In order to surprise the Kokumas, the team split up and crawled through the brush of the mountainside. It had rained overnight, and the ground was muddy and slippery. Apana was first to get up there, his clothes all wet and soiled. Approaching the house with quiet steps, he surprised Mr. Kokuma coming out of the outhouse, still tying his pants as he walked. At the sight of the officer, Kokuma rushed for a rifle stashed near the front door, but Apana cut him off. The two men immediately became locked in battle. Kokuma somehow got hold of a sickle, and he started slashing and thrusting like a madman. Apana was cut several times across the arms and face. At last he knocked the sickle out of the leper's hand and handcuffed him.

Before his teammates arrived, Apana proceeded to look for Kokuma's wife. The fight outside had already roused her from sleep. As Apana entered the house, she, like her husband, made a run for a rifle leaning against a wall. As she dashed by him, Apana grabbed her flowing hair and pulled her back. Enraged, she turned around and attacked him like a wildcat. The fight, as Apana later declared, was "more terrible than with her husband." When his fellow officers at last came to his aid, Apana was about to "sink with exhaustion." The two lepers, according to a police report, were arrested, taken to the police station, and later deported to Molokai.[8]

Fortunately, unlike Koolau, Apana himself did not contract leprosy, despite such close encounters. But the Kokuma confrontation left a permanent imprint on him. Photos from his later years clearly show a scar above his right eyebrow, a souvenir from the sickle attack.

Apana's bravado and bravery would soon win the confidence of his superiors. At some point, he was promoted from street officer to detective, despite the fact that he had no formal education and could read no English or Chinese. Becoming a detective sealed Apana's fame in the annals of history.

9

Double Murder

HONOLULU POLICE DETECTIVE DIVISION, ON THE STEPS OF THE OLD DOWNTOWN STATION; IN FRONT ROW, FAR RIGHT, IS CHANG APANA. AUGUST 6, 1911

(Courtesy of Honolulu Police Department)

Murder like potato chip—cannot stop at just one.
—Charlie Chan

IN A DRAMATIC chapter of the first Charlie Chan novel, *The House Without a Key* (published in 1925), the young Bostonian John Quincy is chased by a criminal gang late at night through a maze of mean alleys in downtown Honolulu, in a neighborhood known as the

River District. Spanning the banks of the Nu'uanu Stream—crime-infested Chinatown to its west and equally rough sections of Iwilei to its east—the River District appears to the blue-blooded Bostonian as a nightmare:

> There in crazy alleys that have no names, no sidewalks, no beginning and no end, five races live together in the dark. Some houses were above the walk level, some below, all were out of alignment. John Quincy felt he had wandered into a futurist drawing. As he paused he heard the whine and clatter of Chinese music, the clicking of a typewriter, the rasp of a cheap phonograph playing American jazz, the distant scream of an auto horn, a child wailing Japanese lamentations. . . . Odd painted faces loomed in the dusk: pasty-white faces with just a suggestion of queer costumes beneath. A babel of tongues, queer eyes that glittered, once a lean hand on his arm.[1]

John Quincy is almost shanghaied.

Foreshadowing the hard-boiled streets of Raymond Chandler's Los Angeles or the symbolic underworld of Roman Polanski's *Chinatown*, Honolulu's rough neighborhoods, described poetically by Earl Biggers as if he had seen them in an opium-induced dream, were the locus operandi of newly promoted Detective Chang Apana. Even the names of these areas betrayed their infamy: Tin Can Alley, Blood Town, Mosquito Flats, and Hell's Half Acre. Whores, pimps, thugs, footpads, bootleggers, dopers, and gamblers swarmed these blocks of slums. In his later years, with a twinkle in his eyes, Apana would reminisce about the time when the Iwilei section was the mecca of crime and the saloons were wide open. "Those were the days," Apana said, "when the police patrol wagon was busy and the riot calls were frequent."[2]

Sometime in the early 1910s, Apana joined the crime-busting squad, a team led by Captain Arthur McDuffie and comprising half a dozen detectives and officers, including John Kellett, George Nakea,

Oliver Barboza, Kam Kwai, and driver Henry Kualii. Like Steve McGarrett's *Hawaii Five-O* quartet a half-century later, McDuffie's group would cruise around town in a black Packard, scouting for trouble. Their car had a special device that enabled the driver to open all four doors at the same time with a click, and the team members would simultaneously leap out into action.[3]

The cases they took up ranged from bootlegging and drug trafficking to missing persons to homicide. With no need for dramatic embellishment, some of these cases would be readymade material for Charlie Chan novels, or, later, *Hawaii Five-O* episodes. (As we will see later, Biggers was first inspired by an obscure article about an opium arrest made by Apana.) In a few cases, missing persons would never be found, despite the team's efforts; in many others, dangerous jailbreakers would be apprehended and killers swiftly brought to justice.

One year, just as the islands were preparing for the big Independence Day celebration, a popular mainland girl named Frances Ash was reported missing from Waikiki Beach. "The news of the disappearance reached the police station early in the morning," read the front-page article in the *Honolulu Star-Bulletin*, "and Chief of Detectives Arthur McDuffie, together with his aides, John Kellett and Apana, came out in a high-powered machine."[4] They searched every hotel room along the beachfront and sent a team of lifeguards, including the brother of famed surfer Duke Kahanamoku, into the water with canoes and surfboards to look for the girl. The search went on for days, but no trace of Miss Ash was ever found.

While such a case required substantial organizational legwork for Apana and his colleagues, others demanded courage, as in the ability to stare down the barrel of a gun and not blink. Apana once joined McDuffie and Kellett in capturing a Korean who had broken out of jail. "They finally located their quarry, hiding under a house," read a police report. "When he was ordered to come out he replied with a fusillade of shots, one of the shots boring the palm of Kellett's hand, the others missing by narrow margin, the other two officers."

In a lull between shots fired by the escaped felon and the officers, Apana snuck around the side of the house, while the other two officers held the fugitive at bay. When Apana pounced on the prisoner, the Korean's gun went off, sending a bullet into Apana's left arm. He was in the midst of a life-or-death struggle when the other officers came to his rescue and subdued the fugitive. Apana took only a week in the hospital to recuperate from the gun wound.[5]

Newspaper reports confirm that Apana's life was anything but boring. On the morning of May 1, 1913, for example, McDuffie, Kellett, and Apana came upon a scene of utter horror at a Chinese store in Kalihi: The bodies of Lim Ah Kim and his new young wife, Lum Shee, were lying on the floor in a crimson pool. Their throats were slashed, and they had suffered multiple stab wounds. The stench of death permeated the store, which had doubled as a residence. A black cat, too frightened to mew, shivered in the corner behind a rice sack, its dark fur stained with blood not yet coagulated. Mr. Lim had been a prominent merchant. His wife, a beautiful twenty-year-old, was pregnant. The cash register had been rifled, a steel safe damaged, and the bedroom drawers ransacked. The officers also found bloodstained footprints on the floor; some indistinct bloody fingerprints on the bed, the safe, and a number of other places; and a heavy hammer bearing the marks of a bloody hand. All signs pointed to robbery as the most likely motive.

Police followed a tip to a nearby gambling room, located in a small shack within a few feet of the store. Declared by neighbors as the rendezvous of soldiers attached to the military post at Fort Shafter, the room had windows covered with khaki uniforms. The murdered storekeeper reportedly had just been paid for the groceries furnished to Fort Shafter's messes, and he was thought to have carried about $600 in cash. But further investigation by McDuffie and his team found no evidence linking the gamblers to the carnage.[6] Other neighbors, however, told police that four Filipinos had been seen near the store on the day of the murder. A description of the men was given to the police: one of the quartet was said to have been wearing a grayish sweater with a red border.

A break in the case came the next day, when a woman phoned McDuffie with information she thought suspicious but "not very important." She was a roomer at the Elite Hotel and had seen a Filipino man trying to wash some stains off his sweater in a third-floor bathroom of the hotel on the night of the double murder. McDuffie and Apana immediately acted on the tip and located the owner of the sweater, Domingo Rodrigues, a servant in the officers' mess at Fort Shafter.

More than a decade later, when Biggers, at the height of his literary career, visited the islands and met with Apana, "the real Charlie Chan" would tell Biggers about the Rodrigues nabbing. When the two officers first approached him, the suspect withstood the questioning well, until Apana drew attention to Rodrigues's new shoes. "Why you wear new shoes this morning?" became the punch line of the whole case. The suspect balked, turned around suddenly, and tried to escape. Swift as a shadow, Apana beat him to the door and blocked the exit. Rodrigues pulled a knife from his pocket and lunged at Apana. The blade slashed open Apana's sport coat, close to his stomach, but fortuitously it landed in his broad leather belt. When the knife hit the brass buckle, Apana grabbed Rodrigues's right wrist and gave it a twist. Once the knife fell to the ground, the "desperado" was arrested. A subsequent search of Rodrigues's room yielded a pair of blood-soaked shoes, a stained sweater, and a pair of trousers smeared with human blood. Soon the other members of Rodrigues's gang—Miguel Manigbas, Hildago Bautista, and Celestino Manalo—were also arrested.[7]

The four Filipinos confessed to the killing, but each pointed the finger of guilt at others. According to Rodrigues, the four men entered Lim's store on the night of April 30. Miguel asked Lim for some apples, and when the owner turned to get them, Miguel stabbed him in the back. "The Chinese screamed in pain and attempted to defend himself with a hammer. After a desperate struggle he was overpowered and collapsed." Rodrigues declared that Miguel had cut Lim's throat. The storekeeper's wife was roused by his shouts for help. She went to the door, which led to the main part of the store from the bedroom. "She was attacked and slain by a well-directed blow. Her mutilated body was left lying on the floor." The store was ransacked, but the killers were unable to locate any loot other than a paltry $4.20 in the cash register, in addition to a revolver.[8]

Justice was swift for the four Filipinos. They were arraigned on May 22, sentenced to death by hanging (except for Manalo, who had turned state's evidence and was sentenced to twenty years' imprisonment) on June 14, and sent to the gallows three weeks later.[9] In Hawaii, between 1826 and 1913, there were forty-nine documented executions: twenty-six Hawaiians, seven Japanese, five Chinese, four Koreans, four Filipinos, two Puerto Ricans, and one Caucasian. The Caucasian was an illiterate Irish sailor, one John O'Connell. He had jumped ship in 1906 and then kidnapped, murdered, decapitated, dismembered, and disemboweled the son of a prominent haole family.[10]

On the morning of July 8, 1913, about a hundred people witnessed the hanging of the three Filipinos at the Oahu prison yard. As the noose was adjusted and a black cap drawn over his head, Domingo Rodrigues shouted to the crowd in broken English that he was being sent out of the territory because he had accidentally killed a man. These were the last words uttered by any of the trio before the traps were sprung one after another on the scaffold.[11]

Beginning with this triple hanging, Hawaii would see in subsequent years a sharp increase in the executions of Filipinos. Following in the paths of Chinese, Japanese, and Koreans, Filipinos were the latest additions to the plantation workforce, and they were on the lowest rung of the islands' social and economic ladder. From 1914 to 1957, the year Hawaii outlawed the death penalty, twenty-six civilians were hanged, of whom twenty were Filipino. The others were two Koreans, two Japanese, one Puerto Rican, and one Hawaiian; not a single white man was among them.[12] Racism had obviously tipped the scale of justice even in the land of aloha.

After the hanging, members of Honolulu's Chinese community paid $2 to $5 for pieces of the hanging rope, mementos that would grace their ancestral halls for generations to come.[13] They also presented Chief McDuffie with a diamond-studded gold badge, "as a mark of esteem and appreciation of McDuffie's efforts in effecting the prompt capture of the quartette of Filipinos."[14] There was no mention of Apana in this recognition, but Apana's reward would come in a different form—one longer lasting and more glittery than a badge studded with precious stones. For that, we need to look at the character he inspired and the man who created Charlie Chan.

PART TWO

CHARLIE CHAN'S POP

EARL DERR BIGGERS AT HIS PASADENA, CALIFORNIA, HOUSE, LATE 1920S

(Courtesy of Lilly Library, Indiana University)

10

The Other Canton

THE SAXTON HOUSE, CANTON, OHIO *(Photo by author)*

This is America—a town of a few thousand, in a region of wheat and corn and dairies and little groves.
—Sinclair Lewis, Main Street, *1920*

PERMIT ME TO digress just a bit from the story of Chang Apana and Charlie Chan. In the late 1980s, I was a student of English literature at Peking University in China. During my sophomore year, in the spring of 1989, student protests broke out. Calling for democracy and freedom of speech, hundreds of thousands of students paraded through the streets of Beijing and staged demonstrations at Tiananmen Square. A hot-blooded youth despite my academic ambition, I joined the protests and camped out every day at the square, where, only two decades earlier, millions of Red Guards, participating in the Cultural Revolution, had jingoistically waved copies of Chairman Mao's *Little Red Book of Sayings*, shouted slogans, and pledged their allegiance to the Communist Party's Great Helmsman. Our own protests and sit-ins, slightly less frenzied, went on for months, but Deng Xiaoping's Communist regime turned a deaf ear to our political demands.

Hearing about the turmoil in the capital city and concerned for my safety, my family lured me out of Beijing under a false pretense: they sent me a telegram claiming that my mother was "gravely ill." When I arrived in my hometown after a three-day journey, I was surprised to see my mother standing in front of our house, looking as healthy as a newlywed and smiling as if she had just won the lottery. On that same night, June 4, troops and tanks rolled into Beijing, killing hundreds of demonstrators—an event remembered today as the Tiananmen Square Massacre. My mother might have felt fortunate that her youngest son had stayed out of harm's way, but the tragedy in Beijing vanquished my realistic hopes for the future of China. Two years later, I left China and landed in, of all places, Tuscaloosa, an Alabama college town. A comparison is futile here, because nothing like it exists in the People's Republic of China. Imagine, for example, leaving Manhattan and arriving in Manhattan, Kansas; or leaving Moscow and ending up in Moscow, Idaho. This is not to say that the experience would necessarily be unpleasant, but one's mind boggles and the senses gasp in the new air of change.

The Deep South certainly has its charms. Alabama, as Carl Carmer puts it, is "a land with a spell on it—not a good spell, always. Moons, red with the dust of barren hills, thin pine trunks barring horizons, festering swamps, restless yellow rivers, are all parts of a feeling—a strange certainty that above and around them hovers enchantment—

an emanation of malevolence that threatens to destroy men through dark ways of its own."[1] Carmer was a Yankee author who taught English at the University of Alabama in the 1920s, at the height of the Ku Klux Klan reign of racial terror and violence. At the time of my arrival in the summer of 1991, Tuscaloosa had already lost the malevolent luster depicted by Carmer, but the Heart of Dixie still was a shock for me. Having grown up in China's homogeneous society, I felt disoriented (in more ways than one) when I was suddenly thrown into an environment where race, to put it mildly, matters.

Yellow, as I was to find out, is not a visible color in the land where Uncle Tom's cabin used to stand. Three decades after the civil rights movement, the historical effect of biracial segregation remained so strong that Asians, as the third race, simply fell into a vacuum. "You are either a white man or a nigger here," a white Baptist minister once infamously said.[2] While blacks still bore the brunt of racial discrimination, Asians were regarded more or less as foreigners, offscreen Charlie Chans, so to speak. Out of desperation and economic necessity, I opened SWEN, a Chinese restaurant in Northport, just across the Black Warrior River from Tuscaloosa, and worked for two years as co-owner, manager, chef, delivery boy, waiter, dishwasher, and kitchen hand. Owning a fast-food joint did nothing to enhance my social status; on the contrary, it had the opposite effect. Ever heard of Chinese haute cuisine? It does exist, but Chinese food in great swaths of America is still associated with the image of lowdown chop-suey joints that once populated Western mining towns in the nineteenth century, and it's tough to shake off that stigma in the Deep South. As a result, during those two years when I made soup and fried rice every morning, delivered boxes of steaming food all over town, and mopped the tiled floors of my restaurant's kitchen every night after closing, I constantly felt like a bottom-feeding fish, one that cannot see the light of day in the muddy pond of America.

After struggling for three years in Alabama, I decided to go to graduate school rather than return to China.

In August 1994, having imbibed these new American vapors for a few years, I felt emboldened enough to make my first cross-country drive from Tuscaloosa, a town of tall pines and red clay now adjacent to the newly chosen American headquarters of Mercedes-Benz, to Buffalo, a faded remnant of a bygone age of Rust Belt glory, where I would study for my Ph.D. in English. Behind the wheel of my beat-up blue Toyota hatchback, I came upon a sign that said, "Canton," about an hour after I passed Columbus, Ohio, on Interstate 71. For a second, I thought I was dreaming, but then my senses got hold of me. Still, I was intrigued by the Chinese-sounding name and hit by the distinct feeling of nostalgia, a yearning for a homeland I had once sworn I would never return to. Chinese names, I knew, were popular among those who were planning American towns in the early nineteenth century. The China trade, which had brought silk, porcelain, and tea from Canton to America, would inspire, as it turned out, the adoption of "Canton" as the name for more than thirty American municipalities. Another thirty, if not more, were dubbed China, China Grove, China Hill, or Pekin. Was this because nineteenth-century settlers wished to create an ersatz feeling that they were in some exotic, faraway land?[3] This was the case for Ohio's Canton, which was founded in 1805. When surveyor Bezaleel Wells divided the town's land, he named it after the Chinese city as a memorial to John O'Donnell, a China trader he had admired. O'Donnell, who owned a Maryland plantation also named Canton, had been the first person to transport goods from China to Baltimore.

At the time of my first cross-country drive, I did not know much about Charlie Chan, let alone Earl Biggers. Nor was I aware of the uncanny coincidence that, while the original Charlie Chan had grown up in a rural village near Canton, China, the man who created the fictional Chinese detective hailed from the woods near a city that bears the same name—though the two Cantons are, both geographically and symbolically, at opposite ends of the earth. Only later would I learn that Biggers had spent his childhood near Canton, Ohio, tumbling in the weeds and haystacks among the oak groves and cornfields that were whizzing by my Toyota on that summer day in 1994.

In order to make ends meet as a graduate student in Buffalo, I had to work busy shifts as a deliveryman at a Chinese restaurant and as a security guard at a Korean-owned wig store in a rundown neighborhood. To relieve the tension, I went book-hunting at estate and moving sales on weekends. Once the so-called Queen City of the Great Lakes but then a virtual ghost town whose population had diminished either through aging or migration to warmer climes, Buffalo had much to offer in antique furniture and used books. At an estate sale inside an old Victorian house, I found something curious—a twin set of Charlie Chan books: crimson, hardboard-covered reprints with five novels bound into two volumes, handsomely titled *Charlie Chan's Caravan* and *Charlie Chan Omnibus*. There was even a handwritten dedication in red wax pencil in one of the volumes: "Hurry and get well, Irving, we miss you—Eddie and Jean." A get-well gift from many years back—the Grosset & Dunlap reprints dated to the 1940s. I took the "caravan" and "omnibus" home for a dollar each. I never figured out who Irving was and whether Charlie Chan had facilitated the desired recuperation, but I became an avid fan of Charlie Chan, renting all the movies I could find at video stores, reading all the novels, and constantly looking out for those cheap paperbacks as well as rare editions.

Through increasingly obsessive research, I found out more about the man who had created Charlie. Earl Derr Biggers was born on August 26, 1884, in Warren, Ohio, "a town of a few thousand," as Sinclair Lewis would put it. After the Revolutionary War, the fledgling state of Connecticut was bizarrely extended to include a 120-mile-long strip of land in northeastern Ohio, which would become known as the Connecticut Western Reserve. In 1798, a wealthy man named Ephraim Quinby bought 441 acres of land in the area and built the town of Warren. Nestled close to the pencil-sharp state line dividing Ohio from Pennsylvania, Warren was called "the Capital of the Western Reserve" in the early nineteenth century. But the epithet rang hollow; two nearby cities, Cleveland and Pittsburgh, with their proximity to lake and canal shipping, stole the limelight and emerged as the Ohio Valley's crown jewels. Warren was left with the false grandeur of its nickname and the emptiness of the promise. At the time of Biggers's birth, Warren had become a prosaic midwestern town of mills, factories, and foundries. With elm-lined streets and a Romanesque courthouse facing a public square of war memorials and patriotic bunting each Fourth of July, it could have been plucked from a Sinclair Lewis *Main Street* tableau. Earl's father, Robert J. Biggers, was a hardworking factory engineer who was able to provide handsomely for his wife, Emma, and their only child.[4]

Like so many children who are born into provincial insularity but grow up to become writers or artists, young Biggers was inspired by his avid reading. Newspaper comic strips were his favorite. According to his recollection, "As soon as I could write connected sentences, I appropriated the characters from Palmer Cox's *Brownie* series, and wove about them many startling romances." He would read these aloud to his grandmother.[5] Aspiring to be a writer, he founded at Warren High School a monthly magazine titled *The Cauldron.* "The first issue led off with a grandiose editorial in which I split three infinitives," he later reminisced, "and used the verb *lay* where I should have used *lie.* I was an author!"[6]

Despite his imaginative powers, young Biggers was stubbornly wedded to the truth. A case in point: There was a haberdashery on the street where the Biggers family lived. Business was dropping off, and the owner hired some New York City slickers—in recollection, Biggers called them "Potashes and Perlmutters," after two Jewish shopkeepers featured in comic novels by Montague Glass—to help boost the sales. The haberdasher also knocked on Biggers's door and asked if the young boy would like to work as a clerk on Saturdays. Biggers agreed and began work on a Saturday. By noontime, the gentlemen from the big city took the haberdasher aside and demanded that Biggers be let go, for he had been, like the boy in "The Emperor's New

Clothes," telling the truth about the goods to the customers and ruining the tall tales of these New York shysters. He was summarily fired.

Years later, when Biggers was working as a columnist for a Boston newspaper, he again got sacked, in his own words, "for telling the truth in my dramatic criticisms." Such unfortunate run-ins with truth-telling made Biggers wiser, and he decided to stick to storytelling from then on. Reflecting about them at a dinner party that celebrated the successful production of his first play in Pittsfield, Massachusetts, in 1912, he said, "It was about that time I decided to let Truth remain crushed to earth—and become a liar on a large scale. And from that time on I have lied ambitiously with what success—the future alone will prove."[7]

Young Biggers seems to have explored his local area and was well acquainted with the two nearby cities, Canton and Akron, as his later writings would show. In *Charlie Chan Carries On* (published in 1930), Ohio, a state that has produced a passel of U.S. presidents, figures prominently in a murder mystery on a global scale. The plot involves a killer stalking a U.S. tour group on a globe-trotting vacation. The first victim—a Detroit automobile executive—is found strangled in a ritzy London hotel, his hand clutching a key marked "Dietrich Safe and Lock Company, Canton, Ohio," obviously inspired by Diebold Safe and Lock Company. Two prominent characters, Akron rubber baron Elmer Benbow and his socialite wife, Nettie, seem to be an amalgamation of Seiberlings and Firestones—founding families of the Goodyear and Firestone tire companies, respectively. Other connections to Canton and Akron include characters named Spicer and Everhard, both recognizable names of pioneering clans in the early days of the Buckeye State.[8]

The most interesting connection is perhaps the name of Charlie Chan. It is a common assumption that Biggers based his character on Chang Apana. But during the time Biggers was growing up, there actually was a Chinese man named Charlie Chan living in Akron. Listed as thirty-six years old in the 1900 census, Chan was, coincidentally, also born around 1864 in Canton, China. He immigrated to the United States as a teen and opened a laundry in Akron in the late 1890s. Located downtown at 40 North Howard Street, the laundry doubled as Chan's home. He ran the business for about fifteen years.

It turns out that Akron's Charlie Chan, unlike many Chinese immigrants in the nineteenth century, was not a mute witness to history. According to a 2008 report, the *Akron Beacon Journal* interviewed Chan for an article about China's Boxer Rebellion, the uprising against foreigners and imperialistic aggression in the summer of 1900. The unnamed reporter, almost as if anticipating Biggers, decided to write in dialect: "Chan was busy, but he came out from the rear of his laundry long enough to be interviewed. He was told that there was a great war raging in China and he was asked to say something about the Boxers. 'War! War in China! Me no care. Me safe. China bad. Me no go back China.' "[9]

While the passage of more than a century prevents us from knowing whether this was Chan's real sentiment, we do know that his laundry was in a prominent location within walking distance of the train station. If Biggers hopped aboard the Pittsburgh, Akron & Western Railroad, he could get to the big city in two hours, and he would not have missed seeing Charlie Chan's laundry sign.

In September 2008, fourteen years after I first saw the road sign for Canton on my northward migration, I flew from California to Indiana to examine Biggers's papers in the Lilly Library at Indiana University in Bloomington. Arriving on a Saturday, aware that the library would not open until Monday, I rented a car at the Indianapolis Airport and drove toward Ohio's flatlands for a closer look at the state that now is called not only "Mother of Presidents" but also the venerable home of Charlie Chan's creator.

As soon as I left the airport, I encountered an almost impenetrable thunderstorm. The skyline disappeared, and all I could see was the blurred glow from the taillights of the car immediately in front of me. Having becoming inured to the seemingly eternal California sunshine, I had forgotten how nasty a Midwest storm could get, and how quickly it could dissipate, especially at that time of year.

After a night at a most hospitable Super 8 Motel in Columbus, I resumed my pilgrimage the next morning, the first day of autumn. Driving past the vast cornfields, where remaining patches of green were melting fast into a sea of gold, I could sense that the sun, having already surpassed the Hawaiian Islands, was inching across the equator on its annual journey south.

My first stop of the day was Canton, that American homage to my homeland. Arriving in the midwestern town on a Sunday morning was like walking into a deserted movie set during a production break: all the props were there, but not a soul was to be seen. Downtown Canton, with its cluster of concrete office buildings, limestone churches, and faded Victorian houses, reminded me of Buffalo, albeit on a smaller scale. I remembered the many Sundays when I had strolled down Main Street to Buffalo's deserted business district, where the stony façades of the Guaranty (now Prudential) Building, the Central Terminal, and art deco City Hall stood as mute witnesses to the glorious past of that Queen City. Canton's Saxton House interested me most, for I knew it had a tragic connection to Buffalo. The three-story Victorian, on the corner of Market Avenue and Fourth Street, had been the home of Ida Saxton McKinley and her husband, William McKinley, before his 1896 election to the presidency. In September 1901, while attending the Pan-American Exhibition in Buffalo, President McKinley was assassinated by anarchist Leon Czolgosz. The grieving First Lady withdrew to her home in Canton, where she died just six years later.

Biggers had just begun his junior year at Warren High School at the time of McKinley's assassination. After lying in state at both Buffalo's City Hall and the White House, the president's body was returned for burial to Canton, where thousands of Ohioans lined up to pay final tribute to their native son. We do not know whether Biggers, living only forty miles away, was one of the mourning spectators.

In the unlikely event that he wasn't, he most certainly was riveted by the dramatic events unfolding in his corner of the world. Judging from his choice of postgraduate careers in journalism and playwriting, we can be sure that affairs of such magnitude and theatricality as McKinley's death and the execution of his assassin would leave an indelible impression on his young mind and give him an early taste for the thrill of dramatic news.

My next stop was Akron. In particular, I was hoping to find the site where Ohio's Charlie Chan had run his laundry business. Prior to the trip, I had used Google Earth to pinpoint the spot and map out the route, but when I arrived at 40 North Howard Street, all I saw was a deserted lot covered with litter and weeds, adjacent to a barn-like building with boarded-up windows. At a fork just down the road stood a nightclub with a comical façade: the one-story brick structure was painted in spotted yellow, rather like SpongeBob SquarePants. Not too far from the highway, I did see railroad tracks, and I imagined what a curious sight it would have been for a nineteenth-century train passenger to spot Mr. Chan's laundry sign in the American heartland.

My final stop of the day was Biggers's birthplace. To get to Warren, I had to turn east on Interstate 76 and then take a local westbound highway a few miles past Youngstown, where in 1878 a twenty-one-year-old young man named Clarence Darrow had just begun his law practice. Darrow would one day become the nation's first celebrity attorney, but his spectacular career would end after losing the infamous Massie Case in Hawaii in 1932, a trial so sensational and so rife with racial tension that it might be called a harbinger of the O. J. Simpson trial more than sixty years later.

Driving on rural Route 82 after Youngstown, I was reminded of the landscape in a realist novel. Sleepy hamlets broke the monotony of expansive corn- and wheatfields. In and out of view came huddled wooden houses framed by their parched lawns and broken wooden fences, and occasionally, trailers scattered behind clumps of oaks and birches. Barns and silos, standing back from the road in the shrouds of thin mist, looked like giant toys in a fairyland dreamed up by some kids but then abandoned after play.

Warren, I must confess, was not quite as grand as I had imagined. The proverbial "diamond in the rough" label would not apply to the hometown of the famous author. As a midwestern town on the fringe of the Rust Belt, Warren showed evidence of decline. Traces of old mills and factories, formerly the lifeblood of the city, were still visible here and there, including a rusty railroad track that seemed to have been unused for years. Pothole covers protruded in the middle of the streets as if someone had started to pull them up for scrap metal but was interrupted.

After driving around aimlessly, I turned to the Warren–Trumbull County Public Library. Perched at the corner of a main thoroughfare and shaded by large elm trees, the library was a two-story brick building with a huge parking lot. At the entrance were racks of used paperbacks and dusty VHS tapes for sale, all donated or withdrawn from circulation. Approaching the information desk, I asked the bespectacled, white-haired librarian about their E. D. Biggers holdings.

"Who?" she responded.

I repeated the name and emphasized that Biggers was a hometown author and the creator of Charlie Chan. This, however, elicited little enthusiasm, though my mention of Chan made her look at me as if I were a Chinese orphan looking for my long-lost father. She typed in the name on a computer terminal to search the database. There was only one item, a Chan novel, in the library's collection, and it was a 1970s paperback reprint. Sensing my disappointment, she kindly told me that I might be able to find something in their History and Genealogy section upstairs. She pointed her finger toward the stairwell in the middle of the room, "That lady up there knows a lot and might be able to help you. But her office is closed on Sunday."

This information put an abrupt end to my pilgrimage of the day. Feeling let down, I decided to reward my efforts with a Chinese buffet before returning to Bloomington. When I got to the Golden Dragon (I'm always amazed by the names given to Chinese restaurants in

America), situated in the corner of a nondescript shopping plaza with a red Chinese paper lantern hanging outside its door, it was already past the lunch rush. Only a few diners still lingered in this forty-seat dive. A big man, with a sizable beer belly, a ponytail, and wearing a black Jesus and Mary Chain band T-shirt, was brooding over his dessert—chunks of cantaloupe and almond tofu. When he lifted his face and stared at the stacks of empty plates and crumpled napkins that mounted before him, he smiled like a hunter pleased with game birds bagged on a good day. Two teenage girls, one wearing braces, were giggling over their fortune cookies. The food trays on the buffet island had run low at this hour. I filled my plate with the few remaining options and sat down near the window.

Wistfully chewing my beef broccoli and *kung pao* chicken, I looked out at the deserted parking lot and the red lantern swinging gently in the breeze. The lantern had the Chinese character "Fortune" printed upside down on its sides and a bunch of golden threads tied together as the tail. The Chinese word for "upside down" is *dao*, a homonym of the word for "arrival." "Fortune" written upside down means "fortune arrives." This lantern reminded me of a curious object in Sinclair Lewis's *Main Street* that appears only once in the book and remains unelaborated by the narrator. Early on in the novel, Carol Milford, a footloose, free-spirited student at Blodgett College, is invited to dinner at the home of Mr. and Mrs. Marbury, a couple who epitomize small-town America's cultural narrowmindedness and smug complacency. The Marburys, writes Lewis, "regarded Carol as their literary and artistic representative. She was the one who could be depended upon to appreciate the Caruso phonograph record, and the Chinese lantern which Mr. Marbury had brought back as his present from San Francisco."[10] Like a recording of Enrico Caruso's voice, the Chinese lantern is a perfect souvenir from cultural excursions that nice folks take outside God's Country. Mr. Marbury is an insurance salesman; he must have bought the lantern in San Francisco's Chinatown on a business trip. A gilded bust of a half-naked laughing Buddha would be too pagan for a Bible-worshipping home like the Marburys'. A lantern is just about right.

Looking at the lantern, I had an epiphany. Until then, I had tried to track the story of Charlie Chan from one Canton to another, from colonial Hawaii to postbellum Ohio. I had always wondered how Biggers, a boy from a milquetoast midwestern town, could have created a Chinaman so alive, so distinct from almost everything in the environment that had nourished his creator. I realized, sitting in that aromatic dining room of the Golden Dragon, that Charlie Chan to Biggers's Ohio was the Chinese lantern to Lewis's Main Street America. He was a whiff of Oriental mystique blown into the insular flatland.

On my way back to Indiana, I turned on the radio. A previous driver, or maybe the rental-car company, had preset the radio to local Christian music and gospel stations. In between evangelical rock and Bible readings, there was also some news, which that day was dominated by America's economic meltdown. The national unemployment rate had just breached the 6 percent mark. Even though that percentage remained a far cry from Great Depression levels, the economists interviewed on the news broadcast all predicted that the worst was yet to come. It seemed inevitable that the rural area through which I was driving, hit hard by the Great Depression, would again bear the brunt of the impending recession. That 1929 stock-market crash, as we will see, caused no small havoc in the life of Earl Biggers.

It was sunset when I crossed the state line separating Ohio from Indiana. Shadows grew longer on the ground. The last rays of the sun burned the edges of the clouds as hot as prairie fire. Over the western horizon, atop rolling hills, the sun hung like a Chinese lantern, about to be extinguished.

11

Lampoon

The Signet House, Cambridge, Massachusetts

(Photo by Ian Graham, courtesy of the Signet Society)

I park my car in Harvard Yard.
—Anonymous

At the dawn of the twentieth century, Harvard University was in the waning days of what George Santayana termed "The Genteel Tradition." The unprecedented forty-year reign of President Charles W. Eliot would come to an end in 1909, six years after Earl Biggers graduated from Warren High School and matriculated at Harvard. In 1910, William James, father of American psychology and pragmatism, would die. Santayana himself, who had arrived on a horse and buggy as an immigrant from Spain, would resign from his professorial post at Harvard in 1912 and leave the country for good.

Popular culture, eroding the gap between the high-brow and the low-brow, also made inroads into the ivory tower alongside the Charles River. Biggers, a youngster from the cornfields of Ohio—short, round, dark, bright-eyed, with a friendly manner—was perhaps the best representative of such a change of tide in American culture. The freshman Biggers showed little passion for the classics. In a few years, the fifty-volume *Harvard Classics*, edited by Charles Eliot, would grace the living rooms of American households aspiring to the upper class. Eschewing the likes of *Dr. Eliot's Five-Foot Shelf*, Biggers preferred Rudyard Kipling and Richard Harding Davis, and he considered Franklin P. Adams a better storyteller than Oliver Goldsmith. A professor who heard his announced preferences in class bemoaned, "Oh, Biggers, Biggers, why will you be so contemporary?!"[1]

On evenings when refined Harvard classmen were reciting Keats and Shelley to one another over shots of brandy and sherry, they would jokingly urge Biggers to leave the room.[2] When T. S. Eliot, who entered Harvard during Biggers's senior year, was contemplating the composition of "The Love Song of J. Alfred Prufrock," in which the speaker is too nervous to approach women at a party, Biggers had an entirely different literary treatment of the same topic. In Eliot's poem, now a classic of high modernism, the "I," balding and thin-limbed, lingers forever over a series of self-doubting questions. Drafts of Eliot's poem were subtitled "Prufrock among the Women." Like Biggers, who might have taken the name "Charlie Chan" from a Chinese-laundry sign seen in his younger years, Eliot was said to have borrowed "Prufrock" from the name of a furniture company called Prufrock-Littau, near his birthplace in St. Louis. But Eliot added a mysterious initial "J" to the fictional name "Alfred Prufrock," just to make it sound more aristocratic. By contrast, Biggers's winning entry in the Harvard *Advocate*'s contest for the best "pick-up" story was sold to a popular magazine for $25.[3] The future creator of Charlie Chan and the future Nobel laureate were obviously traveling on different express trains with not the slightest chance for a collision.

Even though his unabashed populist taste clashed with the literary pretensions of his classmates, Biggers joined several Harvard societies, including the prestigious Signet Club and the *Lampoon*. The Signet, founded in 1870, is perhaps the most elitist literary society on campus. Dedicated to the production of literary work (and later expanded to include music), the Signet boasts members who have defined twentieth-century American literature: T. S. Eliot, Robert Frost, James Agee, Wallace Stevens, Norman Mailer, John Updike, and John Ashbery, to name just a few. The *Lampoon* is decidedly a more mixed bag—its notable alumni include William Randolph Hearst, George Santayana, Robert Benchley, John Reed, Conan O'Brien, and numerous writers and producers of television comedies and feature films that have defined American humor: *The Simpsons, Saturday Night Live, Seinfeld, Futurama,* and *The Office.* The odd mixture in these clubs of future movers and shakers—high and low, elitist and populist—speaks volumes to the reach of the rising popular culture, and to the fact that what Thorstein Veblen called the "leisure" class was losing its monopoly over American culture.

I will never forget my first and only visit to the Signet Club. It was in the spring of 2000, my first year as an assistant professor at Harvard. One of my students, a Signet member, had invited me to lunch at the clubhouse on Dunster Street. Entering this charming yellow house tucked away on the fringe of Harvard Square, I noticed an ornate coat of arms, the signet ring, hanging above the front door, where I was greeted by my student and her fellow club members—all undergrads except for one elderly gentleman, who was standing in the far corner of the reception room. When I inquired about the many dried roses hanging on the walls, my student explained that it is the tradition of the society that, upon induction, each new member receives a red rose. It is to be kept, dried, and returned to the society upon publication of the member's first substantial literary work. Particularly noteworthy to me was T. S. Eliot's rose, enshrined with his original acceptance letter.

My student, a six-foot blonde whose elegant manners recalled, say, a charming heroine from a Henry James novel, continued to give me the inside scoop about Signet treasures, such as the famous pipe once owned by William Faulkner that allegedly had been used by some adventurous undergrads to smoke pot; and the handwritten poem by Santayana in the ladies' room, to which I would, regrettably, have no access.

It was right at this point that the elderly, gray-haired gentleman approached me and introduced himself: "How do you do? S— P—, '57." The diplomat part of me quickly shook his extended hand, and I was able to reply, "Hi, I'm Yunte Huang. Nice to meet you." But part of me was rendered speechless. Other than the formulaic, "Nice to meet you," applicable almost anywhere, I had no answer to his self-introduction, "S— P—, '57." For me to say, "Yunte Huang, Peking University, '87," would have seemed to challenge the niceties of the exchange. His "'57" meant that he was a member of the class of 1957, of no other university than Harvard. What's absent in the information should be taken for granted—an implied context of parlor talk, hidden as a secret badge but obvious as daylight. Making this succinct self-introduction, either he assumed I was a member of that community who would be able to reply without ambiguity—"Yunte Huang, '87"—or he was putting me on the spot by asserting his insider status.

Between our introductions, a gulf had opened, a chasm so wide that neither of us seemed able to reach over and compare notes from our life experiences. He was, as I learned from our brief chat in the room decorated with dried roses, a retired English professor from a Boston-area college. He had been educated at Harvard, both as an undergrad and as a graduate student, and had been a member of the Signet since his junior year. By contrast, I suspect I must have seemed to him like a social upstart, getting to where I was not by entitlement but by luck—or, even worse, by the magic wand of equal opportunity.

He could hardly have known that I grew up in a rural village in southeastern China, and even though I went to China's foremost university, that would not, in many American eyes, really count. After I came to the United States, the cycle seemed to repeat, as I started almost from scratch in Tuscaloosa. I am one of those against whom Henry James, the old gentleman's favorite author, once warned in his 1905 Bryn Mawr College commencement speech—those immigrants who came to this country, sat up all night, worked mindlessly, and then played to their hearts' content with the English language. The fact that I was assigning my Harvard undergraduates to read Gertrude Stein—"a horrible prose writer," as the old gentleman sniffed—was perhaps proof enough of my poor taste and the sad state of Harvard education. As for other authors whose work I taught in my classes, such as Maxine Hong Kingston, Theresa Cha, and Leslie Marmon Silko, he had either never heard of them or would not, as he remarked with polite nonchalance, "consider them as worthy of studying."

James's friend, Henry Adams, whose classic autobiography reveals, among other things, how a Harvard education failed to prepare him for new problems in American culture, put his finger on the issue when he described a scene of symbolic confrontation between immigrant upstarts and people of entitlement like himself. Returning in 1868 from Britain, where he had gone to avoid fighting in the Civil War, Adams, upon witnessing the influx of immigrants at the docks in New York City, described his feelings this way:

> One could divine pretty nearly where the force lay, since the last ten years had given to the great mechanical energies—coal, iron, steam—a distinct superiority in power over the old industrial elements—agriculture, handwork, and learning—but the result of this revolution on a survivor from the fifties resembled the action of the earthworm; he twisted about, in vain, to

> recover his starting-point; he could no longer see his own trail; he had become an estray; a flotsam or jetsam of wreckage; a belated reveller, or a scholar-gipsy like Matthew Arnold's. His world was dead. Not a Polish Jew fresh from Warsaw or Cracow—not a furtive Yacoob or Ysaac still reeking of the Ghetto, snarling a weird Yiddish to the officers of the customs—but had a keener instinct, an intenser energy, and a freer hand than he—American of Americans, with Heaven knew how many Puritans and Patriots behind him, and an education that had cost a civil war.[4]

Just as James was alarmed by the mongrel crowds of dagos, Danes, Irish, and the like, Adams felt defeated by the hordes of Yiddish-sputtering Eastern European Jews who seemed much more energetic and instinctual than he, "American of Americans," who surely ought to be entitled to the leadership and hence championship in the game of life.

On that particular day at the Signet clubhouse, I felt neither humiliated nor proud in front of that old gentleman, "S— P—, '57." I was actually thinking about Earl Biggers, an author I had then just started researching. I wondered how Biggers, a so-called rube from Ohio, felt when he first stepped in the club that eventually elected him an honorary member in 1908, a year after his graduation. Biggers, a small-town midwesterner whose parents had had to borrow money to send him to college, had to climb the social ladder through sweat and toil, unlike the two blue-blooded Henrys.

The lunch was delicious, like most Harvard meals, until they get repetitious and tiresome. Garden salad, grilled salmon, scented rice, and broccoli that was always a bit overcooked. And the conversations continued to be polite and jolly, like well-polished English prose.

12

The Raconteur

EARL DERR BIGGERS, CIRCA 1907 *(Courtesy of Lilly Library, Indiana University)*

Boston, a city most cultivated, where much more English words are put to employment than are accustomed [in Honolulu].
—Charlie Chan[1]

A YOUNG BUCKEYE boasting no family wealth or connection, Earl Biggers went through ups and downs in his immediate post-Harvard career. His first job was as a night police reporter at the *Cleveland Plain Dealer*, a regional newspaper that he had read every morning while growing up in nearby Warren. He did not last long at the job, however: he was a better storyteller than a journalist. The newspaper, said the editor, had no room for "a reporter who embroiders fiction out of facts," especially when the facts were police matters.[2]

After another brief stint as a manuscript reader for the Indianapolis-based Bobbs-Merrill Company, which would later become his publisher, Biggers returned to New England in February 1908 and worked for the *Boston Traveler.* His daily column, improbably titled "The Fact Is," contained humorous absurdities, sharp-tongued opinions, and sarcastic doggerel. In one of the columns, he penned what he called a "lyrical roast," a stinging review of current "worst bestsellers":

Peter de Puyster Blottingplad,
Who wrote "Marie, the Subtle Sinner,"
Does his best work when he has had
Plenty of artichokes for dinner.

Mabel Redink, the "girl Dumas,"
Who mingles history with fiction,
Reads books on corporation law
In order to improve her diction.

Samuel Gray, who's all the rage,
Because he has convulsed the nation,
Spends hours before a monkey's cage
Gathering loads of inspiration.

Thus is our sadness put to rout
By publishers—kind gloom dispellers—
Who send us cheery news about
The folks who write the worst bestsellers.

These Alice-in-Wonderland–like rhymes are followed by odds and ends of ordinary absurdities accompanied by deadpan witticisms:

> A Brooklyn man ate a beer glass—which no doubt proved food for reflection.
>
> Six playing cards on a plain board mark a grave in Arizona. Doubtless by this time the late lamented realizes the error of holding more than five cards in a poker game.
>
> "The Good Old Ways"—It gives us great joy to note that a citizen of Mingo, Okla., whipped out his trusty six-shooter the other day and shot the mustache off another citizen. The good old ways are too seldom practiced for the inspiration of the "deadeye Dick" school of fictionists. We sincerely hope that the gentleman who lost the mustache appreciated the fact that he had a mighty close shave.[3]

These humorous punch lines were undoubtedly great practice for Biggers's later work on Charlie Chan novels, in which the wisecracking detective charms readers with such rat-a-tat one-liners as "Truth, like football—receive many kicks before reaching goal," "Some heads, like hard nuts, much better if well cracked," and "Every maybe has a wife called Maybe-Not." A famed raconteur among his friends and associates, Biggers took whimsical pleasure in running the humor column, a job he compared to making faces in church. "It wasn't fun," he said, "and it offended a lot of very nice people."[4]

The same went for his next job as the drama critic at the paper. His lampooning reviews annoyed many theater owners and producers, who demanded he be fired. The axe eventually fell on a snowy night in January 1912. Coming back to Boston after a Christmas visit in Warren, Biggers learned that the newspaper had been sold. The editor handed him a cigar.

"What does this mean?" asked Biggers. "Was I fired last Saturday, or is it next week?"

The editor, who had been trying to protect him but had now failed with the new owners of the paper, told him that it was last Saturday.[5]

Walking out of the office and into a blizzard, Biggers was wearing an elegant fur-lined coat with a handsome raccoon collar, which he had just bought on the installment plan.

"I didn't have a job," as he recalled later in a mock interview with a parrot on the eve of publication of his second Charlie Chan book, *The Chinese Parrot*, "but I had the coat."[6]

Indeed, Biggers had even more ambitious personal plans: he was contemplating marrying Eleanor Ladd, a New Englander who wrote columns for the *Boston Traveler* under the pseudonym of Phoebe Dwight.

Back in his room at Mount Vernon Place, a Harvard graduate with no immediate prospects of employment yet with a bride in the offing, Biggers knew he had to earn his living somehow. So he sat down near the coal grate and started to write his first book, *Seven Keys to Baldpate*. Like many authors who are quite particular about how and where they write—Truman Capote wrote lying down, with a typewriter and a cigarette and coffee; Gertrude Stein wrote behind the wheel of her Ford Model T; and Vladimir Nabokov wrote standing up and on index cards—Biggers had his own eccentricities. He liked writing with moonlight streaming in through the casement (one wonders now if he only wrote when the moon was out) and a sack of peanut brittle at his elbow. Working at a pace of one chapter a day, and rewriting at the same speed, Biggers was no procrastinator: he finished the mystery novel in less than three months. Two weeks later, Bobbs-Merrill, where he had once worked and had befriended editor David Laurance Chambers, agreed to publish the book.[7]

Set in a deserted summer mountain resort in the dead of winter, *Seven Keys to Baldpate* involves an author, Billy Magee, who seeks peace and quiet in order to write his next book. Up to this point, Magee has been a successful writer of popular literature, "the sort of novels sold by the pound in the department stores . . . wild thrilling tales for the tired businessman's tired wife—shots in the night, chases after fortunes. Cupid busy with his arrows all over the place! It's good fun, and I like to do it. There's money in it."

"But now and then," Magee confesses, "I get a longing to do something that will make critics sit up—the real thing. . . . Now I'm going to go up to Baldpate Inn and think. I'm going to get away from melodrama. I'm going to do a novel so fine and literary that Henry Cabot Lodge will come to me with tears in his eyes and ask me to join his bunch of self-made Immortals."[8]

The reference to Lodge, one of Harvard's most famous graduates, a symbol of the upper echelon of American culture in the early twentieth century, represents a dilemma that would dog Biggers throughout his writing career. As much as he claimed to prefer popular literature to the classics, despite his evident knack for pulp or popular writing, Biggers also wanted to be a "serious" writer. In his twenty-fifth Harvard class-reunion report, the then-famous author admitted, "I am quite sure that I never intended to travel the road of the mystery writer."[9]

In *Seven Keys to Baldpate,* Magee is merely a mouthpiece for his creator, who at this time was forced by necessity to write nothing but a novel that would be sold by the pound in the department stores and newsstands. And the mystery at Baldpate Inn is the kind of thrilling tale that its protagonist ostensibly tries to avoid writing: explosions in the dark, a large fortune sought after by dueling parties, love at first sight, secrets buried in the bosom of time—all the ingredients for concocting a fantastic melodrama. But this proved lucrative, providing enough money to enable Biggers, with an advance from Bobbs-Merrill, not only to keep the fur coat on his back but also to marry Eleanor Ladd and move to a posh neighborhood in Pelham Manor, just outside of New York.

"What saved my life and my coat," as Biggers confessed to the interrogating parrot, "was *Seven Keys to Baldpate*!"[10]

On the day of his debut novel's publication in 1913, the *Boston Herald* published an article, "Earl Derr Biggers Now a Real Novelist," which contains a piece of Biggersian doggerel in honor of the former humor columnist, the famed Boston raconteur:

Biggers, once dramatic critic,
Without the usual fetters,
Has just earned the title
Of, "Jack-of-all letters."

A poet, critic, humorist,
And writer of short stories,
His novel which has just appeared,
Has dimmed his other glories.

The book has humor, love and strife,
But one above all deserves the prize,
A character that's drawn from life
She is not hard to recognize.[11]

Anticipating the golden age of the American mystery, *Seven Keys to Baldpate*, which predates S. S. Van Dine's *The Benson Murder Case* (1926) by more than a decade, was an instant success. Reviews were glowing, as exemplified by the one in the *New York Times*: "The brilliant way in which Mr. Biggers has written this, his first novel, gives promise of excellent things to come in his career as a novelist."[12] Dramatic rights were acquired by George M. Cohan, who produced the play on Broadway for a 320-performance run. At least seven film adaptations of the novel were subsequently released, making Biggers a nationally known author.[13] But these "fifteen minutes of glory" were no comparison to the lasting fame that Charlie Chan would bring him.

13

The House Without a Key

J. A. Gilman residence, Honolulu, 1908. The house was part of the hotel run by Mrs. La Vancha Gray in the 1920s

(Photo by L. E. Edgeworth, courtesy of Bishop Museum)

In an obscure corner of an inside page, I found an item to the effect that a certain hapless Chinese, being too fond of opium, had been arrested by Sergeants Chang Apana and Lee Fook, of the Honolulu Police. So Sergeant Charlie Chan entered the story of The House Without a Key.

—E. D. Biggers

After the success of *Seven Keys to Baldpate,* Earl Biggers continued to produce at a rapid pace. In addition to writing short stories for the *Saturday Evening Post,* the *American Magazine,* and the *Ladies' Home Journal,* he also published *Love Insurance,* a romantic farce, in 1914, as well as *Inside the Line,* a play. *The Agony Column,* a novella, quickly followed in 1916. Particularly during the last part of that decade, he concentrated on drama and collaborated with a number of Broadway and Hollywood producers. "At one point," according to his biographer Barbara Gregorich, "Biggers was writing and rewriting two plays a day, attending rehearsals for one in the morning, the other in the afternoon."[1] Such a frantic pace wreaked havoc with his health, resulting in a doctor's recommendation of a long, therapeutic vacation, which took him to the sandy white beaches of Waikiki.

Biggers arrived in Hawaii in April 1920, at a time when narcotic arrests and police graft scandals were making daily headlines in Honolulu newspapers. Standing at the crossroads of the Orient and the United States, Hawaii was then a major transit point as well as a destination for opium traffic. According to an article published in the *Honolulu Advertiser,* dope traffic had the islands in its "horrid grip." By 1924, an estimated two thousand addicts in Hawaii were spending $6,000,000 a year on opium.[2]

"Officers Seize Opium; Arrest Two Japanese," screamed one headline in the *Advertiser* on March 9, 1920. In this bust, federal agents confiscated $7,200 worth of opium. On April 7, Arthur McDuffie's team uncovered another opium store and found eight tins of narcotics in a garage. But the biggest headline of those spring months was the arrest of Moses Needham, captain of police in Honolulu, for failure to report opium confiscation. According to an *Advertiser* article on March 23,

> Captain of Police Moses Needham was arrested at 3 o'clock yesterday afternoon on Alakea Street by United States Marshal

> J. J. Smiddy on a warrant which charges that on the evening of February 29 he took from a Chinese six tins of opium and $211 in cash and failed to make a report of the matter to the headquarters. Needham's bond was fixed at $1,000 and he was released from custody at 3:45 o'clock yesterday afternoon at the marshal's office.[3]

These news stories clearly made an indelible impression on Biggers, who was relaxing his nerves under the tropical shade in Waikiki: his first Charlie Chan novel, *The House Without a Key*, involves opium trafficking on the islands. Biggers stayed for three months at one of the cottages run by Mrs. La Vancha Maria Chapin Gray on the beachfront that still bears her name—Gray's Beach. When he first checked in, Biggers asked for the key to the cottage. "What key?" retorted Mrs. Gray. In those days, no one in Waikiki would lock their doors. That brief exchange—culture shock for a Bostonian—would eventually inspire the title of the first Chan book.

Biggers was sitting on the lanai of the cottage one evening. A tropical scene of "semi-barbaric beauty" unfolded in front of him that he would later immortalize at the very beginning of *The House*:

> It was the hour at which [Miss Minerva Winterslip] liked Waikiki best, the hour just preceding dinner and the quick tropic darkness. The shadows cast by the tall cocoanut palms lengthened and deepened, the light of the falling sun flamed on Diamond Head and tinted with gold the rollers sweeping in from the coral reef. A few late swimmers, reluctant to depart, dotted those waters whose touch is like the caress of a lover. On the springboard of the nearest float a slim brown girl poised for one delectable instant. What a figure! . . . Like an arrow the slender figure rose, then fell; the perfect dive, silent and clean.[4]

A strong swimmer who can make a silent, clean dive turns out to be the novel's cunning killer. As the crepuscular light faded in front of his lanai, Biggers saw the looming outline of a ship anchored not too far offshore. It must be a ship that had arrived too late to be cleared by the authorities to dock at the harbor, he thought, just as would occur with the steamer that transported the murderer in his novel. The ship's lights twinkled in the vast expanse of a darkening ocean. To his left, Biggers could see the winking yellow eye of the Diamond Head Lighthouse; to his right, the lanterns of swift Japanese sampans glowed intermittently. An idea suddenly dawned: he could write a novel in which the killer swims ashore from a ship docked beyond the harbor, commits the murder, and then swims back to the ship, allowing himself a perfect alibi. The idea became the basis for the murder plot in *The House Without a Key.*

At this point, there was still no Charlie Chan. If the novel was conceived on the cool lanai of Mrs. Gray's beach cottage in the spring of 1920, Chan would be born four years later in the stuffy, hushed reading room of the New York Public Library—or at least that was Biggers's claim.

Having conceived of this new novel, the workaholic Biggers could no longer sit still, despite his doctor's orders to take a break from writing. He tried to rent an office in downtown Honolulu, but the owners of the few vacant places looked askance at Biggers—renting a business office in order to write a book must have been too exotic an idea for the locals. So Biggers ended up renting a room in a dingy, small hotel. Having put his desk and typewriter there, Biggers would go downtown at about nine every morning, feeling good in the cool breeze. It got hot fairly quickly in Honolulu after sunrise, and before long the harsh sun would sap his energy. The hotel room had a cozy double bed, and the temptation to lie down for just a few minutes was too strong. A nap that started out in midmorning often ended in time for supper, a tropical phenomenon experienced by John Quincy in *The House,* when he first landed in the lotus land: "Lazy, indeed. John Quincy had a feeling for words. He stopped and stared at an agile little cloud flitting swiftly through the sky—got up from his chair to watch it disappear over Diamond Head. On his way back to the desk he had to pass the bed. What inviting beds they had out here! He lifted the mosquito netting and dropped down for a moment."[5] Thanks to the distracting balmy weather in Hawaii, Biggers did not complete his Waikiki murder mystery there. Instead, he finished it at a lodge in Williamstown, Massachusetts, during the long, cool summer of 1924.

Upon returning from Hawaii, Biggers continued to mull over the Waikiki novel while selling his short stories. On October 23, 1922, Biggers wrote to his editor, Laurance Chambers, "I am, as I told you on the street, contemplating a novel—a mystery story of Honolulu, which I have promised to the *Post* as a serial. I have it pretty well worked out, and expect to go to work on it after I do about two more short stories to get money enough to keep me going while engaged with the longer work."[6]

Two months later, Biggers reported to Chambers on the progress of the novel, which he tentatively titled *Moonlight at the Crossroads*:

> I enclose a couple pages regarding the projected novel. . . . I have a large list of characters with which to play here—army people, traders, planters. An Americanized Chinese house boy—the star pitcher on the All-China baseball nine—the lawyer for the opium ring—an Admiral of the Fleet who introduced the two-step to Honolulu society in the days of King Kalakaua—an old Yankee from New Bedford who came over sixty years before, married a Hawaiian, and never went back—a champion Hawaiian swimmer—beachcombers—the picturesque keeper of a run-down hotel at the beach who is the younger son of a good English family—his daughter—the president of the Japanese bank.[7]

Still there was no Charlie Chan.

In the winter of 1923, Bigger's health declined again, leading him to consider selling his house in Pelham Manor and moving to warmer climes for good. As he wrote to Chambers, "I haven't been quite so well as I hoped, but it may be that the coming of spring will finally drive out the poisons, tonsorial and otherwise. . . . The doctor says I should never spend another winter in a cold climate, and was particularly anxious for me to get away this winter. But alas, no one has bought the house, and I seem marooned here."[8]

The following summer brought good news. "The house deal was settled yesterday," he wrote Chambers on June 11. "Hope to have a good manuscript for you soon." While en route to the Berkshires, his usual summer hideout, Biggers stopped by the cavernous New York Public Library to do some reading and refresh his memories of Hawaii. It was in the Reading Room, while browsing through a big pile of Hawaiian newspapers, that Biggers supposedly came across the name of Chang Apana: "In an obscure corner of an inside page, I found an item to the effect that a certain hapless Chinese, being too fond of opium, had been arrested by Sergeants Chang Apana and Lee Fook, of the Honolulu Police. So Sergeant Charlie Chan entered the story of *The House Without a Key*."[9]

If Biggers's claim were true—that the chubby Chinese detective, who would charm millions of readers and viewers, was indeed born in that dim, hushed Reading Room—then Charlie Chan certainly would be in good company. As the Great Depression sent the country into a tailspin, a generation of 1930s writers, including Henry Miller and Henry Roth, would make good use of the Reading Room inside Forty-second Street's stone-lion–guarded building. Chan would have been born, then, in the same cradle as Miller's semiautobiographical alter ego and Roth's Yiddish-speaking David Schearl.

Biggers's claim, however, cannot easily be verified.

My careful examination of the two major Honolulu newspapers being published in 1924, the *Honolulu Advertiser* and the *Honolulu Star-Bulletin*, failed to locate the item Biggers specified. The only Apana news that came close was an equally obscure item published in the "Brevities" section of the *Honolulu Star-Bulletin* on June 6, 1924, which reads: "Arrested for Assault—Tong Kut Lum, alleged assailant of Lai Tin, was arrested this morning by Detective Chang Apana.

He is alleged to have struck Lai yesterday, following an altercation. Both men were members of a Chinese theatrical company. Tong was charged with assault and battery."[10]

While it is quite possible that Biggers was reading newspapers from previous years, further evidence from the Honolulu Police Department seems to suggest that Biggers might have conflated events. In a letter dated February 26, 1979, Earl Thompson, assistant chief of the Administrative Bureau of the HPD, replied to a query from a Mr. J. David Reno of Boston, Massachusetts, obviously a Charlie Chan aficionado: "Regarding your inquiry of Lee Fook, complete checks of our records fail to identify this person as a police officer with our department."[11]

Without Lee Fook, the news item regarding Apana and Lee making opium arrests appears as fishy as the fifth ace on the river.

Just to be thorough, I also checked with the New York Public Library and was told by their research division that there was no record of the library's having subscribed to either of the two Hawaii newspapers before 1924.[12]

Such a legalistic attachment to historical facts may take just a bit of the romance out of Charlie Chan's legendary birth. But, regardless of how or where Biggers first encountered Chang Apana, it is certain that Charlie Chan arrived fully formed—like Athena emerging from the head of Zeus—in that distant summer of 1924. And those summer months, as we will see, proved to be a turning point in American culture.

PART THREE

CHARLIE CHAN, THE CHINAMAN

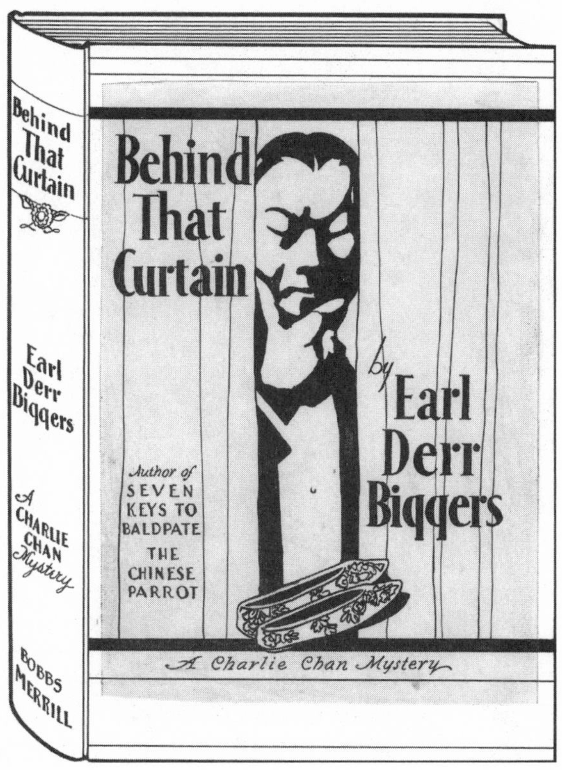

COVER DESIGN FOR E. D. BIGGERS'S *BEHIND THE CURTAIN*, 1928

(Courtesy of Lilly Library, Indiana University)

14

The Heathen Chinee

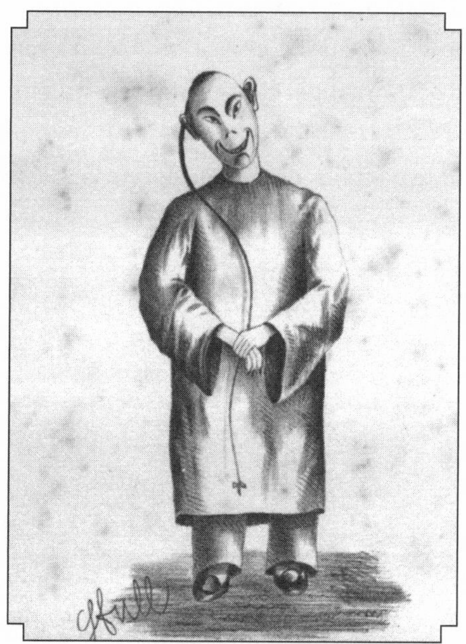

BRET HARTE, "THE HEATHEN CHINEE," 1870

(Courtesy of Poetry and Rare Books Library, University at Buffalo)

Ching Chong Chinaman sitting on a fence
Trying to make a dollar out of fifteen cents.
Along came a choo-choo train
Knocked him in the cuckoo brain,
And that was the end of the fifteen cents.
—American children's jump-rope song from a less-enlightened era

THE FIRST CHARLIE Chan book, *The House Without a Key*, was published in March 1925. A quarter of the way through the novel, Charlie Chan makes his inconspicuous entrance as a minor character, literally as "the third man," the Chinaman:

> As they went out, the third man stepped farther into the room, and Miss Minerva [Winterslip] gave a little gasp of astonishment as she looked at him. In those warm islands thin men were the rule, but here was a striking exception. He was very fat indeed, yet he walked with the light dainty step of a woman. His cheeks were as chubby as a baby's, his skin ivory tinted, his black hair close-cropped, his amber eyes slanting. As he passed Miss Minerva he bowed with a courtesy encountered all too rarely in a work-a-day world, then moved on after Hallet. . . . "But—he's a Chinaman!"[1]

Chan's idiosyncratic, ungrammatical speech is apparent from the beginning. His first utterance, like a newborn's first cry, is unmistakably pidgin English: "No knife are present in neighborhood of crime."[2]

Charlie Chan's unceremonious debut is a prelude to his tortured legacy in American culture, a legacy that at once endears and offends millions. Depending on one's persuasion, Biggers's first description of Chan yields very different readings. Chan is "fat," which means he is either chubby and lovable or oafish and ugly. He walks "with the light dainty step of a woman," which means he is unobtrusive and agile, or he is effeminate. His close-cropped black hair suggests his neatness or lack of status. "His amber eyes slanting" projects a sense of realism to some, but a degree of repulsion to others, since "slanting" sounds pejorative. His courteous bow indicates politeness to some but docility to others. Chan's ungrammatical speech, reminiscent of fortune-cookie witticisms, sounds hilariously funny to many but racially parodic to others.

All things Charlie, it seems, are radically polarizing.

But we are already ahead of ourselves in the story. Let us backtrack and look more closely at Charlie Chan's literary debut, at a time in the mid-1920s when the Chinaman grabbed the attention of the reading public and film audiences nationwide, an era when American children chanted, "Ching Chong Chinaman sitting on a fence," as they jumped rope on the streets, the chant being their first exposure to "Oriental" culture.

Charlie Chan, as we know, was not the central character in Biggers's early conception of the novel. Biggers originally opened the story in San Francisco, and two newspapermen there, both white, were the designated heroes. "Sergeant Charlie Chan entered the story of *The House Without a Key*," as Biggers recalled, "supposedly a minor character, a mere bit of local color."[3] As the writing progressed, however, Chan modestly but firmly took the spotlight. And as soon as Biggers's story ceased running serially in the *Saturday Evening Post*, "Say—when are we going to have another Charlie Chan story?" became a popular cry, suggesting that Biggers's magazine excerpts had an electrifying effect on readers, in much the same way that earlier Americans had crowded the New York docks to get the next installment of a Dickens novel more than half a century earlier.

A flood of letters descended on Biggers following the selections in the *Saturday Evening Post*, and his readers clamored for Charlie Chan to take center stage. Biggers soon realized that Chan, like a monkey on his back, could never be killed off. Much as Sherlock Holmes dogged Sir Arthur Conan Doyle (in fact, Doyle even tried to kill him), Charlie Chan would remain forever linked to his creator.

But why? What made Charlie Chan so appealing to the reading public of the 1920s? Why was he so popular on the silver screen in America and beyond? The answer lies, I believe, both in the kind of Chinaman that he is and in the kind of nation that America had become during the "tribal twenties."

Just as Biggers's first descriptive passage portends the troubled legacy of Charlie Chan, Miss Minerva's exclamatory sentence, "But—

he's a Chinaman!"—led by a conditional "but" and broken by a dash—identifies the peculiar aura of his appeal. Indeed, a *Chinaman*, a loaded word in the English language, can now be applied to one character who can carry the whole burden of being a Chinaman.

So, what is a Chinaman?

Actually, we cannot ask such a timeless question, for the image of the Chinaman changes over time. As an English word, *Chinaman* was first used as a neutral term for a Chinese male. Occasionally, it even referred to a man from the Far East, including Japanese and Korean men. Unlike *Frenchman* or *Englishman*, however, the connotation of *Chinaman* turned negative in the nineteenth century as anti-Chinese sentiments gained currency in the United States.

As in Hawaii, Chinese immigration to the United States had been sporadic before the mid-nineteenth century. Sightings of individual Chinese were reported in Pennsylvania as early as 1785, but it was the discovery of gold at John Sutter's mill in 1848 that suddenly spiked the number of Chinese arriving in North America: 325 in 1849, 450 more in 1850, 2,716 in 1851, and 20,026 in 1852. By 1870, there were about 63,000 Chinese in the United States, and 77 percent of them were in California.[4]

At first, Chinese were welcomed in America, especially in California, which had just joined the Union in 1850. The Chinese arrivals were routinely reported in the *Daily Alta California* as increases to a "worthy integer of population." In his January 1852 address to the state's legislature, Governor John McDougall praised the Chinese immigrants as "one of the most worthy class of our newly adopted citizens." But as the competition in the goldfields became more intense, the tide soon turned against the Chinese, and these affectionate feelings turned sour. Only four months after Governor McDougall's speech, the California legislature, at the urging of white American miners, passed the foreign miners' license tax, which required a monthly payment of three dollars from every foreign miner who did not desire to become a citizen. Since a 1790 federal law had already denied "nonwhite persons" their eligibility for citizenship, Chinese miners became the main target of the tax. From 1852 to 1870, California collected $5 million from the Chinese, a sum representing between 25 and 50 percent of the state's revenue.[5]

When Ralph Waldo Emerson wrote in 1854, "The disgust of California has not been able to drive or kick the Chinaman back to his home"—a sentence cited today by the *Oxford English Dictionary* as the first recorded American use of the word *Chinaman*—the New England sage seemed well informed about the events in the Wild West. White Californians' resentment and discrimination toward the Chinese were indeed on the rise. The following stanza from a gold rush song entitled "California As It Was and Is," published by John A. Stone under the pseudonym "Put" in 1855, precisely captures the anti-Chinaman sentiments of the era:

I remember, I remember when the Yuba used to pay,
With nothing but a rocker, five hundred dollars a day.
We used to think 't'would always last, and would, with perfect ease,
If only Uncle Sam had stopped the coming of Chinese.

Here the blame of an idealized California's passing was laid on the newly arrived, the Chinese FOBs ("fresh off boats"), whose presence in the foothills along the Yuba River was a common sight in the heyday of the gold rush.[6]

Other songs of the period caricatured the Chinaman directly, mimicking his pidgin speech, such as this one entitled "Hong Kong":

My name is Sin Sin, come from China
In a bigee large shipee, commee long here;
Wind blow welly muchee, Kick upee blubelly
Ship makee Chinaman feelee wellee queer.
Me fetchee longee a lillee gal nicee
She com longee to be my wife
Makee bigee swear to it all her life.[7]

This kind of pidgin imitation of Chinese, while enriching the English language with such neologisms as "ching chong," "ka-ching," and "chop chop," would grow into a time-honored tradition in American popular literature. Eventually, it would become fodder for Earl Biggers as he crafted the idiosyncratic speech for Detective Charlie Chan.

As Emerson keenly observed, however, white resentment and ridicule did not stop the Chinese from coming, in part because there was such great demand for cheap labor, especially in the West. In February 1865, the Central Pacific Railroad hired fifty Chinese workers to lay the tracks for the transcontinental line going east from Sacramento. The company had made the hire on a trial basis, because construction boss James Harvey Strobridge, "a tough Vermonter of Irish ancestry," considered the Chinese men too small—most of them weighed scarcely a hundred pounds. Started in early 1863, the work on the western end of the transcontinental line had become too hard and dangerous as the tracks reached the Sierra Nevada, and many of the Irish workers had quit. Desperate to find replacements, the company's superintendent, Charles Crocker, decided to try the Chinese, who had been driven out of the minefields. A former gold miner, Crocker was a huge man who had a reputation for roaring "up and down the track like a mad bull." He reminded Strobridge that although they might not look as sturdy as the young lads from Ireland, the Chinese "had built the longest stretch of masonry in the world": the Great Wall.[8]

Reluctantly, Strobridge gave the fifty men their so-called Chinaman's chance but soon found them to be, as Crocker put it in a report, "nearly as equal to white men in the amount of labor they perform." Leland Stanford, owner of the company, also praised the Chinese workers as "quiet, peaceable, industrious, economical—ready and apt to learn all the different kinds of work." By the fall of 1865, the company had hired 3,000 Chinese, and more were on their way from Canton. Within two years, 12,000 Chinese were employed by the Central Pacific, representing 90 percent of the entire workforce. These thousands of men contributed physical labor, technical skills, and even their lives to a railroad project that eventually would transform America. One observer of the construction site described the Chinese workers as "a great army laying siege to Nature in her strongest citadel. The rugged mountains looked like stupendous ant-hills. They swarmed with Celestials, shoveling, wheeling, carting, drilling, and blasting rocks and earth." The winter of 1865–66 was particularly brutal, with a record forty-four snowstorms that piled snowdrifts more than sixty feet high. Avalanches, a constant threat on the job, buried camps and crews. Not until the following spring would the thawing corpses be found, standing upright, "their cold hands gripping shovels and picks and their mouths twisted in frozen terror."[9]

In the spring of 1869, the railhead crossed into the salt flats of Utah and pushed toward Promontory Point, where the Central Pacific Railroad would meet the Union Pacific Railroad coming from the east with its Irish crews. As the two grading gangs—"Irish workers heading west and Chinese workers heading east"—drew close, competition turned ugly. Resenting the Chinese for taking their fellow countrymen's jobs, the Irish, themselves often targets of ethnic bias, "secretly placed a charge of blasting powder so that it blew up Chinese workers." On May 10, 1869, the last rail was laid down, the last spike—a golden spike—was rammed home, and engines of the two companies moved forward until they touched. To commemorate the completion of the first railroad to span the North American continent, the cheering crowd gathered for an official photo. In this picture, however, there is not a single Chinese face.[10]

The end of the transcontinental railroad project also meant unemployment for the thousands of Chinese workers. Many of them went to San Francisco, a city that, in the words of Will Rogers, "was never a town." After growing exponentially during the heat of the gold rush, San Francisco by 1870 had developed into "a locus of industry," becoming the ninth-biggest manufacturing city in the United States. The Chinese population of the city had also soared, from 2,719 in 1860 to 12,022 in 1870. Most Chinese immigrants in America crammed into crowded urban neighborhoods and made their living in retail business, service, vice, or entertainment within the confines of Chinatowns. In San Francisco, they also fanned out and sought employment in the city's booming manufacturing industry. By one account, nearly half of the workers in San Francisco's factories in 1872 were Chinese.[11]

For employers, the advantage of hiring Chinese laborers was all too obvious: they were cheaper than white workers. Just as Mark Twain had pointed out in one of his Hawaiian letters, "You will not always go on paying $80 and $100 a month for labor which you can hire for $5." While Twain's numbers sound a bit exaggerated, it is a fact that by hiring the Chinese workers, the Central Pacific Railroad was able to reduce its labor costs by one-third. The competition from cheap Chinese workers produced white-labor resentment, as it had done previously in the mines. Racial antagonism was further exacerbated by the business owners' practice of using Chinese replacements as a wedge for breaking strikes led by white workers. As a result, anti-Chinese riots erupted constantly in the American West, a region already notorious for violence.

While it is impossible to know how many Chinese were murdered or brutalized in isolated areas where the rule of law was a phantom, some of the worst outrages did not go unnoticed. The earliest recorded urban anti-Chinese riot took place in 1871 in Los Angeles, then a sleepy town of 5,728 souls, when twenty-one Chinese were shot, hanged, or burned to death by white mobs. One historian lists thirty-one California urban centers that experienced burnings of Chinese stores and homes and expulsions of Chinese residents in the 1870s. During an 1880 riot in Denver, a mob shouted death threats to the Chinese, overwhelmed the eight police officers on duty, and destroyed most of the buildings in Chinatown. Then they wrapped a rope around the neck of a Chinese laundryman, dragged him through the streets, and kicked and beat him to death. In another incident in 1885 in Rock Springs, Wyoming, a mob of 150 disgruntled white miners, armed with Winchester rifles, stormed into the

Chinese quarter. They killed twenty-eight Chinese, wounded fifteen, and burned much of the district to the ground. According to one eyewitness, "the Chinamen were fleeing like a herd of hunted antelopes, making no resistance. Volley upon volley was fired after the fugitives. In a few minutes the hill east of the town was literally blue with hunted Chinamen." Some linguists believe that the word *hoodlum* comes from the anti-Chinese cry of "huddle 'em," a signal for mobs to surround and harass the Celestials.[12]

Vigilante violence was coupled with a series of anti-Chinese ordinances and legislation enacted by cities, states, and Congress. In the 1870s, San Francisco passed a number of ordinances with the stated intent to "drive [the Chinese] to other states to be their own educators against" further Chinese immigration. The Cubic Air Ordinance called for each tenement to have at least 500 cubic feet of air for each inhabitant. The city officials enforced the ordinance only in Chinatown and arrested not the predominantly white landlords but the Chinese tenants. The Laundry Ordinance set licensing fees punishingly high for Chinese laundries, charging them $15 every three months but only $2 or $4 for laundries run by whites.[13]

In the state of California, following the 1852 foreign miners' license tax bill, the legislature passed an 1855 law entitled "An Act to Discourage the Immigration to this State of Persons Who Cannot Become Citizens Thereof." In 1862, newly elected Republican governor Leland Stanford, whose railroad company would soon become the largest employer and exploiter of Chinese labor, used his inaugural address to decry "the presence among us of a degraded and distinct people," and to call for "any constitutional action, having for its object the repression of the immigration of Asiatic races." In the same year, the legislature passed "An Act to Protect Free White Labor against Competition with Chinese Coolie Labor, and Discourage the Immigration of Chinese into the State of California." While an 1849 state statute had already provided that "No Black or Mulatto person, or Indian, shall be allowed to give evidence for or against a white man," an 1854 ruling by the California Supreme Court added

Chinese to the list and barred them from testifying.[14] Most states had in the nineteenth century adopted the 1661 Maryland law against miscegenation, but the California version was designed to include the Chinese in the prohibition. As a white politician warned in 1878, "Were the Chinese to amalgamate at all with our people, it would be the lowest, most vile and degraded of our race, and the result of that amalgamation would be a hybrid of the most despicable, a mongrel of the most detestable that has ever afflicted the earth." Two years later, the California legislature passed a bill to ban the marriage of any white person with a "negro, mulatto, or Mongolian."[15]

Although some of these racist laws, such as the foreign miners' license tax, were voided by the federal Civil Rights Act (the Enforcement Act) of 1870, the anti-Chinese movement gained momentum in post–Civil War America. As economic depression hit the country and led to job losses and labor strikes, Chinese immigration became a national issue. In 1879, President Rutherford B. Hayes—who had won the highly disputed 1876 election by one electoral vote but lost the popular vote to his opponent—placed what he called "the Chinese Problem" within the broad context of racial relations in America. He argued that the "Chinese invasion" was pernicious and should be discouraged. "Our experience in dealing with the weaker race—the Negroes and Indians," he said, was not encouraging. The Chinese appeared to be a bigger threat because they were seen as intelligent and competitive, and their population was increasing. "I would," Hayes concluded, "consider with favor any suitable measures to discourage the Chinese from coming to our shores."[16] Although Hayes ultimately would veto the so-called Fifteen Passenger Bill, which only allowed fifteen Chinese per ship to enter the United States, a landmark immigration bill was passed by Congress in May 1882, during the term of President Chester A. Arthur. Known as the Chinese Exclusion Act, the bill suspended the immigration of Chinese laborers for ten years and reconfirmed the inadmissibility of Chinese for citizenship. Renewed in 1892 and then extended in

1902 until its repeal in 1943, the exclusion led to a sharp decline in the Chinese population: from 105,465 in 1880 to 89,863 in 1900 to 61,639 in 1920.[17] The bill was the first significant restriction on free immigration in U.S. history and the first immigration law to target a specific ethnic group. In the words of Senator George Frisbie Hoar, a Massachusetts Republican who was one of a handful of the bill's opponents, "Chinese exclusion represented nothing less than the legalization of racial discrimination." Hoar's stance made him a target for scorn, especially in the western states. He was burned in effigy in Nevada, and California newspapers labeled him a "dwarf" and a "chicken-hearted Puritan of the east."[18]

Recently, historians have pointed out that the exclusionist policy had as much to do with class tensions as with race. Ronald Takaki, in his monumental study of Asian American history, writes:

> In fact, there was very little objective basis for the Congress to be worried about Chinese immigrants as a threat to white labor. The Chinese constituted a mere .002 percent of the U.S. population in 1880. Behind the exclusion act were fears and forces that had little or no relationship to the Chinese. . . . The Chinese Exclusion Act was in actuality symptomatic of a larger conflict between white labor and white capital: removal of the Chinese was designed not only to defuse an issue agitating white workers but also to alleviate class tensions within white society.[19]

Whether class tension, economic necessity, or outright racism was the real cause for the passage of the bill—most likely it was a combination of all three factors—the Chinese served as highly visible scapegoats for the social ills in the decades following the Civil War. Not surprisingly, the white working class resented "cheap Chinese labor" way out of proportion to the actual number of Chinese laborers. Nowhere was this racist sentiment captured more colorfully and cogently than in the poem "The Heathen Chinee," by F. Bret Harte.

Like his close friend Mark Twain, Harte was otherwise sympathetic to the plight of Chinese workers in the Western states, but he was also responsible for a work that would greatly enrich American racist vocabulary, particularly pertaining to the Chinese. Also known as "Plain Language from Truthful James," the narrative poem, first published in September 1870 in *Overland Monthly,* was originally meant to be a parody of racial animosity toward the Chinese. It began with a plain-speaking "Truthful James" as the narrator:

Which I wish to remark—
And my language is plain—
That for ways that are dark
And for tricks that are vain,
The heathen Chinee is peculiar,
Which the same I would rise to explain

The second stanza introduces a prototype of a Chinaman whose name will become a "John Doe" for all Chinese in racist literature:

Ah Sin was his name;
And I shall not deny
In regard to the same
What that name might imply,
But his smile it was pensive and child-like
As I frequent remarked to Bill Nye.

The trio—James, Bill Nye, and Ah Sin—taking a break from their backbreaking toil in the minefield, are playing a card game, euchre, in which Ah Sin claims to be a beginner:

It was August the third
And quite soft was the skies,
Which it might be inferred

That Ah Sin was likewise;
Yet he played it that day upon William
And me in a way I despise.

Which we had a small game,
And Ah Sin took a hand;
It was Euchre. The same
He did not understand;
But he smiled as he sat by the table,
With the smile that was child-like and bland.

Bill, it turns out, is cheating, hiding cards inside his sleeve:

Yet the cards they were stocked
In a way that I grieve,
And my feelings were shocked
At the state of Nye's sleeve;
Which was stuffed full of aces and bowers,
And the same with intent to deceive.

But for some reason, Ah Sin seems to have beginner's luck, soundly beating them both:

But the hands that were played
By that heathen Chinee,
And the points that he made,
Were quite frightful to see—
Till at last he put down a right bower,
Which the same Nye had dealt unto me.

And here comes the moment of enlightenment: a question that would later be quoted over and over in the annals of American foreign-labor policy, a refrain that can still be heard today:

Then I looked up at Nye,
And he gazed upon me;
And he rose with a sigh,
And said, "Can this be?
We are ruined by Chinese cheap labor?" . . .

At this point, a mob, led by indignant Bill Nye, beat up Ah Sin, that heathen Chinee, who is actually a better cheater but has played dumb. According to Truthful James, Ah Sin has stacked twenty-four packs of cards up his sleeve. "I state but the facts," James claims.

Which is why I remark,
And my language is plain,
That for ways that are dark,
And for tricks that are vain,
The heathen Chinee is peculiar—
Which the same I am free to maintain.[20]

Truth be told, Harte, who had reported sympathetically about the Chinese for newspapers in the region (Mark Twain lost his job because he did the same), intended the poem to be a satire about racial prejudice held by the likes of Truthful James and Bill Nye rather than an outright caricature of Ah Sin. The Irish working class, targets of ethnic slurs themselves, were often portrayed in literature of the period as the main instigators of racial discrimination against the Chinese, their chief competitors for menial jobs in minefields and railroads.

The poetic irony, however, was completely lost on mostly white readers who embraced Harte's poem not as a satire but as an accurate depiction of the Chinese. Soon reprinted in the *New York Evening Post, Prairie Farmer, New York Tribune, Boston Evening Transcript, Providence Journal, Hartford Courant,* and *Saturday Evening Post,* Harte's poem became a defining piece that shaped the American conception of the Chinese, making Harte one of the most popular American writers in 1870.

Harte himself would in later years call the poem "trash," "the worst poem I ever wrote, possibly the worst poem anyone ever wrote."[21] But the damage was done, the image was sealed for American posterity, and key phrases from the poem have become commonplace sayings in American life since then. As a heathen Chinee, Ah Sin wears a queue, waxing tapers on his fingernails, with a soft, childlike expression; he cheats in "ways that are dark" at a card table and ruins American prospects with "Chinese cheap labor" in the workplace.

Poems and songs such as "The Heathen Chinee" appeared at a time when popular music was attracting a mass audience and songsters were crafting new tunes to satisfy demand. These ditties were recited and sung around campfires, in parlors and saloons, and at political rallies. Harte's poem, in particular, was recited in public among opponents of Chinese immigration. Eugene Casserly, a senator from California who was "vehemently opposed to the admission of Chinese labor," wrote Harte to thank him for supporting his legislative agenda.[22] The profound ways in which a poem like "The Heathen Chinee" had molded American minds and attitudes would only be matched by the influences of Charlie Chan novels and films, which struggled against the legacy of earlier songs and poems.

In 1931, when Earl Biggers was contemplating the title for his sixth Charlie Chan novel, he had actually considered adopting Harte's "Heathen Chinee" catchphrase, "Ways That Are Dark." The idea had originally come from a press agent at the Fox Film Corporation (predecessor of Twentieth Century-Fox). In February 1931, Fox was producing a movie version of Biggers's fifth Chan novel, *Charlie Chan Carries On*, with the Swedish actor Warner Oland debuting in the leading role. In his communication with Biggers, Willoughby Speyers of Fox's press department wrote, "Incidentally, could you use the Bret Harte—heathen Chinee phrase of 'Ways that are dark' as a possible title for some forthcoming exploits? It doesn't seem to have ever been used as a film title, though of course it may have been used for a book."

Two days later, Biggers wrote to Laurence Chambers at Bobbs-Merrill: "The enclosed letter from the Fox press department is in answer to some data about Charlie I sent them at their request. . . . 'Ways That Are Dark' is not a bad title for a mystery, but I feel sure it must have been used before. Besides, it might be dangerous to accept a title from a press agent."

Sensing an opportunity, Chambers immediately looked into the matter and within days sent Biggers a reply: " 'Ways That Are Dark' is a pretty slick title, and the *Publishers Weekly* office says it has not been used before on a book."[23]

The idea stuck with Biggers for quite a while when he was working on what eventually would be published in 1932 as *Keeper of the Keys*, in which a main character is a Chinese houseboy named Ah Sing. Biggers explained to Chambers why he had opted not to adopt Harte's phrase, even though he had named a character after the poem's protagonist: "I think KEEPER OF THE KEYS the best title. For a while I feared it might tip off the ending. But I guess we can chance that. I'll hold WAYS THAT ARE DARK up my sleeve. I fear that, used on this one, it would shove Ah Sing into too much prominence. I don't want him to overshadow Chan."[24]

Charlie Chan might have narrowly escaped a damning title for his last story and avoided the humiliation of being outshone by Ah Sing, but the American cultural landscape offered few hiding places where he could avoid racial humiliation and negative stereotypes. Museum exhibitions and minstrel shows, for example, provided prominent, pre-cinema venues for the display of visual caricatures of exotic Chinese. In 1784, the same year the *Empress of China* docked in Canton, Peale's Museum in Philadelphia displayed Chinese curiosities among its collections of objects from Africa and India. Among the items were everyday utensils, weapons, and bric-a-brac. Best of all was a collection of wrappings used to bind Chinese women's feet and accompanying tiny shoes and slippers.[25] The success of Peale's soon inspired similar exhibit openings elsewhere, including Salem, Massachusetts, and New York City. But what astounded the museum world half a century later was the appearance of Chang and Eng, the "Siamese twins."

Born in Siam (now Thailand) of Chinese ancestry in 1811, the Bunker brothers were joined at the sternum by a piece of cartilage with a fused liver. They were discovered by British merchant Robert Hunter and taken, like zoo specimens, on a world tour. The twins, combining the exotic with a rare physical anomaly, were first displayed in 1829 at Peale's, where they caused a stir, especially in a century when the study of phrenology was very popular. After successfully touring the United States and England for a decade, the twins "retired" to Wilkesboro, a county seat in western North Carolina, where they established themselves as landed Southern gentry. They purchased two farms, built two separate residences, and became slaveholders. In 1843, Chang and Eng married the Yates sisters, Sarah and Adelaide, and between them fathered twenty-two children. The twins died on the same day in 1874, Chang first and Eng a few hours later.

The "freak shows" of the Siamese twins only sensationalized the perceived Chinese exoticism. Their later attempt to live a normal life through gentrification did nothing to normalize the image of the Chinaman in the public eye. Their marriages to the Yates sisters, especially, heightened a fear of miscegenation among whites. Hinton Rowan Helper (1829–1909), a famous abolitionist during the Civil War who later became a white supremacist, was one such American statesman whose ideological views might have been affected by racial anxieties. Growing up in the county adjacent to where the Bunkers had settled, the young Helper, "in addition to sharing the salacious but almost universal fascination with the imagined sexual practice of the twins and their wives, resented the fact that the Siamese twins were land owners of substance and slaveholders to boot, while Helper's own family found itself in reduced financial circumstances on its small farm as the result of his father's early death."[26] The local gossip mills churned out juicy and lurid stories about how the Bunker wives squabbled, forcing the conjoined twins to set up two households within miles of each other and to alternate spending three days at each home and each conjugal bed.

In his influential book *The Land of Gold* (1855), written before his abolitionist treatise, *The Impending Crisis of the South* (1857), made him a household name, Helper, in the words of Robert G. Lee, "is obsessed with the presence of the Chinese as a deterrent to the immigration of respectable white women and thus a barrier to 'normal' family development."[27] Perhaps with images of the Siamese twins in mind, Helper ridicules the Chinese:

> [John Chinaman's] feet enclosed in rude wooden shoes, his legs bare, his breeches loosely flapping against his knees, his skirtless, long-sleeved, big-bodied pea-jacket, hanging in large folds around his waist, his broad-brimmed chapeau rocking carelessly on his head, and his cue [queue] suspended and gently sweeping about his back! I can compare him to nothing so appropriately as to a tadpole walking upon stilts.[28]

Like the Siamese twins, the John Chinaman referred to in Helper's passage was a stock character in minstrel shows of the mid-nineteenth century. Before he was replaced by the more sinister "Ah Sin," "John Chinaman" had been the "John Doe" for all Chinese. Performed in "yellowface" on the minstrel stage, John Chinaman often integrated the pidgin mimicry as portrayed in songs and rhymes with the freak-show quality of the Siamese twins. A variation of the "Hong Kong" song quoted earlier in this chapter features John Chinaman lamenting the loss of his "lillie gal" to minstrelsy's archetypal white working-class hero, Mose:

> *Me stopee long me lillee gal nicee*
> *Wellee happee Chinaman, me no care,*
> *Me smokee, smokee, lillie gal talkee,*
> *Chinaman and lillee gal wellee jollee pair.*

. . .

Me catchee white manee lillee gal talkee
Kiss-kiss lillee gal, give her lots of smack.

At this point, the chorus joins in and attributes John Chinaman's loss of love to his grotesque dietary choice:

Me likee bow wow, wellee goodee chow-chow,
Me likee lillee gal, she likee me
Me fetchee Hong-Kong, whitee man come long,
Takee lillee gal from a poor Chinee.

Many minstrel shows, such as the duo of Charley Fox and Frank Dumont, made John Chinaman as well as Siamese twins part of their comedy routines.[29]

All of these popular cultural representations joined forces to create a demeaning stock image of the Chinaman: a yellow coolie who is either an emaciated walking chopstick or fat and greasy like an oafish butcher. With slits for eyes and a bland, round face, he wears a pair of blue pantaloons and a skullcap, his long queue swinging like a rat's tail. What comes out of his mouth, if he speaks at all, is pidgin English, grating singsong of dubious significance.

Such is the caricature of the Chinaman that Charlie Chan sets out to undo. But before we look at Chan's globetrotting career, we have yet to account for another super-Chinaman who is often regarded as Chan's "evil twin," Dr. Fu Manchu.

15

Fu Manchu

BORIS KARLOFF IN *THE MASK OF FU MANCHU*, 1932 *(Courtesy of Everett Collection)*

I made my name on Fu Manchu because I know nothing about the Chinese.
—Sax Rohmer

"IMAGINE A PERSON, tall, lean and feline, high-shouldered, with a brow like Shakespeare and a face like Satan, a close-shaven skull, and long, magnetic eyes of the true cat-green. Invest him with all the cruel cunning of an entire Eastern race, accumulated in one giant intellect, with all the resources of science past and present, with all the resources, if you will, of a wealthy government."[1]

Such is the insidious image of Dr. Fu Manchu, created in the early part of the twentieth century by the British writer Sax Rohmer. Compared to the genial, soft-spoken Charlie Chan, who uses his Oriental wisdom to fend off menaces to mainstream, white culture, Fu Manchu epitomizes the East's threat to the West. Made in the heyday of the Yellow Peril, Fu Manchu is no small-time cardsharp like Ah Sin or whiny weakling like John Chinaman. Instead, he is a daunting enemy who can be defeated only by the very best deputy of the West: Special Commissioner Nayland Smith of Scotland Yard. Like Steve McGarrett's far more contemporary archrival, Wo Fat, Fu Manchu is an agent of the Chinese government who moves about, wraithlike, within the opium dens, subterranean passages, and loathsome dungeons of the modern metropolis. As readers learn, his feline claws can penetrate the rosy bosom of the pristine English countryside or that cradle of Western democracy, the White House. A scientific wizard with incredible expertise in chemistry, medicine, engineering, botany, and zoology; an omniscient hypnotist who can control one's mind for hours or days on end; and a skilled linguist who speaks English impeccably but with an odd choice of words—Fu Manchu is, in sum, a superman with a satanic heart.

How did this improbable Chinaman come about?

If one thinks it curious that Charlie Chan's initial incarnation may have been in the Reading Room of the New York Public Library, think again: Fu Manchu, according to Sax Rohmer, was born on a Ouija board.

Like his creation, Rohmer was a lifetime devotee of occultism. Born Arthur Henry Ward on February 15, 1883, in Birmingham, England, Rohmer grew up in South London with an alcoholic Irish mother and a hardworking stonemason father. In his early years, he suffered from that strange affliction called somnambulism (a malady that may partly account for his penchant for creating nightmarish atmospherics in his writing). While sleepwalking, Rohmer once pounced on his father and nearly choked him to death. Another time, he tried to pull his wife, Elizabeth, out of bed because he dreamed that she was about to be run over by a car.

Rejecting all mainstream religions, including the Roman Catholicism of his Irish heritage, Rohmer joined the Hermetic Order of the Golden Dawn, a secret society whose members included William Butler Yeats, among other luminaries. He was also admitted, along with Rudyard Kipling, to the Rosicrucian Society, an influential international sect founded with the belief that a fund of secret wisdom could be handed down through the ages and transmitted only to the initiated. He had kept his memberships secret even from his wife, who shared his belief in supernatural powers but would only learn of his affiliations with these societies after his death.

Before achieving fame with Fu Manchu, Rohmer made a meager living as a freelance writer, selling stories to magazines and journals. Like Biggers, Rohmer also had a brief stint as a reporter for a newspaper, the *Commercial Intelligence*; and, like the father of Charlie Chan, the creator of Fu Manchu was also fired for his propensity to embroider facts. These are no trivial similarities. The ability to conjure up a character from another culture and to make a career out of such cultural ventriloquism requires a particularly healthy imagination.

Uncertain about his future, Rohmer cajoled Elizabeth into helping him experiment with a Ouija board. Having established "contact" with the mysterious being, which answered "yes" or "no" to a few preliminary questions, Rohmer went to the heart of the matter with a straight question: "How can I best make a living?" To the astonishment of the couple, the pointer, according to Rohmer's protégé and biographer, Cay Van Ash, "moved rapidly over the chart and, not once, but repeatedly, spelled out: C-H-I-N-A-M-A-N." The incredulous couple "looked at each other and shook their heads. They had not the faintest idea what it meant."[2]

The strange missive from "the Unknown" was soon deciphered

when Rohmer received a magazine assignment to write a feature story on a "Mr. King" in London's notorious Limehouse District. Around the turn of the twentieth century, the mere mention of the term *Limehouse* would conjure up images readymade for Victorian horror novels: "A vista of dark streets, shadowy yellow-faced forms, the brief flash of a knife blade, a scream in the night, a bloated corpse fished up from the murky waters of the Thames." Such snapshots might appear to be merely clichéd will-o'-the-wisps concocted by second-rate writers with Oriental fantasies, but, as Van Ash wrote, "Before the First World War, it was a fact that the warren of narrow streets and alleyways in the neighborhood of West India Dock Road, Pennyfields, and Limehouse Causeway formed a no-man's-land which honest citizens hesitated to penetrate after dark. It was a fact that the Metropolitan Police honored the area with double patrols."[3]

The "Mr. King" whom Rohmer was supposed to track down was allegedly "a considerable property owner, a known drug trafficker and, according to rumor, the guiding hand in half of the underworld activities of Limehouse."[4] But no one seemed ever to have met him. Looking for the elusive King, Rohmer would disappear in Limehouse for days and mingle with the most unlikely cocktail of humanity. Without question, Rohmer, inspired by the Victorian occult, was a man on a mission, as suggested by his peculiar pseudonym: "Sax," suggesting "Saxon," means "blade" in the Anglo-Saxon language; "Rohmer" is a homophone of "Roamer." Sax Rohmer, then, was an errant Saxon knight on a quixotic quest.

Rohmer's connection to Limehouse was Fong Wah, a storeowner who purveyed strange delicacies dear to the Chinese palate: bamboo shoots, shark fins, water chestnuts, lily roots, seaweed, bird nests, and preserved eggs. A tall and elderly man with a finely lined face that looked like a map of Asia, Fong Wah was rumored to have been the executioner of Hankow in his early days. Not averse to distaff pleasures, he even took on a fourth wife young enough to be his granddaughter.[5] Rohmer's friendship with the executioner-turned-merchant did not, however, bring him any closer to the elusive Mr. King; the mere mention of the name was enough to make Fong Wah go mum or change the subject.

As the deadline for the commissioned piece pressed ever closer, Rohmer became as desperate as an ant in a hot wok. His penchant for creative embroidery took over and saved him from certain failure. Based on a few facts that he had gathered about the tongs and other secret organizations in Limehouse, Rohmer began to fantasize a scenario:

> Supposing, I asked myself, a number of those sinister organizations—perhaps, even, all of them—were in turn responsible to the direction of some super-society? Such a society would hold the power to upset Governments, perhaps change the very course of civilization. . . . I began to wonder what the president of my imaginary super-society would be like, what manner of man could dominate that would-be shadowy empire. He would have Caesaresque qualities. He must be a man of great scientific culture, a genius.[6]

But Rohmer's imagination stopped there, as he could not visualize the appearance of such an Oriental "King." He knew that "conditions for launching a Chinese villain on the market were ideal."[7] Memories of the two violent and sanguinary Opium Wars that had wracked China were still fresh among the British public. The more recent Boxer Rebellion, during which many Anglo-Europeans in China were singled out and killed by the rebels, had set off fear of a "Yellow Peril," a phrase coined by German Chancellor Otto von Bismarck. And sensational reports on Limehouse's crimes and grime had always riveted the public's attention. All Rohmer needed to do was put a face on the sinister figure he now imagined.

One day, Fong Wah finally rewarded Rohmer for his patience by tipping him off about the possible appearance of "a very strange man who sometimes visits Limehouse." Rohmer got the cue and waited in the shadow of a dingy little alley at the specified hour. After a long wait, a shiny limousine pulled up before a mean-looking house, and a uniformed chauffeur jumped out and opened the car door for his passengers. "A tall, dignified Chinese, wearing a fur-collared overcoat and a fur cap, alighted and walked in," Rohmer recalled years later. "He was followed by an Arab girl wrapped in a grey fur cloak. I had a glimpse of her features. She was like something from an Edmund Dulac illustration of *The Thousand and One Nights*." When the house door was opened and the light flooded out, Rohmer caught a glimpse of the face of the man in the fur cap. In that instant, Rohmer's imaginary monster, Dr. Fu Manchu, sprang to life.[8]

Fu Manchu thus was born in the fall of 1911, less than three years before an assassin's bullet would plunge Europe into war. The first in the series of Fu Manchu stories was called "The Zayat Kiss," referring to the evil doctor's use of a scorpion as his devious method of killing. Playing on Oriental fantasy, Rohmer concocted a legend about travelers who stopped by *zayats*—resthouses along caravan routes in Burmese jungles—and then were found dead. Nothing indicated the cause of death but a little mark suspected to be a scorpion sting—hence, "the zayat kiss." A fictional re-creation of the worst colonial nightmare, the Asian jungle now struck back at the center of the empire, and the evil doctor, representative of the Asiatic race, brought the kiss of death into the tranquil bedrooms of British homes. First a letter dipped in a rare perfume was mailed to the potential victim. Then, on the night the letter arrived, one of Fu Manchu's trained dacoits (bandits) would bring a scorpion into the room where the victim was sleeping. The lingering traces of perfume on the victim's hand would attract the scorpion, leading to a fatal strike.[9]

First serialized in *The Story-Teller* in October 1912 and then published in June 1913 as a book under the title of *The Mystery of Dr. Fu-Manchu,* the ten episodes of this evil-Chinaman saga seized the English imagination. The xenophobic fear instigated by the fictional character represented the anxiety and paranoia of a jittery nation on the eve of a global war. Fu Manchu was not just a single Chinaman who, like Ah Sin, has "tricks that are vain" and "ways that are dark." He was an instigator and leader of what Rohmer described as a "Yellow Movement"; his murderous agents included an assortment of dark-skinned Orientals and such other exotics as Thuggs, dacoits, Arabs, Africans, and Greeks. "In the Fu-Manchu stories," a scholar once wrote, "Rohmer has produced Europe's worst nightmare, a global insurgency intent upon turning the tables of world domination."[10]

First serialized in the American magazine *Collier's Weekly, The Mystery of Dr. Fu-Manchu* was released in the United States as a book in September 1913 under that most verbose of titles, *Insidious Dr. Fu-Manchu: Being a Somewhat Detailed Account of the Amazing Adventures of Nayland Smith in His Trailing of the Sinister Chinaman.* The novel appeared less than two years before the film release of *The Birth of a Nation,* based on Thomas Dixon's best-selling 1905 novel. Set during the Civil War and directed by D. W. Griffith, the 190-minute silent movie is noted not only for its innovative technical and narrative achievements but also for its controversial treatment of white supremacy and its sympathetic account of the rise of the Ku Klux Klan. Blacks, played by white actors in blackface, are portrayed as barbaric rapists threatening the virtues of white women and the sanctity of the civilized white world.

The introduction of an equally threatening Chinese villain only reinforced racist fears. Not surprisingly, the Fu Manchu book became as popular in the United States as in Britain. The book was reprinted at least twenty times. By the 1970s, more than forty hardcover and paperback editions of the first Fu Manchu novel had appeared in the two countries.

Success ignited Rohmer's literary passions. The outbreak of the Great War provided a greater impetus, as xenophobia spread like a virus. In rapid order, *The Return of Dr. Fu-Manchu* (also known as *The Devil Doctor*) appeared in 1916 and *The Hand of Fu-Manchu* (also known as *The Si-Fan Mysteries*) in 1917. Needing to up the ante, Rohmer created these sequels in which Fu Manchu's team of running dogs perpetrates new murders with even more exotic and devious methods. In one episode, Fu Manchu kills a character "carrying a cane with a knob in the shape of a snake's head." The satanic mastermind replaces the cane with "a hollow tube holding a live adder, its head in the place of the knob." In another vignette, he trains a murderer who is an Abyssinian half-man, half-baboon with human intelligence and animalistic strength and agility. On other occasions, Fu Manchu frightens victims to death by broadcasting an eerie echo, while at other times he kills with a peculiar poison, "the flower of silence," against which the only antidote is the Buddhist chant, "Sakya Muni."[11]

These fantastic tales were catnip for early masters of the silent-movie era. Not surprisingly, the evil doctor would appear in yellowface. The first Fu Manchu movie, *The Mysteries of Dr. Fu Manchu,* was made in Britain in 1923, starring Harry Agar Lyons, who reprised his role the following year in *The Further Mysteries of Fu Manchu.* The first Fu Manchu talking film was made in Hollywood by Paramount Pictures in 1929. *The Mysterious Dr. Fu-Manchu* starred Warner Oland. Having previously played a patriarchal Jew in Al Jolson's *The Jazz Singer* (1927), Oland padded his credentials so well with his superb yellowface that he would soon be picked to star in Charlie Chan films. For a year or two, Oland shuttlecocked between the two Oriental roles—a menacing villain with an evil design on the West and a smiling detective applying Chinese wisdom to Western criminology. Hardly flummoxed by the need to inhabit two divergent characters, Oland starred in *The Return of Dr. Fu-Manchu* in 1930 and then "carried on" his yellowface stunt in *Charlie Chan Carries On* the next year. He worked at Fox in the Chan film *The Black Camel* later in 1931 and then went back to Paramount for the Fu Manchu sequel, *Daughter of the Dragon.*

The most famous incarnation of Fu Manchu was the 1932 MGM film *The Mask of Fu Manchu,* featuring Boris Karloff. The story involves Fu Manchu's attempt to recover the legendary sword and armor of Genghis Khan, whose conquest of the West in the Middle Ages was an inspiration for the evil doctor. Karloff, fresh from his breakout role in the 1931 *Frankenstein* movie, played Fu Manchu as an Asian Frankensteinian monster so skillfully that he propelled both the character and the film into cult status. With its campy humor, Grand-Guignol sets, and torture sequences, *The Mask* featured Myrna Loy as Fu Manchu's daughter, Fah Lo See, with whom he appears to have an incestuous relationship.

In later decades, Asian American critics would note the references to incest and other sexual transgressions ascribed to Fu Manchu and often commented on the demeaning depictions of Asian men. "Unlike the white stereotype of the evil black stud, Indian rapist, Mexican macho," Frank Chin writes, "the evil of the evil Dr. Fu Manchu was not sexual but homosexual. . . . Dr. Fu, a man wearing a long dress, batting his eyelashes, surrounded by muscular black servants in loin-cloths, and with his bad habit of caressingly touching white men on the leg, wrist, and face with his long fingernails, is not so much a threat as he is a frivolous offense to white manhood."[12]

Sadly, fictional representation, no matter how false or tortured, has a strange way of making a claim on reality. By 1932, Fu Manchu had become a household name, and many even believed in his physical existence, in the same way that the British Post Office was for years saddled with letters addressed to Mr. Sherlock Holmes at 221B Baker Street. At the peak of Fu Manchu's notoriety, a threatening letter once was sent to an employee of the U.S. State Department and signed "President of the Si-Fan." The FBI conducted an investigation but could find no information about this secret organization.[13] As recently as 2008, during the Summer Olympics in Beijing, the fourteen-time gold-medalist swimmer, Michael Phelps, was reported to have shaved off his "Fu Manchu beard" prior to the games to ensure top speed in the water. Yet the same menacing beard had returned a few months later, when a British tabloid showed him smoking a bong. Perhaps it was this satanic growth of facial hair that caused the hapless Phelps to try weed? What is more certain is that the Chinaman image of Fu Manchu, like that of Charlie Chan, is firmly ingrained in popular cultural memory.

In his lifetime, Rohmer, the Saxon knight on a mission, wrote thirteen Fu Manchu books, making him one of the most widely read and highly paid writers of popular fiction in the world. As an author who made a career out of fictionalizing the "inscrutable" and "insidious" East, Rohmer died in 1959 in an ironic way: While traveling in the United States, Rohmer caught what the alarmed news media called the "Asiatic flu." The illness would begin as a feverish cold and pass quickly, "leaving the victim in an odd state of weakness during which the slightest overstrain produced complete and fatal collapse. Nothing quite like it had appeared before; no one seemed to know anything about it."[14] Coming out of Asia, this incurable, mysterious flu claimed the lives of many victims, including Rohmer, the man who specialized in making the Orient demonic.

"I made my name on Fu Manchu because I know nothing about the Chinese," Rohmer once famously said. "I know something about Chinatown. But that is a different matter. Nowadays, I like to think that a Chinese and a Chinaman are not the same thing."[15] Despite the author's disclaimer, Fu Manchu the Chinaman, inspired by that most reliable of prognostications, the Ouija board, has lived on as a Chinese archetype in popular culture. And Rohmer insisted that the conflation of image and reality, stereotype and type, was not the work of him or his fellow travelers: "When I began writing, 'Chinaman' was no more than the accepted term for a native of China. The fact that it has taken on a derogative meaning is due mostly to the behavior of those Chinamen who lived in such places as Limehouse."[16] Such a double demonization—portraying London's Chinese citizens as bad and blaming the negative image on their bad behavior—was typical of the Chinatown literature of the twentieth century's early decades. It would, however, provide a fitting contrast for Charlie Chan. As we will see, the honorable detective from Honolulu would have to compete with the evil doctor in a struggle for center stage, to determine which Chinaman would become foremost in the West's popular imagination.

16

Charlie Chan, the Chinaman

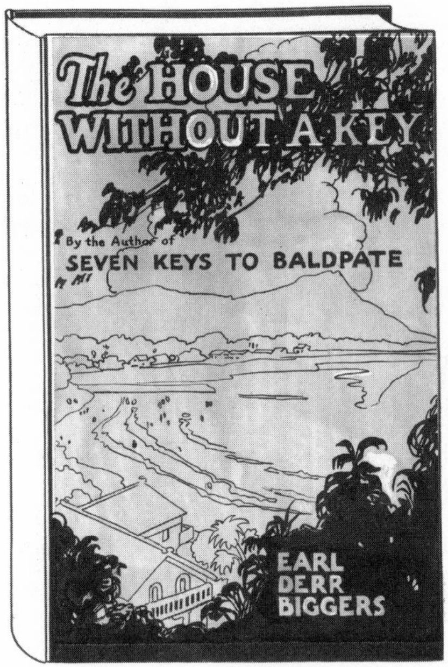

COVER DESIGN FOR E. D. BIGGERS'S *THE HOUSE WITHOUT A KEY*, 1925

(Courtesy of Lilly Library, Indiana University)

World is large, me lowly Chinaman.
—Charlie Chan

IT WAS CALLED the Jazz Age, an era that commenced with the 1918 Armistice and ended with the Great Crash of 1929. The American nation experienced social changes and dislocations as profound and unsettling as any since the Civil War. Perhaps no change was as dramatic as the proliferation of the automobile, which brought an end to the horse-and-buggy era. The national registration of motor vehicles rose from fewer than six million to more than twenty-three million. Industrial production increased overall by almost 50 percent, the national income grew from $79.1 billion to almost $88 billion, and the purchasing power of American wages increased at a rate of 2 percent annually. Stimulated by salesmanship and advertising, Americans bought newfangled automobiles, radios, washing machines, refrigerators, toasters, sewing machines, and vacuum cleaners at a rate that challenged the capacity of the country's fast-expanding factories. During this period of unprecedented prosperity and consumption, America, to quote F. Scott Fitzgerald, "was going on the greatest, gaudiest spree in history."[1]

Such a rosy picture of the Roaring Twenties cannot, however, overshadow the fact that this was also one of the most racist and xenophobic eras in American history. Nostalgic images of flappers can be most misleading. Not everyone danced as fast as they could. Nativist frenzy, Ku Klux Klan activity, and the passage of the infamous 1924 Johnson-Reed Act—all contributed to the era's reputation as a narrow-minded "tribal period." It is remarkable, then, that the fictional Charlie Chan would enter the American imagination when xenophobia was so prevalent. For this reason, many of his detractors have regarded Chan as no more than a "personality reduced to a Chinese takeout menu," a Yellow Uncle Tom, the flip side of that racist coin with the insidious Fu Manchu in the front. But Charlie Chan should not be confused with Fu Manchu, and such reductive portrayals miss the subtleties and complexities of Chan as a unique Chinaman.

Like a multilayered Chinese box, Chan is a character whose strength and virtue extend well beyond a mere chimera of the benign Chinaman in Western fantasy. Like all racialized figures—including Uncle Tom, Aunt Jemima, John Chinaman, Ah Sin, Nigger Jim, and Fu Manchu—Chan bears the stamp of his time, a birthmark that encapsulates both the racial tensions and the creative energies of a multicultural nation. Strikingly, the Chan character—the consummate Chinaman—entered the world as the 1924 Immigration Act (Johnson-Reed Act) was being signed into law.

The passage of this 1924 exclusionary act resulted from several key factors, including the rise of nativism, America's transition from an agricultural to an industrial nation, and the changing structure of global geopolitics. Nativism—defined as an intense opposition to internal minorities on the ground of their presumed "foreign" connections—has a long and tortured history in American culture.[2] Sometimes barely distinguishable from racial prejudice, nativist sentiments found ample expression in the anti-Chinese, anti-Irish, and anti-Italian movements of the nineteenth century. At the dawn of the twentieth century, especially during the Progressive Era, nativism lost some of its energy as many chose to celebrate America as a melting pot. But the outbreak of World War I put an end to the American dream and unleashed strong waves of patriotism and xenophobia. Demand for unity, hatred of Germans, and fear of Bolshevism each contributed to nativism's resurgence, a sentiment that lingered on even after the war. Theodore Roosevelt's famous motto of "America for Americans," the grassroots campaign of "100 Per Cent Americanism," and the rather comical renaming of sauerkraut as "liberty cabbage," were just a few symbols of the nationalist fervor of the time.

In fact, with the war as catalyst, nativism developed unstoppable momentum. In 1916, Madison Grant, a leading nativist, published *The Passing of the Great Race,* a book that would set the benchmark for the era's racial discourse. Grant argued passionately that there is a three-tiered hierarchy of Mediterraneans, Alpines, and Nordics within the white race; Americans are Nordics, and any mixture with the other two would lead to a destructive process of "mongrelization."[3] New editions of Grant's book appeared after the war and enjoyed a substantial vogue, selling about sixteen thousand copies between 1921 and 1923. Major newspapers and journals published editorials endorsing the book. America's most widely read magazine, the *Saturday Evening Post* (in which Charlie Chan would make his debut when *The House Without a Key* was serialized in 1925), actively and consistently commended Grant's racial doctrines in the years leading up to the Johnson-Reed Act.[4] As the spiritual bellwether of nativism, Grant inspired a bevy of popular writers and academic scholars, among whom the most influential was Lothrop Stoddard. A Massachusetts lawyer with a Ph.D. in history from Harvard, Stoddard published *The Rising Tide of Color Against White World-Supremacy* in 1920. Drawing on Grant's three-tier theory, Stoddard suggested that the Nordics, as the best stock, should be preserved by way of eugenics. Stoddard was less concerned about variety within the white race, however, than about the threat coming from the colored races. He warned that the rapid multiplication of the yellow and brown races would soon enable them to overwhelm the white world and topple white supremacy.

Simultaneous with these articulations of racism from the late 1910s to the early 1920s was the founding, or resurrection, of a series of nativist, antiforeign organizations, including the American Protective League, American Legion, American Defense Society, and the Ku Klux Klan. The Klan, a long-defunct sect originally organized by ex-Confederates during Reconstruction to intimidate carpetbaggers and Negroes, suddenly came to life in late 1915, the year D. W. Griffith's *The Birth of a Nation* was playing to great fanfare in movie theaters everywhere. Under the leadership of William J. Simmons, a former salesman and a mellifluent orator, the Klan spread like wildfire. By late 1923, the organization was claiming an aggregate membership of close to three million, with regional operations and affiliates in almost every state. The original mission of the Klan was to perpetuate white supremacy by putting down Negroes. In its twentieth-century reincarnation, however, the Klan had a much wider spectrum of agendas, ranging from anti-Catholicism and anti-Semitism to Anglo-Saxon pride and hatred of foreigners. It comprised, in John Higham's words, "the whole range of post-1919 nativism." As a formidable force in national politics, the Klan became a major voice in calling for immigration restriction in order to keep the nation "free from all mongrelizing taints."[5]

In addition to these nativist pressures, tremendous advances in mechanization also enabled industries to reduce their reliance on immigrant labor. It was during the 1920s that America made a key transition from an agricultural society to an industrial one. In that decade, industrial capitalism matured to the point where more economic growth would come from technological advances in mass production than from continued expansion of manufacturing labor.[6] In the past, it had been in the interest of big businesses and industries to lobby for more lenient immigration policies, but with machines replacing muscles on an unprecedented scale and efficiency accelerating as never before, they now had no more incentive to battle against exclusionist bills. Mechanization also brought an unintended benefit: machinery, as one business editor observed astutely, " 'stays put.' It does not go out on strike, it cannot decide to go to Europe, or take a job in the next town."[7]

While domestic affairs on the ideological and economic fronts both favored exclusionism, global politics also contributed to the cause of immigration restriction. Xenophobia, which had reached a feverish pitch during the war, did not simply die out in November 1918. The dream of international collaboration, as reflected by Wilsonian idealism, was also short-lived; no sooner was the Treaty of Versailles signed than the League of Nations began to crumble. The result, according to Higham, "was an intense isolationism that worked hand in hand with nativism. By mid-1920, a general revulsion against European entanglements was crystallizing. . . . Policies of diplomatic withdrawal, higher tariffs, and more stringent immigration restriction were all in order."[8]

In the spring of 1924, with the blessing of President Calvin Coolidge—as bedrock a Calvinist as any president in the twentieth century—the bill ultimately called the Immigration Act was introduced by Representative Albert Johnson and Senator David Reed.

Given the anxious climate of this time, it passed Congress with overwhelming support. President Coolidge, who had already lent his name to the nativist cause in a popular 1921 article on the Nordic theory and immigration restriction, swiftly signed the bill into law on May 26.[9] Adopting the concept of national-origin quotas for the first time in U.S. immigration policy, the Immigration Act had three main components: restricting immigration to 150,000 people a year, establishing temporary quotas based on 2 percent of the foreign-born population in 1890, and excluding from immigration all persons ineligible for citizenship. It rejected the melting-pot concept of the previous decades and constructed a vision of the American nation that embodied a hierarchy of races and nationalities, serving mainly the interests of white Protestant Americans from northern European backgrounds, the Nordics.

While the first two components of the law were meant to drastically reduce the number of immigrants from southern and eastern Europe—the Mediterraneans and the Alpines—the last component in effect barred half of the world's population, the Asiatics. But the law achieved more than exclusion; it did significant cultural harm from within. In fact, in 1924, "Asiatic" was a newly minted racial category, codified only a year earlier by the U.S. Supreme Court in *U.S. v. Thind.* Denying eligibility for citizenship to Bhagat Singh Thind, an Indian who claimed to be a white person based on his Aryan and Caucasian roots, the Court made a leap in racial logic in its ruling and lumped all peoples of Asian countries under the category of "Asiatic," even though Chinese, Japanese, Indians, Koreans, Thais, Indonesians, and others represented discrete ethnic groups and, anthropologically speaking, different racial groups.[10] Riding on the tailwind of this ruling, the 1924 Immigration Act conveniently condemned all Asians to the status of permanent foreigners. For those already living in the United States, their ties to their homelands were in effect severed, as other family members could not gain entrance to American shores, and they themselves could not become U.S. citizens.

The passage of the Immigration Act, in the words of influential nativist Captain John Trevor, "marks the close of an epoch in the history of the United States." Or, as Higham wrote in his classic work on American nativism, *Strangers in the Land*, "The country would never be the same again, either in its social structure or in its habits of mind. Although immigration of some sort would continue, the vast folk movements that had formed one of the most fundamental social forces in American history had been brought to an end. The old belief in America as a promised land for all who yearn for freedom had lost its operative significance."[11]

It was at this turning point in American culture that Charlie Chan, the aphorism-spouting Chinaman, entered the arena. I am not alluding to a cause-and-effect relation between President Coolidge's signing of the bill in May and Biggers's adding the Chan character to his novel-in-progress in the summer of that year; crude historical determinism is mostly a self-fulfilling prophesy, an insult to the magic of literary imagination. It cannot escape even a casual reader, however, that Charlie Chan bears the distinctive mark of the time: his exotic manners, his pidgin speech, his multitudinous family, and even his anti-Japanese sentiments. All are symptoms of a culture that had just closed its doors to the so-called foreigners.

For readers of the *Saturday Evening Post*, the buzz over immigration must have still been ringing in their ears when the chubby Chinese detective materialized on the magazine's pages. Over the years, the *Post*, drumming for immigration constraints, not only had published editorials replete with quotes from Madison Grant and his ilk but also had hired Kenneth Roberts to do a series of immigration stories condemning "the good-for-nothing mongrels of Central America and Southeastern Europe." In the days leading up to the passage of the Johnson-Reed Act, Roberts practically camped in the congressional committee's offices while working on his immigration articles for the *Post*.[12] Years later, Earl Biggers would claim that it was the enthusiastic reader responses to *The House Without a Key* that had pushed him to write more Chan novels. Obviously, in creating Charlie Chan, Biggers had his finger on the pulse of the nation.

As we saw in chapter 14, when Charlie Chan makes his debut in the novel, he is described as a fat man with the chubby cheeks of a baby and the dainty step of a woman. His exotic appearance—ivory skin, short black hair, and slanting amber eyes—is so shocking to Miss Minerva Winterslip that she cannot help exclaiming, "But—he's a Chinaman!" Later in the book, Biggers continues to play up the motif of Chan's foreignness, his marked difference from characters with distinctively Anglo-Saxon names and cultural backgrounds, such as Minerva Winterslip and John Quincy. A blue-blooded Bostonian, John Quincy is initially skeptical of a Chinaman's ability to find his uncle's murderer. "Damn clever, these Chinese!" he tells his aunt, Miss Minerva. "You don't mean to say you've fallen for that bunk. They seem clever because they're so different."[13] "Racial difference" was a nativist shibboleth used to reject the melting-pot concept and justify racial exclusion.

Even as he slowly warms up to Chan and recognizes the talent of the Chinese detective, Quincy still feels an insurmountable racial and cultural barrier between them. In the course of the investigation, Quincy discovers that his uncle Dan used to be a "blackbirder"—a slave and coolie trader—in the Pacific, a sordid past that may have had something to do with Dan's murder. But, sitting across a table from Chan at a dingy Chinese restaurant in Honolulu, Quincy hesitates to reveal the vital information that may help solve the case. He is concerned that the revelation would hurt his family pride in front of a Chinaman: "His dilemma was acute. Must he here in this soiled restaurant in a far town reveal to a Chinaman that ancient blot on the Winterslip name?" Ignoring Chan's earlier warning—"All cards should repose on table when police are called upon"—Quincy keeps mum and causes considerable delay in the case.[14]

Toward the end of the book, when the murder mystery is about to be unveiled, Quincy arrives at Chan's home on an urgent errand. Entering the bungalow on Punchbowl Hill, Quincy observes the detective in all his foreignness: "In this, his hour of ease, he wore a long loose robe of dark purple silk, which fitted closely at the neck and had wide sleeves. Beneath it showed wide trousers of the same material, and on his feet were shoes of silk, with thick felt soles. He was all Oriental now, suave and ingratiating but remote." The interior decoration of Chan's house widens the cultural gap between the two men. "Beneath the picture stood a square table, flanked by straight, low-backed armchairs. On other elaborately carved teakwood stands distributed about the room were blue and white vases, porcelain wine jars, dwarfed trees. Pale golden lanterns hung from the ceiling; a soft-toned rug lay on the floor. John Quincy felt again the gulf between himself and Charlie Chan."[15] The seemingly unbridgeable difference resonates with a poetic line by Rudyard Kipling, a line frequently quoted by American nativists in their push for exclusion: "East is East, and West is West, and never the twain shall meet."

Nothing, however, marks Chan's foreignness more than his pidgin speech and his rat-a-tat fortune-cookie aphorisms. As a character, Charlie Chan belongs in the pantheon of überdetectives with the likes of Sherlock Holmes, Philip Marlowe, and Hercule Poirot—all wise gentlemen with unforgettable idiosyncrasies. Holmes, a cocaine addict, is the incarnation of human rationality, verging on cold-bloodedness. Marlowe, Raymond Chandler's hard-boiled private investigator, has a knack for flushing out liars and a thing for ladies' legs. And Poirot, Agatha Christie's eggheaded, toupee-topped, and mustachioed Belgian sleuth, takes funny penguinlike steps and acts like a seasoned, hot-tempered hairdresser with finicky habits.

Among this elite crowd, Charlie Chan wears a uniquely ethnic badge: his Chineseness, which is manifested above all in the manner of his speech. While the imitation of Chinese pidgin had a long tradition in American popular literature that went back to the days of John Chinaman and Ah Sin, Earl Biggers took the linguistic mimicry to a new level. In *The House Without a Key*, Chan's ungrammatical first utterance, like the first note of a musical composition, sets the tone for the singsong, Peking Opera–like vocalization we will hear from him thereafter: "No knife are present in neighborhood of crime."

This is followed immediately by a verbal tussle between Chan and the prejudiced Miss Minerva:

> "The person who did this must be apprehended," she said firmly.
>
> He looked at her sleepily. "What is to be, will be," he replied in a high, sing-song voice.
>
> "I know—that's your Confucius," she snapped. "But it's a do-nothing doctrine, and I don't approve of it."
>
> A faint smile flickered over the Chinaman's face. "Do not fear," he said. "The fates are busy, and man may do much to assist. I promise you there will be no do-nothing here." He came closer. "Humbly asking pardon to mention it, I detect in your eyes slight flame of hostility. Quench it, if you will be so kind. Friendly cooperation are essential between us."[16]

As we see, Chan's sentences often lack subjects, nouns lack articles, and verbs are not conjugated correctly. His grammar is so comically and idiosyncratically mangled that it soon becomes a trademark of Chanism. In the 1976 spoof *Murder by Death,* a movie with an all-star cast (Truman Capote, Peter Sellers, Peter Falk, James Coco, Eileen Brennan, and so on) and ample pastiches of supersleuths (Sidney Wang/Charlie Chan, Sam Diamond/Sam Spade, Milo Perrier/Hercule Poirot, and others), Chan's habitual slaughtering of English grammar finally prompts a retort from Capote's wall-mounted moose head: "Use the article!"

Interestingly, Chan's troubles with grammar—or what he calls "my reckless wanderings among words of unlimitable English language"[17]—enable Biggers to craft some Chanisms that border on comedy, absurdity, and poetry. "Endeavoring to make English language my slave," as Chan tells John Quincy, "I pursue poetry."[18] A grandmaster of circumlocution like Henry James might even envy Chan some of his colorful sentences, such as: "Relinquish the firearms, or I am forced to make fatal insertion in vital organ belonging to you," "Let us not shade the feast with gloomy murder talk," "Story are now completely extracted like aching tooth," and "Is it that you are in the mood to dry up plate of soup?"

Among the famous fictional detectives, Hercule Poirot perhaps comes closest to Chan in also having a distinguishable, though not as memorable, manner of speech. Agatha Christie, a British hospital nurse during World War I, created Poirot's character in her first novel, *The Mysterious Affair at Styles,* published in 1920. Even though there is no evidence that Christie and Biggers influenced each other in any way, they did have something in common on their résumés: both became best-selling authors by creating a distinctively "foreign" detective character in an era when wartime xenophobia was a very recent memory. Like pidgin-speaking Charlie Chan, Christie's Belgian sleuth, when agitated, also flounders in a comical version of English: "I demand of you a thousand pardons, monsieur. I am without defense. For some months now I cultivate the marrows. This morning suddenly I enrage myself with these marrows. I send them to promenade themselves—alas! not only mentally but physically. I seize the biggest. I hurl him over the wall. Monsieur, I am ashamed. I prostrate myself."[19]

Occasionally, there are also linguistic infelicities in Poirot's speech, as seen in the following dialogue:

> "I thank you, no," said Poirot, rising. "All my excuses for having deranged you."
>
> "Not at all, not at all."
>
> "The word derange," I remarked, when we were outside again, "is applicable to mental disorder only."
>
> "Ah!" cried Poirot, "never will my English be quite perfect. A curious language. I should then have said disarranged, *n'est ce pas?*"
>
> "Disturbed is the word you had in mind."[20]

Poirot is allegedly well read in British Romantic poetry: he once exposes the cover of a suspect posing as a John Keats expert by intentionally misquoting from memory a line by Percy Shelley; and he is often seen reading a volume by William Wordsworth. Given such a literary background, Poirot's linguistic blunders seem much less credible than those verbal slips of Charlie Chan, who allegedly received no formal education but worked his way up in the world from the humble position of a houseboy.

In addition to their shared linguistic difficulties, the Belgian and Chinese detectives have something else in common: their penchant for proverbs. But this seeming similarity will ultimately set them apart. Unlike Chan's Chinese aphorisms, Poirot relies exclusively on well-known English proverbs as he addresses native English speakers. "And there came your proverb," Poirot once said to an Englishman, "the death of the goose that laid the golden eggs." Or, another time, "It's better late than never, as you English say." Due to their familiarity, Poirot's proverbs sound very plain and their meanings quite precise.

By contrast, Charlie Chan's pseudo-Confucian aphorisms, which he dishes out as the occasion demands, are often intended more to baffle than to enlighten his interlocutors. Their confounding effect derives less from the semantic opacity of these sayings than from the unfamiliarity of their origin. In *The House Without a Key*, most of Chan's fortune-cookie sayings may be easy enough to understand semantically, such as "Patience are a very lovely virtue," "A picture is a voiceless poem," and "Appearance are a hellish lie." What makes them sound grating on a reader's ear is their unfamiliarity in the English language, a sense of being off-key that is compounded by the pidgin. It takes a cosmopolite like Miss Minerva to figure out both the philosophical meaning and the Confucian origin of a quote like "What is to be, will be." Others are not so lucky. In *The Black Camel* (published in 1929), for example, Chan confronts an arrogant and insulting suspect by pulling out a spicy item from his proverbial stock:

> Jaynes pushed forward. "I have important business on the mainland, and I intend to sail at midnight. It is now past ten. I warn you that you must call out your entire force if you propose to keep me here—"
>
> "That also can be done," answered Charlie amiably.
>
> "Good lord!" The Britisher looked helplessly at Wilkie Ballou. "What kind of place is this? Why don't they send a white man out here?"
>
> A rare light flared suddenly in Charlie's eyes. "The man who is about to cross a stream should not revile the crocodile's mother," he said in icy tones.
>
> "What do you mean by that?" Jaynes asked.[21]

Chan seems to know the effect of his talk, which is at best only half-comprehensible to many of his listeners. He enjoys forcing people to ask, as Jaynes does, "What do you mean by that?" or "What does it mean in English?" although he is speaking English, pidginized English. The psychological advantage he gains by baffling people is one of his hidden weapons in the sleuthing business. "The secret," as he tells a fellow police officer in *Keeper of the Keys*, "is to talk much, but say nothing."[22]

Charlie's secret seems to work against the grain of common assumptions about aphorism. Like its cousins—maxim, proverb, adage, epigram, axiom, dictum, and so on—aphorism is meant to achieve the greatest meaning with the fewest words. Civilizations were founded on the cornerstones laid by great thinkers whose doctrines have been crystallized into a body of memorable sayings, such as Heraclitus's "You cannot step twice into the same river," and Confucius's "The nature of man is always the same; it is their habits that separate them." The post-Renaissance, early modern world also boasted such master aphorists as Francis Bacon, Montaigne, Goethe, and even Benjamin Franklin, born in Boston in 1706. Bacon, for instance, writes specifically of aphoristic virtue:

> The writing in aphorisms hath many excellent virtues, whereto the writing in Method doth not approach. For first, it trieth the writer, whether he be superficial or solid: for Aphorisms, except they should be ridiculous, cannot be made but of the pith and heart of sciences; for discourse of illustration is cut off: recitals of examples are cut off; discourse of connection and order is cut off; descriptions of practice are cut off. So there remaineth nothing to fill the Aphorisms but some good quantity of observation: and therefore no man can suffice, nor in reason will attempt to write Aphorisms but he that is sound and grounded.[23]

Bacon's notion exemplifies the traditional belief that behind the seeming fragmentation of aphorisms lies a larger truth. And such a mother ship of truth guarantees the integrity of these adorable, spattering babies of wisdom, babies who can see through the emperor's new clothes.

Benjamin Franklin, who published the *Pennsylvania Gazette* (which the *Saturday Evening Post* claims as its forerunner), is perhaps the most significant aphorist in American history. As "Poor Richard" Saunders, Franklin composed, recast, or simply plundered countless aphorisms and stuffed them into his tremendously popular books. Many of these sayings, such as "God helps them that help themselves" and "A penny saved is a penny earned," have been built into the foundation of American wisdom. Most readers of the *Post*, nurtured in their youth on Franklin's aphorisms, must have found it striking to read a Chinaman's proverbial wisecracking in the magazine's pages. There is wisdom in Chan's sayings. In fact, many Chanisms are quite profound and funny, such as "Aged man should not consort with ruffians. Eggs should not dance with stones," "Talk will not cook rice," "Can you borrow a comb in a Buddhist monastery?" and "The fool in a hurry drinks his tea with a fork." But most Chanisms, contributing significantly to the charm of the character, sound too much like their generic cousins, fortune cookies, which are more symbols of exoticism than carriers of wisdom. In an age that had just legally codified Asians as foreigners, a pidgin-speaking, aphorism-spouting Charlie Chan would fit the label of "foreigner" like a glove.

In addition, Charlie Chan's obvious dislike for the Japanese reveals him as a product of the age. In remarks such as "Cooking business begins to get tiresome like the company of a Japanese," Chan conveys anti-Japanese sentiments that may at first seem representative of the age-old animosity between the Chinese and the Japanese. However, considering the geopolitical climate of the 1920s, Chan was perhaps more a spokesperson for American rather than Chinese anti-Japanese racism. With the rise of Japan as a modern global power, the United States increasingly regarded this Asian nation as a menacing competitor. The Japanese were the main Asian target for the 1924 Immigration Act, because a series of anti-Chinese laws had, since 1882, effectively halted Chinese immigration. Chinese, thus, were no longer a threat, and the Yellow Peril found a new incarnation. This distinct anti-Japanese streak in the Chinese detective would continue to manifest itself in later Chan films, especially those produced during World War II.

It is obvious that the character of Charlie Chan did not emerge from a vacuum. Inspired by the colorful exploits of the real-life, legendary Detective Apana, the fictional Chan was a creation that embodied the Zeitgeist of America in the 1920s. As he burrowed deeper into the American psyche, and as American culture underwent transformations over the ensuing decades, Charlie Chan would always stay on top of his game—as the iconic Chinaman.

17

Kaimuki

CHANG APANA'S HOUSE, KAIMUKI, HAWAII *(Photo by author)*

He don't like us violate the law. He arrests his own brother even, you know.
—Walter Chang, referring to his uncle, Chang Apana

WHEN THE FIRST Charlie Chan novel was published in 1925, Chang Apana had already become the "Grand Old Man," a nickname given him by his fellow officers at the Honolulu Police Department. According to John Jardine, who had joined the force two years earlier, at the age of twenty-two, and would later become a famous detective himself, Apana was "no longer sent out on 'live' cases but remained at the station to supervise trusties assigned to clean up the place."[1] "If the local police station is always ship shape," said a Honolulu Police Department report, "it is the quiet efficiency of Chang [Apana] that is responsible."[2] When he did get called upon, the case usually would involve Chinatown or Chinese. The publication of *The House Without a Key* made Apana even more famous: Honolulu residents soon figured out the striking resemblance between Charlie Chan and their local legend. From then on, Apana became known as "Charlie Chan," a moniker he readily accepted with a smile. He would happily autograph the Chan novels for any admiring locals and curious tourists. In recognition of his great service and superb performance, Apana was promoted to Second Grade Detective on April 1, 1925, followed by another promotion to First Grade Detective three years later.

Young Jardine recalled that the table in the detectives' room had an ornamental top made from black-and-white dominoes and mahjongg pieces that Apana and others had seized in gambling raids in Chinatown. A reticent man, Apana disliked bragging about his illustrious past. "He has been in on the inside of many of the big cases at the police station," reads an HPD report about Apana, "but no leaks have ever been traced to him." When he did talk about some of the old cases from years back, Jardine said, "Young men like myself liked to listen."[3] But even when the stories were told, Apana tended to err on the sketchy side; when his younger colleagues pestered him for more details, Apana would shake his head and say, "I could do it again. Just wait till they need a good man in an emergency."[4]

Under Captain John Kellett, the Detective Division consisted of twenty members, a mixture of old-timers like Apana and young rookies like Jardine. The diverse backgrounds of these detectives made the division look like the struggling League of Nations. John Nelson McIntosh had been born in Ireland and served in constabularies in South Africa and New Zealand before joining the force in Honolulu. Thomas J. Finnegan, another Irishman, had been a constable in Dublin before coming to Hawaii. Juan Oxiles had been a policeman in his native Philippines. Harry K. Noda, the smallest man on the entire force, who "looked half-asleep most of the time [but] in fact missed very little that went on," was of Japanese ancestry. And Kam Kwai, who had been a member of the force since 1910, was half-Chinese and half-Hawaiian.[5] All the detectives could speak at least two languages; one of them, named Stein, was fluent in eight languages. Jardine was the son of a Portuguese sailor who had come to the islands on a whaler. To become a cop, Jardine had had to take a physical exam and a written test in spelling, geography, and history at the eighth-grade level—a sign that things had changed at the HPD since the days when Apana, an illiterate man, had been allowed to join the force. As a rookie cop, Jardine walked some of the toughest beats in the city, including Aala Park and Hell's Half Acre. Within a year, he was promoted to the Detective Division and began to learn the tricks of the trade from Apana and other veterans, one important technique being the necessity to cultivate stool pigeons. The HPD might have instituted educational requirements for hiring officers, but it still lagged in adopting modern scientific methods of crime detection and evidence analysis. The first lie detector, a small machine retired from service by the Berkeley, California, Police Department, did not arrive at the HPD until the spring of 1924.[6] So, over the years, according to the recollection of fellow officer Joaquin Lum, Apana had received most of his clues from "an elaborate network of informants."[7] "Just like the harness cops," Jardine wrote in his memoir, "the detectives built their own strings of stool pigeons. A man was only as good as his stool pigeons were."[8]

Even though Apana was now at a remove from the sprawl of the street, he remained an inspiration and a role model for the department. In 1925, according to newspaper accounts, a new wave of hooliganism and violence hit Honolulu. Young gangsters were hanging around street corners and attacking unescorted women and servicemen on shore leave, so the HPD organized a "whipping squad" to clean up the streets. Under the leadership of Sergeant Antone Louis, five detectives (Jardine, John R. Troche, Oliver Barboza, George Nakea, and Joe Munson) were equipped with blacksnake whips that coiled around their waists, Apana-style. For a while, the squad was quite effective in breaking up the gangs. As Jardine recalled, "Young thugs who felt like heroes fighting clubs and fists with clubs and fists squealed like naughty children when they were on the receiving end of blacksnake whips. And we were pretty good. We got so good we could flick small specks off the seats of hoodlums' pants." Unfortunately, two detectives one day accidentally flicked the wrong youngster while pursuing a bunch of hoods and were charged with assault and battery. They were convicted in court and fined $100 each, and that was the end of the "whipping squad." Undeterred, Jardine still considered Apana-style crime fighting more humane and effective than other methods, especially in dealing with youngsters. "It's better," he said, "to whip a young man than to have to shoot an older one."[9] Apana would agree with that.

Like Charlie Chan, who has multiple offspring, Apana had a large family. After the death of his second wife, with whom he had three children, he had married her younger sister, Annie Lee Kwai, in 1914. Among Apana's three marriages, this was the only one recorded, with the marriage certificate revealing that the Catholic wedding was held on April 12 at Our Lady of Peace Cathedral in downtown Honolulu. Father Reginald Yzendoorn, a Sacred Hearts priest, officiated, and witnesses were Alfred F. Ocampo and Anna Kepano.[10] With Annie, Apana would have six more children. All told, he had ten children by the time of his death, while his fictional double sired a baker's dozen.

Born in 1895, Annie was about twenty-five years younger than Apana. An extant photo of Annie, taken in 1932 with Apana and three of their children (Annie, Alexander, and Rose), shows a beautiful young woman wearing a flowery dress and a broad-brimmed hat, looking confident, strong, full of pep. Since Apana never learned to drive, preferring instead the less mechanical, *paniolo* modes of transportation (a horse or a horse-drawn buggy), Annie was the family chauffeur. When in his wife's car, Apana always sat in the right front passenger seat, his right hand holding onto the canvas top of the car, "as if expecting it to blow off at any minute."[11]

Chang Apana was a very strict man, both with himself and with the people around him. He kept a regular daily schedule and would cook and serve family meals at the same time every day. Anyone who was tardy would be out of luck. Friends and relatives trying to curry favor with him in police matters, such as traffic tickets or car licenses, were often disappointed. "He don't like us violate the law," recalled his nephew, Walter Chang. "He arrests his own brother even, you know. He's a very strict man. That's what, you know. You can't beat the man, very strict." When suitors of his daughter Cecelia came to call at the house, Apana sometimes would give them the third degree.[12]

Apana especially disliked gambling, a social disease prevalent among the Chinese. According to Gilbert Martines, the Apana family moved in 1922 from downtown Honolulu to the outskirts for reasons related to gambling. Living in town might have made it easier for Apana to go to work, but it also gave Annie the convenience of socializing with her friends, who appeared addicted to mah-jongg. Like stud poker and fast-drawing cowboys, mah-jongg and Chinese ladies are inseparably linked. Even though Annie and her friends played for pennies, Apana came down hard on gambling of any kind, and he became furious with his wife. To get Annie "away from the undesirable influences" of her friends, he moved the family from downtown Morris Lane to Waialae Avenue in Kaimuki, which was considered to be "the country" at that time.[13]

IN JUNE 2008, during a research trip to Honolulu, I went to visit Apana's house at 3737 Waialae Avenue. As soon as the sun rose from behind craggy Diamond Head and transformed Waikiki Beach from its predawn monochrome to a colorful postcard, I left my hotel on Kalakaua Avenue and walked windward along Kapahulu Avenue. A plumeria-scented ocean breeze blew gently at my back. Large monkey-pods stood by the roadside under majestic canopies, their blossoms flaming like sunrise clouds.

Densely populated today, Kaimuki is no longer the prim countryside to which the Apana family moved in the 1920s, but it has remained one of the most multiracial residential areas in Hawaii. My barber in Santa Barbara, a man named Dean who grew up in Honolulu, has repeatedly told me while swooshing his sharp scissors close to my ears, about the Chinese *chow fun* and Vietnamese *pho* he used to have at places in Kaimuki.

That June morning, I was not looking for a homey dive for *chow fun* or *pho.* I had Apana's last address memorized, but I had miscalculated the distance when perusing the map. What I had figured to be a mere thirty-minute walk lasted for more than an hour. I soon realized that Waialae Avenue, Kaimuki's main thoroughfare, runs all the way from Waikiki toward the coral reefs on the east, and Apana's house is at the farther end of the avenue, near the ocean.

Typical of Honolulu weather, the temperature rose quickly as the sun edged higher in the sky. Walking block after block in the direction of the sun and the sea, I passed by modest-looking shops, fruit stands, markets, fast-food restaurants, bus stops, and telephone booths. The word *Kaimuki* in the Hawaiian language means "the ti oven." It is believed that in the old days, the Menehune (Hawaii's legendary little people) chose this area of rocky hills as a stronghold where they could safely make their famous ti ovens and not be molested by the Kamapuaa (pig gods) during the night. After the haoles arrived, they set up a semaphore signal station on Kaimuki Hill. In 1887, a rich German from Kauai, Daniel Paul Isenberg, bought a plot of land at Waialae and developed an extensive ranch for cattle, alfalfa, and racehorses. In 1898, during the real-estate boom following Hawaii's annexation to the United States, Kaimuki became the first major subdivision in Hawaii. The 1900 Chinatown fire, described in chapter 6, sent some residents to this area to build their new homesteads and businesses. By the time the Apana family moved here in 1922,

Kaimuki had become a quiet suburb with affordable, small bungalows scattered throughout the formerly barren, red-dirt land.[14]

Close to the Apana house was the Sacred Hearts Academy, an impressive white building with a stone terrace leading up to an arched façade. Founded in 1909, this was where Apana's three daughters had once gone to school. On days when Annie's car was not available, a police paddy wagon would arrive at the house to pick up Apana for work and also drop off the girls at the academy, where their schoolmates would wonder what the girls were doing in a police wagon.[15]

A few blocks down the street, where one could begin to glimpse the turquoise ocean shining under the tropical sun, stood a humble, two-story wood-frame house at the corner of Waialae Avenue and the uphill Fourteenth Avenue. Built in a plain plantation style, the house was nestled among brick-red vines of bougainvillea and the green shade of a mai-say-lan tree about to bloom. A metal mailbox sitting atop a low brownstone wall read: "3737," Apana's last address before he died. Right next to it was another mailbox, somewhat older, with the number "3737A," indicating an apartment attached to the rear of the house. There used to be a cottage behind the house, and when girls from the detention home sometimes came to help the Apanas with domestic chores, they would bunk in the cottage.[16]

The mai-say-lan tree—if it was indeed the same tree that had once stood in the Apana's garden—has an interesting history. *Mai-say-lan* is the Cantonese name for what is called *mi lan* in Mandarin Chinese. Also known as *Aglaia odorata,* mock lemon, or Chinese perfume plant, mi lan is a popular tree in southern China. When it blooms, the flowery bulbs look like little grains of yellow rice (hence the name *mi,* meaning "rice") and emit a distinct sweet aroma. The chain-smoking Apana invented a unique way of enhancing his favorite Chesterfield brand. He would put the cigarettes in a can containing a mixture of tea leaves and mai-say-lan flowers. Over time, the mingled fragrance would seep into the Chesterfields and float in the air when he smoked the cigarettes.[17]

Behind the mai-say-lan was a narrow front lanai, built of beams painted in coffee brown and partly shaded by two barren white trellises. As an illiterate man, Apana used to have his daughter Rose read to him on the lanai after dinner.[18] (Incidentally, Charlie Chan's eldest daughter, who is said to be an avid reader of movie magazines, also happens to be named Rose.) One can easily imagine a scene of domestic bliss: an aging father, a former rough-and-tumble *paniolo* and now a grizzled detective, who had endured multiple stab wounds and gunshots, listening to his teenage daughter reading stories to him in a language he did not completely understand. The parental pleasure obviously would not be found solely in the stories themselves, but more in the satisfaction of knowing that his daughter was growing and learning.

The scene reminded me of my own daughter, Isabelle, and the times we had spent together. When Isabelle was still living with me in Santa Barbara, I used to get up every morning to make her breakfast—pan-fried mini-pancakes, scrambled eggs, and a glass of warm soy milk—and then drive her to school. The fifteen-minute drive along the foot of the Santa Ynez Mountains was my favorite. As we passed the orange groves and rolling hills, Isabelle would sit to my right, telling me about her dreams of the previous nights and things she had learned at school. And she would ask me millions of questions. Since she had learned to speak Chinese first, she was still struggling with English then. Every day, I was delighted to notice new English words she had picked up; every new word was an instant enlargement of her world, like tree rings or Emerson's circles that grow wider and wider.

Thinking of Isabelle, I envied Apana his domestic bliss, his precious time with his daughter.

In between Rose's stories, promptly at nine o'clock, Apana would go inside and bake goodies—cornbread, pudding, or jelly rolls. While waiting for the pastry to be done, the father and daughter would resume their ritual of reading or holding long chats in the midst of the sweet smell drifting out from the kitchen. According to Rose, her father would "tell her of his hopes that she would go to college some day." (Charlie Chan's daughter Rose, like many of her siblings, does go to college, in California.)[19]

From where they were sitting, they could see the dark profiles of the ridges to the north of Kaimuki. Today those ridges are covered with houses. And to the east, where Waialae disappeared into the night, the ocean glistened with silvery fish-scale waves. The yellow lanterns of Japanese sampans twinkled like fireflies under the moon. In Apana's day, motorcars were still too rare to disturb the underdeveloped, rustic Kaimuki at such late hours. Only the tick-tock hoofbeats and squeaking wheels of a buggy would now and then interrupt the calm of the night.

The nights at Apana's house, however, were not always so peaceful. Opium dealers would stop by and try to bribe the detective into revealing the locations and times of pending busts. There had been many graft scandals at the HPD in the early decades of the century, resulting in the arrest and firing of several of Apana's associates and superiors. Chief of Detectives Arthur McDuffie resigned in 1923 after being implicated in a scandal. His successor, Captain John Kellett, was indicted for graft in 1927, while a few years later, Kam Kwai, Apana's close associate, was accused but cleared of corruption. As the longest-serving officer at the HPD at the time of his retirement, Apana had maintained a remarkably pristine record. When those offering bribes showed up at his door, Apana would scream at them and send them away.[20]

Walking around the house that morning, I thought about knocking on the door and trying to speak to whoever was living there. But I realized that eight o'clock on a Sunday morning might be too early to barge into a strange house and ask questions, especially questions about residents who had lived there about eight decades earlier. I had been circling the residence for more than twenty minutes, and no one seemed to be up and about; the only movement was a white satin curtain behind a slightly opened upstairs window that bowed waywardly as the morning breeze came and went.

At one point, an old Asian woman emerged from a bungalow next door, dragging behind her a fallen bougainvillea twig. As she put the dry twig into a trash can by the street, I approached her. She was startled, and when I tried to speak to her in English, she shook her head and said something that sounded like Vietnamese. Then she quickly went back inside.

Across the street was a bus stop, so I went there and waited, trying to decide what to do next. Suddenly, my cellphone buzzed; it was my daughter, Isabelle, calling from her home in Austin, Texas. "Daddy, aloha!" she yelled cheerfully. Before my trip, I had sent her a book from her favorite Juni B. Jones series, called *Juni B. Jones, First Grader: Aloha-ha-ha!* We started chatting about what she had read in the book, and I told her I would send her a postcard from Hawaii. We had made a pact that every time I went on a trip, I would send her a postcard from each city I visited. Within a year, she had received about half a dozen cards from all the places I had visited for lectures and readings: snowy Boston (her birthplace), the Liberty Bell in Philadelphia, the Sooner Hotel in Norman, Oklahoma, the Statue of Liberty, the Golden Gate Bridge, and so on.

While we were talking, a bus showed up on the far horizon, like a ship rising from the sea. By the time I said good-bye to Isabelle and to Apana's old home, the bus had arrived and I hopped aboard. As the bus cruised along bustling Waialae Avenue, it was suddenly clear to me, perhaps because of having visited the detective's final homestead, how much of a patriarch Apana had become—not only to the Honolulu police force and his family but now to me as well.

18

Pasadena

Earl Derr Biggers's house, Pasadena, California *(Photo by author)*

I selected Pasadena as the winter home of my family because I consider it a veritable paradise, it has no equal in the world, regarding healthful climate, scenery, vegetation, flowers, shrubberies, fruit and general comfort of living. . . . Pasadena is undoubtedly destined to become a most popular American winter residence.

—Adolphus Busch, 1911

Pasadena, 1924. Bounded by the bold-faced San Gabriel Mountains on the north and a broad valley to the east, the city was reveling in a postwar glamour and opulence that lived up to its name in the Chippewa dialect: "Crown of the Valley."

Spanish missionaries settled here in 1771, first building the San Gabriel Mission. In the early nineteenth century, a steady flow of hard-hit midwestern farmers and ranchers, driven out by harsh winters, arrived in the area to rebuild their lives in more temperate climes. With the coming of the railroad in the mid-1880s, Pasadena changed almost overnight from a loose cluster of ranches and haciendas into a busy resort town, replete with luxurious hotels, palatial mansions, and trolley lines.[1] Attracted by Southern California's climate and scenery, the nation's rich and famous—including Henry Huntington, Walter Raymond, Thaddeus Lowe, and Adolphus Busch—built homes in Pasadena. Orange Grove Avenue, crowded with mansions designed by famous architects, would soon be known as "Millionaires' Row." Made up of what one resident called "the cream of culture, education and refinement of the Eastern cities," Pasadena by 1920 had become the wealthiest city per capita in the United States.

During the 1920s, Pasadena roared in a style that helped give the decade its glow. What is known today as the Rose Bowl Parade had expanded by 1922 from a few flower-bedecked carriages to a tide of motor-driven floats and marching bands. The first national radio broadcast, which described the spectacle, went out over KPSN from the *Pasadena Star-News* building in 1926.[2] The majestic City Hall, designed by Bakewell & Brown of San Francisco, was completed in 1927, the same year the Huntington Library and Art Gallery opened its doors to the public. Living to the full, the city was a center for art deco, jazz, painting, literature, and science.

In late 1924, Earl Biggers, whose chronic health problems forced him to abandon his Brahmin friends in the Northeast, decided to relocate and seek warmth and sunshine in Southern California. The move was made financially possible by the handsome advances he had received from both the *Saturday Evening Post* and Bobbs-Merrill for *The House Without a Key*. Along with his wife, Eleanor, and son Bobby, Biggers arrived in Pasadena in November. "We are settled in Pasadena and it looks good to us," Biggers wrote in a letter dated November 21. "Bobby is in a good school, and I think we will look for a bungalow next year."[3]

The Biggers trio first stayed at the resplendent Maryland Hotel.

Founded in 1903 and then rebuilt after a fire in 1914, the Maryland was the first luxury hotel in Pasadena to remain open throughout the year. Located on Colorado Boulevard between Euclid and Los Robles, it was well known for the separate bungalows that it leased to the most affluent, who wanted both hotel services and private accommodations.[4] After spending Christmas and New Year's at the Maryland, the Biggers family moved into a lovely little bungalow at 609 South Hudson Avenue, right off California Boulevard. Nestled among roses and with two orange trees on the front lawn, it was a comfortable enough house, but Biggers had developed the habit of working in an office rather than at home. Every morning at nine, he walked through Pasadena's sunny streets to a rented office, a small room in a building next to the *Pasadena Star-News.* He kept office furnishings to a bare minimum: one desk, one chair, and one steel filing cabinet. No telephone, no rugs, and no place for a visitor to sit. Pounding away all day at his Remington typewriter in his shirtsleeves, he could hear the clatter of the *Star-News*'s press outside his windows. "I try to imagine," Biggers told a friend, "that I am out to make the next edition."[5]

In this spartan office, Biggers finished writing his next Charlie Chan novel, *The Chinese Parrot.* By insatiable demand, Charlie appeared in the book as the central character, against the background of the stunning beauty of the California desert, which had been introduced to Biggers by a Connecticut senator, Charles C. Cook. As with the first book, the *Saturday Evening Post* serialized the second novel in 1926, and Bobbs-Merrill published it in a hardcover edition. The publisher sold 20,000 copies in six months, a 6,000-copy improvement over *The House Without a Key.*

The year 1926 also saw the publication of S. S. Van Dine's *The Benson Murder Case,* a book often touted as the beginning of the golden age of American mystery. Born Willard Huntington Wright in Charlottesville, Virginia, on October 15, 1888, Van Dine was the son of a rich family that made money from its vast real-estate holdings across California. First educated at St. Vincent College and then Pomona

College, Van Dine entered Harvard in 1906. He was in the same class as T. S. Eliot and three years behind Earl Biggers. Intolerant of professors, Van Dine was soon expelled from Harvard for attending classes with a glass of absinthe perched on his chair to ease the tedium of lectures. In and out of jobs for more than a decade as a journalist, critic, and editor, Van Dine never made a splash in the literary pond until publication of *The Benson Murder Case.* It was said that he had become interested in crime novels after being confined to bed for cocaine addiction. He adopted his pseudonym in part from his mother's maiden name, Van Vranken, and in part because, as he put it, "the steam ship initials summarized my desire to travel and I hoped that *dine* would at last turn into a verb. I had lived so many years without having had it in my vocabulary at all."[6] Indeed, Van Dine would not have to worry about his dinner bill again for a long time. The first edition of *The Benson Murder Case* sold out in the first week, and his next book, *The "Canary" Murder Case* (1927), broke all records for detective fiction, including the works of Arthur Conan Doyle, at the time.

It may be true that Van Dine was more popular than Biggers in those years, but history proves that Biggers's legacy—or, rather, Charlie Chan's—is far more enduring. Published by Scribner's, Van Dine's novels set out to win the cultured public, as did the works of other authors groomed by Maxwell E. Perkins, who had been the editor for, among others, Thomas Wolfe, F. Scott Fitzgerald, Ernest Hemingway, and a young Henry Roth. Van Dine's hero, Philo Vance, is a wealthy, sophisticated New Yorker with a fund of knowledge so arcane that it requires footnotes.[7] In contrast to aphorism-sputtering Charlie Chan, Philo Vance wears his foreign words on his sleeve and pretends to be far more versed in European languages than he actually is. Like T. S. Eliot's Prufrock, Philo Vance is a hero—or, to adopt the modernist parlance, an antihero—of the elite class. He is the inverse of Charlie Chan.

Humble, self-effacing Charlie Chan captured the fancy of readers of a different sort. Forged out of the common stock, Chan has a much wider appeal than aristocratic Vance, and the Chan novels are not blood-dripping thrillers, but rather fine and subtle examples of detective fiction stretching back to Wilkie Collins's *The Moonstone*, with a touch of comedy and romance added for the modern reader. *The Chinese Parrot*, for instance, mixes mystery with Western romance to perfection: California desert, ghost mining town, love story, and gunslinging. Contrary to Van Dine's famously inept claim that "the detective story, in fact, is the only type of fiction that cannot be filmed," *The Chinese Parrot* was readymade for Hollywood, and Chan's adventures in the Wild West drew enthusiastic responses from the mystery/Western–hungry public. As Biggers reported happily to his Bobbs-Merrill publisher:

> I was much surprised a few days ago to open an express and find inside a large and deadly-looking six-shooter, which fairly screamed of the wide open spaces where men were men. It was accompanied by a letter which read: "This Battle Battered Betsy has been through many vicissitudes in many climes. She is rusty and creaks at the knees but will still belch fire and throw a mean bulk of lead. She is good for some years of active service and as a wall flower will defy time. Please accept Betsy as a slight token of my appreciation for the Bill Hart gun boost. Your *Chinese Parrot* is a corker."[8]

In October 1926, with the royalties piling up from his book sales, Biggers bought a lovely Spanish-style home in Pasadena. Located at 2000 East California Boulevard, the house, according to Biggers, "is made of remarkably good materials and is in a section where land values are certain to increase." When I visited the address in the fall of 2008, just a few months after my field trip to Apana's Kaimuki residence, a charming red-tiled, white-stucco–walled house still stood there, looking as if it had just been built.

At the house, Biggers hired a Chinese servant named Gung Wong, about whom he would complain constantly. Despite the relocation to

Southern California, Biggers continued to have bouts of illness and would be bedridden now and then. Wong obviously was not as good a houseboy as Charlie Chan. "During my six weeks in bed," Biggers wrote in 1930, "I came into close contact, for the first time, with our Chinese boy, and I found him an unfeeling little devil—not much of a boost for Charlie."[9]

Thrilled with his success at being a literary Pygmalion, Biggers could no longer confine his Galatea-like invention of Chan to the mere pages between book covers. With Eleanor's help, he featured his invented Chinaman on a New Year's card that read: "For the New Year I warmly wish you plenty rice—since even the sunrise is without beauty to the hungry; plenty health—since even the road down hill is hard for the sick; and plenty peace of mind—since even trouble follows the restless like flies in the fifth month."[10]

When Homer Croy, a freelance writer and Chan aficionado, queried Biggers regarding the origin of the Chinese sleuth, Biggers actually responded with Charlie Chan's idiosyncratic diction, in which the puckish detective carries on a dialogue with his "boss":

> Boss looks me over, and puts me in novel, *The House Without a Key.* "You are minor character, always," he explains. "No major feelings, please. The background is your province—keep as far back as is humanly possible." Story starts to begin serial career, and public gets stirred up. They demand fuller view of my humble self. "What is the approximate date of beginning of next Charlie Chan story?" they inquire of the boss. And is my face red?
>
> Boss glares at me, plenty gloomy. "Good Lord!" he cries, "am I saddled with you for the remainder of my existence?"
>
> "You could be saddled with horse," I bristle.
>
> "But how can I write of Chinese?" he demanded. "I know nothing of same. I could not distinguish Chinese man from Wall Street broker."
>
> "Chinese would be the one who sold you the honest securities," I elucidate.

So the boss writes *The Chinese Parrot,* and *Behind That Curtain. . . .*[11]

Biggers was not alone in assuming the Charlie Chan persona. Apana, as mentioned earlier, was hardly offended by the sobriquet when he was addressed as "Charlie Chan" in the streets of Honolulu. The reification of this literary detective was complete when even officials at the Hawaii Tourist Bureau took part in the game, affecting Chan's accent. George Armitage, head of the bureau, who had been in constant touch with the novelist, once sent Biggers a beautiful painting of Hawaii as a New Year's gift, accompanied by a grammatically bludgeoned letter from "Charlie Chan":

Most Truly Friends:

Most warm congratulations on most fruitful writings which now find place in book stores, news stands and drugs store all over world.

My own pleasure is not to be worded that I, Charlie Chan, are honored to appear in most late book from pen which have made English language and story of mystery her slave and which tell of Honolulu and Waikiki which are spots of heartbreaking charm.

It is greatest privilege for me, I would say, for I am before only policeman on small remuneration living on Punchbowl Hill with my happy wife and children, but fates have been in smiling mood and what we have now are plentiful. At present I have many promotions in Honolulu police department and salary are so ample I have become proud owner of a home in Manoa Valley where rainbow smiles upon me. Children are now in Punahou School and University of Hawaii.

I have unlimited yearning to see you, but duty remains duty so I must keep ever-open eye to detect criminals here. Gratitude are well known to me, however, and Mrs. Chan and I have talked with our children, and your friendship are a happy item on the golden scroll of memory so we ask you to receive a small gift from us. My

University son and daughter are thinking a Hawaiian picture are most appropriate. Some things are not well-known to me, but, quoting old Chinese saying: "A picture is a voiceless poem," so I am bowing before judgment of rising generation.

Forget writing worries in California and come to Waikiki where we can float idle like leaves on stream.

The honor of your company would pleasure me deeply.

My final wish—the snowy, chilling days of winter and the scorching, windless days of summer—may they all be springtime for you.

Your humbly servant,
Charlie Chan[12]

As Biggers told his publisher at Bobbs-Merrill, Armitage's letter was "the best amateur effort in that line which I have seen." High praise, indeed, from the author. But would we wish to consider how many more amateur efforts there have been since? Several generations of American schoolchildren in the coming decades would be the natural mimics of Charlie Chan, whom they saw on screens large and small. Of course, Biggers was fully cognizant of the commercial reasons why the Hawaii Tourist Bureau would want to keep up ties with a writer in Southern California. The future fiftieth state had always been well known for its true aloha spirit, but it had also been one of the savviest U.S. territories in promoting itself to attract traders and tourists alike. Ever since the annexation in 1898, the question of statehood had been in almost every Hawaiian's mind. Territorial status had huge disadvantages. The governor of Hawaii was appointed by the president of the United States. The people of Hawaii could not take part in presidential elections. They could elect a territorial delegate to Congress, but the delegate had no vote in the House of Representatives. Hawaii paid taxes as if it were a state, but it was not entitled to all the federal benefits enjoyed by the states.[13] Therefore, despite the opposition of some powerful local parties, almost every territorial legislature since 1903 had passed resolutions endorsing statehood. The U.S. Congress, however, had not been so keen on the idea of accepting into the Union a state dominated by an Asian population. As a result, the game of courtship and demurrals went on for decades.

Over the years, Hawaii had built an impressive list of authors it could count as either adopted citizens or best friends. In 1908, on the occasion of the completion of Mark Twain's Stormfield residence in Redding, Connecticut, and his seventy-third birthday, the Hawaii Promotion Committee sent him a mantelpiece and wall decoration carved out of Hawaiian koa wood. In return, Hawaii received from America's most beloved writer a phrase that would become the best advertisement for the islands: "The loveliest fleet of islands that lies anchored in any ocean."[14] Jack London was also duly thanked for his thrilling description of surfing at Waikiki, which became instrumental in popularizing Hawaii's "royal sport," even though his candid stories about leprosy infuriated the islanders.

The Charlie Chan books endeared Biggers to the people of Hawaii, and not just the haoles. As soon as the first installment of *The House Without a Key* appeared in the *Saturday Evening Post* on January 24, 1925, the *Honolulu Star-Bulletin* ran a lengthy review under the title "Writer Boosts Hawaii in Tale." It praised Biggers's publication "as good as anything a malihini [outsider] has done since Jack London lived in Hawaii." The anonymous reviewer was impressed that a malihini writer "can spell *pau* and *pilikia* and *wiki-wiki* and *papaya,* and write a story in which not only all these words are correctly used, but one which is full of atmosphere and beauty and romance as well."[15] Upon the publication of the book by Bobbs-Merrill that spring, the same newspaper again gave it a glowing review, noting especially the free publicity for Hawaii in the book: "Biggers' story was of great interest to the island people, especially residents of Honolulu, as it portrayed vividly the life of the city and its customs. No phase of the racial situation, the scenery, climate, music or customs, went without notice by the author. With several places of the city used as settings, Biggers fabricated a plot which contained the elements of a successful one—love and action."[16]

There was, however, some criticism of the book. Besides several factual errors involving Hawaiian names and customs, one chief concern was with Charlie Chan's pidgin English. Chester A. Doyle, a veteran court interpreter who had, in his own words, "years of experience handling oriental criminals for the police department of Hawaii," thought that Biggers's book was "the bunk" and a "literary curiosity." "No Chinese," Doyle stated, "would use the language attributed to the Chinese detective."[17] Biggers replied to the charge in a letter sent to the *Star-Bulletin*: "I am sorry if Honolulu is still distressed by Charlie Chan's way of putting things. As I told you, if he talked good English, as he naturally would, he would have no flavor. . . . In this dilemma, I turned to the way the Oriental mind sometimes works when its owners take pen in hand."[18]

Whether or not Biggers's justification, employing the worst kind of Orientalist cliché, sounded convincing, Hawaii had the author to thank for the boost to its image. In April 1925, the Hawaii Tourist Bureau sent Biggers a huge koa-wood key—twenty-five inches long and six inches wide—with an inscription: "Hawaii is still the House Without a Key; you have it. Use it often."[19] In his reply, Biggers expressed his deep gratitude: "I am proud of the friends I have made in the islands, and prouder of this key than anything that has happened to me in 20 years of writing." He added, "Most people who have been to Hawaii long to return, and in the future I shall long a bit more ardently than most."[20]

True to his words, Biggers would soon return to the islands.

19

A Meeting of East and West

EARL DERR BIGGERS WITH A STAND-IN CHARLIE CHAN, JULY 1928

(Courtesy of Lilly Library, Indiana University)

If Charlie Chan must have an original, he could not have a better one.
—Earl Derr Biggers

CONTRARY TO RUDYARD Kipling's famous claim, the East and West *do* meet.

On June 30, 1928, Earl Biggers and his family sailed for Honolulu on board the *Malolo*. With three best-selling Charlie Chan novels to his credit, Biggers was looking for new material, especially island material, for his future work. Since Chan's two most recent exploits had taken place on the West Coast, fans had been asking when they would see the Honolulu sleuth in action again on his home turf. South Seas romance was, after all, one of the key ingredients in the tangy chop suey that made up a Charlie Chan mystery. As Biggers reminded his publisher when they were still discussing the promotion of the first book, *The House Without a Key*:

> I wanted to talk to you regarding the handling of this book. I haven't any revolutionary ideas, but I felt that in pushing it it might be well to soft pedal murder and play up the setting. I have never mentioned Honolulu to anybody but heard what they said—"Oh, I have always wanted to go there" if they hadn't already been. Mr. Leslie Hood of Vroman's bookstore here, told me the other day that he couldn't ask for a better setting than Honolulu in appealing to his clientele—unless it was Southern California. Of course he had to add that. But I do believe that the biggest point of appeal on this story will be the setting, and it may be that we can break through the ranks and sell a few outside the regular mystery story clientele by the Hawaii appeal. Certainly everyone who has been there will want the book—and there are lots of them. So I felt that in any advertising you might bring in the color stuff I didn't get in the title—as for instance "The House Without a Key" stood by the white beach of Waikiki at the Crossroads of the Pacific, etc. etc. You might advertise it as a "Crossroads Puzzle."[1]

Biggers arrived in Honolulu just in time for the Independence Day fireworks, a long tradition started by American settlers in the early days of Kamehameha the Great. He was given a celebrity's welcome by local residents and organizations. Hawaii newspapers reported his arrival on their front pages, as they did with other famous visitors: "After an absence of eight years, Earl Derr Biggers, famous author of *The House Without a Key, The Chinese Parrot, Behind That Curtain,* in which the now equally famous Chinese detective Charlie Chang [*sic*] solves deep mysteries, returned to Honolulu yesterday." The city did have reason for gratitude, for, as the article continues, "Through Biggers' popular mystery novels, Honolulu has received invaluable publicity all over the world, as Biggers reported that his books have been translated into leading languages of Europe and Chang is now known as well in Moscow as he is in Honolulu or San Francisco."[2]

Biggers stayed at the Royal Hawaiian Hotel (also known as the "Pink Palace of the Pacific"), which had just opened its doors to guests the previous year. With a bright-pink Moorish-style stucco façade, the Royal Hawaiian owed its architectural influence to Hollywood, especially Rudolph Valentino and his Arabian movies, which had inspired a fad for all things Spanish and Moorish in the 1920s. It boasted four hundred large, luxurious rooms and suites. Adding to its exotic charm, the hotel's bellhops all wore pseudo-Chinese costumes. The spectacle that accompanied the opening of the hotel in February 1927 was like a performance at the old Metropolitan Opera House, with a tropical twist. "A huge pageant featured a fleet of Hawaiian outrigger canoes, each of them carrying torch- and spear-bearing warriors in full regalia who were greeted on shore by lei-bedecked native princesses." *Turandot,* completed by Giacomo Puccini that year, could never be so grand. At the black-tie gala inside the lush hotel, all of the twelve hundred guests were haoles except for Princess Abigail Kawananakoa, the last link to the Hawaiian monarchy. On an island where four out of five people were nonwhite at the time, the Royal Hawaiian Hotel was as much a symbol of racial hierarchy as an icon of Hawaiian tourism.[3]

After his arrival, Biggers regularly granted interviews to reporters and toured around the island, sightseeing and lecturing. The Honolulu Advertiser's Club billed Biggers and Miss Jessie de Both, the new director of the club's cooking and homemaking school, as speakers for its monthly meeting in July. Not to be outdone by the ladies, gentlemen at the exclusive Oahu Country Club, gratified by the free publicity Biggers had given their organization in his work, invited him to lunch and a few rounds of golf. The Hawaii Tourist Bureau, as usual, was busy orchestrating all sorts of promotional events, including a quixotic photo-op with a stand-in Charlie Chan.

Set on the airy terrace of the Royal Hawaiian, the picture shows Biggers sitting with a Chinese man dressed in a traditional robe. Between them and their tiger-skin–lined wicker chairs stands a small table on which rests an empty birdcage—suggesting "the Chinese parrot"? Under the tropical sun, Biggers looks immaculately well groomed in his light-toned pongee suit and white leather shoes, beaming with creative energy as he holds a pen and puts both hands on the table, as if in the midst of conjuring up the character sitting right in front of him. The anonymous Chinese man—perhaps one of the hotel's bellhops—dressed in faux Charlie Chan threads, tucks his hands inside the long sleeves of his robe and holds them together over his lap as if doing a curtsy. With close-cropped hair and a Mongolian face, he looks unmistakably Chinese. A marbled terrace, royal palms, flaming flora in the background, and an author and his literary creation meeting over a writing table and a birdcage—the staged picture is fantastically rich in local color and international flavor. The scene easily portrays the fantasy of "East meeting West," much more so than if Chang Apana had been sitting opposite Biggers on the terrace, dispelling the magic with realism.

Beyond the contrived photo-op, however, a real meeting between East and West did occur. On July 5, the second day of his visit, Biggers met up with Chang Apana. In the plush lounge of the Royal Hawaiian Hotel, Biggers graciously received Apana, who had arrived in his usual spick-and-span suit and tie. Chang Joe, Apana's restaurateur nephew, was the interpreter.

By this time, Apana had become a celebrated citizen of Honolulu not only for his guts as a legendary cop but also for his inspiration for the Charlie Chan character. "He was a marked man among tourists," Biggers wrote, as if describing an elephant on an African safari. "He was autographing my books with a flourish. When, at ball games, he walked proudly up and down before the crowds, swinging his famous rawhide whip, hundreds of little Oriental kids shouted in chorus: 'Charlie Chan! Charlie Chan!' "[4]

Biggers was singularly impressed by the man who had inspired his best-selling novels and made him a celebrity author, even though he had always denied publicly that Charlie Chan was based on any real person. "If Charlie Chan must have an original, he could not have a better one," Biggers acknowledged. "For the record of Chang Apana, after nearly forty years on the force, is a record of honesty, faithfulness and courage that Chan himself could well be proud of. He is one public servant who is honored and respected by the entire town."

During their meeting, Apana held out his worn old hands and said, "No money ever stuck to them." The veteran detective rolled up his trousers and revealed deep gashes, long since healed. He also indicated other wounds by pointing to various portions of his body. "Yes, they had tried to do him in—some of them," Biggers wrote. "But most of them feared him mightily; once they saw his hand moving towards the whip at his waist, they fled in droves before him."

Despite the language barrier, which could never be fully overcome by translation (Chang Joe was also illiterate but spoke a little English), Biggers was delighted to see the twinkle of authentic humor in Apana's eyes. "An amiable man," Biggers later recalled, "a man who can laugh even as he reaches for the whip."[5]

The meeting had such an evident effect on Biggers that in the next Chan novel, *The Black Camel,* published a year later, the detective makes his entrance in no other place than the lobby of the Pink Palace. Posing as a Chinese merchant—Apana as a See Yup Man, but in a more respectable costume—Charlie Chan approaches Tarneverro, a fortune-teller who is also wearing a disguise. After a few rounds of brain wrestling, they draw to a tie, with Chan in his usual politeness complimenting the slippery veil-lifter: "Memory of your cleverness will linger in my poor mind for long time to come."[6] In the 1931 film version, the detective's punch line is a Chanish reminder: "Always harder to keep murder secret than for egg to bounce on sidewalk."

AUTHOR MEETS 'LIVE' CHINESE DETECTIVE

Earl Derr Biggers and Chang Apana, July 5, 1928

(Courtesy of Honolulu Star-Bulletin*)*

The meeting between the real Charlie Chan and the author culminated in the two men posing for the camera. As seen in the only surviving copy of the photo, they look into each other's eyes rather than at the camera lens. Apana smiles with his sharp, deep-set eyes and heavily etched cheeks. Biggers looks demure, as if a little taken aback by the searching gaze of the man who has made his career. "I shall go on being grateful to him," Biggers said. "He has turned out to be the ideal 'original' for Charlie Chan."[7]

In the end, it was the staged photo, orchestrated by the Hawaii Tourist Bureau, that was later released and distributed to about fifty newspapers. Perhaps the ideal original did not, after all, look too ideal in the picture. A man dressed in a long silk robe would certainly appear to be more "authentically" Chinese, or more stereotypically Asian and exotic, than a wizened old man in a Western suit and tie. Charlie Chan, as we know, is an exotic Chinaman. Sometimes fiction can make a stronger claim on reality, and for that, nothing can outdo film, which in the late 1920s had just begun to occupy a central position in American cultural life. And it was on the silver screen that the wisecracking fictional Chinese detective would have a most spectacular career.

PART FOUR

CHARLIE CHAN AT THE MOVIES

Kamiyama Sojin as Charlie Chan (alias Ah Kim) in *The Chinese Parrot*, 1927 *(Courtesy of Everett Collection)*

20

Hollywood's Chinoiserie

GRAUMAN'S CHINESE THEATRE, HOLLYWOOD *(Photo by author)*

Hollywood is famous furnisher of mysteries.
—Charlie Chan

THE *NEW YORKER* in 1929 printed a cartoon showing a child standing in a movie-theater lobby and asking, "Mama—does God live here?" The child, clinging to his mother's side, looks awe-struck. The cartoon contains more than just a kernel of truth. "Picture palaces" such as the Roxy, Mark Strand, Capitol, Imperial,

Grauman's Egyptian and Chinese, Tivoli, and Howard—all extravagantly designed with art deco flamboyance or rococo motifs—shot up in such major cities as New York, San Francisco, Los Angeles, Chicago, and Atlanta. They reflected the gaudy splendor and the "unparalleled plenty" of that decade.

The motion picture, having come of age during the Great War, consolidated its position as America's dominant mass medium. What we know of film—as an art, an industry, and a state of mind—all took hold during the decade. Even before the advent of talking pictures, a Hollywood lifestyle had come into being.[1] Before World War I, movies had begun to shed the infamy of their origin in shabby storefront nickelodeons and had become a respectable form of entertainment. It was in the 1920s, however, when movies began to grab the lion's share of what German philosopher and social critic Theodor Adorno would call the "culture industry," taking center stage in the consciousness of the American people.

As Robert Sklar tells us in his classic work, *Movie-Made America*, "every large city and most medium-sized towns boasted at least one brand-new sumptuous picture palace" in the late 1920s. Sklar, one of the best historians of American film, re-creates for us the experience of "going to the pictures" at that time:

> Outside on the sidewalk stood a doorman, attired in frock coat with white gloves, waiting to open your car door and direct you to the ticket booth. If it was raining, he held an umbrella over your head; if snowing, an usher in the lobby rushed forward to brush off your coat. You passed from usher to usher as you moved through ornate lobby corridors, hushed by the atmosphere of an Egyptian temple or a baroque palace that had provided the inspiration for architectural imitation.

Once you entered the auditorium, there was yet another phalanx of ushers. One of them, next to the automatic seating boards, would tell you which seats were empty, and the other, holding a flashlight, would then take you to your seat. "There, after live stage performances, musical interludes played by an orchestra numbering up to thirty pieces, a newsreel and a travelogue, you saw what you had come for—a feature film, accompanied by its own especially arranged musical score."[2]

It was during the time that Sklar calls "the radiant dawn of popular mass culture" that Charlie Chan appeared as an icon in the American imagination. As the honorable detective once said, "A thousand-mile journey begins with one step."[3] His cinematic career, however, had more than one false step, especially during the silent-film era.

In 1926, a year after the publication of *The House Without a Key*, Pathé, a pioneering movie company well known for its newsreels and comedies, produced a ten-chapter serial based on Biggers's book. Directed by Spencer G. Bennett, then known as the "King of Serial Directors," the silent film featured George Kuwa as Charlie Chan. A Japanese actor who had appeared in fifty-eight silent and sound films at the time of his death in 1931, Kuwa could pass muster for the "very fat" Chan of Biggers's novel. Kamiyama Sojin, who in 1927 played Chan in *The Chinese Parrot*, directed by Hollywood's "golden boy," Paul Leni, was described by Biggers as "a corking actor" but "a long, thin, sinister Chink," hardly the fat sleuth of the novel.[4] Biggers might have gotten the physical description right, but Sojin was not a "Chink." Like Kuwa, who also appeared in the film, Sojin was what Biggers might have called a "Jap."

The choice of Japanese actors to play Charlie Chan, given the fact that he is so vehemently anti-Japanese in the novels, might seem odd, but such casting seemed completely understandable at the time. The film industry, especially in the 1920s, abounded with such ironies. Paradoxically, as feelings intensified against foreigners and new immigrants—best exemplified by the sensational Sacco and Vanzetti case—those responsible for the creation of the movie industry (and, in effect, mass American culture) were predominantly foreigners themselves. As David Robinson notes in his monograph, *Hollywood in the Twenties*, it is interesting to consider the "foreign" origins of the people who were responsible for the development of the movies and who ruled the American cinema in the 1920s and beyond. Adolph Zukor, the original founder of Paramount Pictures, was born in Hungary to a Jewish family and immigrated to America at the age of sixteen "with forty dollars sewn in the lining of his suit." Carl Laemmle, founder of Universal, came to the United States from Germany in 1884 and "worked for years in menial jobs." Louis B. Mayer, cofounder of Metro-Goldwyn-Mayer, was born Lazar Meir in Minsk and "started his life in the new world as a beachcomber and scrap dealer." Like his future MGM partner, Samuel Goldfish (later Goldwyn) was also a Polish Jew who left Warsaw on foot, penniless, and started off in upstate New York's garment business. And William Fox, the man who founded the company that would one day produce most of the Charlie Chan films, was born Wilhelm Fried in Hungary; at the age of seven, he had to support his impoverished family by working as a peddler.[5]

In short, the people who built the American cinema were also the very people whom the 1924 Immigration Act now excluded. The other obvious targets of the Johnson-Reed Act were of course the Japanese. Like their Jewish and Eastern European counterparts, the Japanese created a strong presence in early American movies, despite the prevalent racism of the time. The most famous Japanese actor in Hollywood was Sessue Hayakawa. Born Kintaro Hayakawa in Chiba, Japan, in 1889, Hayakawa was the third son of the governor of the prefecture. After failing in his training as a naval officer and a suicide attempt, he came to America in 1911 to study political economics at the University of Chicago. A martial artist, he played quarterback for the university football team and made good use of his jujitsu skills. Hayakawa recalled that period in his memoir, *Zen Showed Me the Way* (published in 1960):

> No matter how big a man came at me in blocking practice, upon contact he wound up flat on the field, out of play. I simply employed *taiatari*, judo body technique. After my first real game, it was noised about the campus that I possessed occult

> power. But a good thing can't last. The second season I played, the members of an opposing team complained. The use of judo or jujitsu was promptly forbidden. Once and [*sic*] a while thereafter, however, in the heat of the game I would forget; and after the University of Chicago varsity was penalized ten and fifteen yards four or five times, I was put off the team. So much for football.[6]

A chance visit to the Japanese Theater in Little Tokyo in Los Angeles sparked his interest in acting, and he adopted a stage name, "Sessue," meaning "snowy island." Hayakawa got his first major role in Thomas Ince's *The Typhoon* (1914). The next year, he starred in Cecil B. DeMille's *The Cheat*, which instantly propelled him to stardom.

A precursor to Rudolph Valentino, Hayakawa became a matinee idol whose exotic appearance suggested forbidden love. According to one seemingly apocryphal tabloid story, Hayakawa one day emerged from a limousine in front of a theater and was about to step into a puddle when "dozens of female fans surrounding his car fell over one another to spread their fur coats at his feet."[7] At the height of his career, he made $5,000 a week, on a par with Charlie Chaplin and Douglas Fairbanks. In 1918, unhappy with the roles he had played in the films and determined to portray a Japanese person "as he really is and not the way fiction paints him," he established his own production company, Haworth Pictures Corporation, which made twenty-three films in three years, amassing $2 million in profit each of those years. Yet his corona shone briefly. In 1922, as racial animosity toward Japanese heightened, and censorship increased after the appointment of William Hays as the president of the Motion Picture Producers and Distributors of America, Hayakawa left the country to pursue his career in Europe and Japan.

A media star, says film historian Richard Dyer, is a paradox in itself, a person who embodies tensions between multiple meanings and affects.[8] Thus, Hayakawa's sensational stardom at a time when anti-Japanese racism was on the rise can be explained in several ways.

Perhaps film from its very beginning has been regarded as a potential threat to traditional values and mainstream beliefs. Especially in its early days, before the adoption of the restrictive Hays Code and other moralistic guidelines, cinema appeared not only as transgressive but outright revolutionary. A plethora of risqué flicks, bloodcurdling horror movies, and vampire fare caused no small disturbance for Main Street America. Hollywood, it appears, has always been a haven for eccentrics and foreigners, a fact that would play into the hands of conservative forces in the days of McCarthyism.

No doubt Hayakawa's popularity also resulted from the "Japan craze" that had begun in the late nineteenth century but lingered on until after World War I. For many decades, Japan's art, architecture, costumes, and lifestyle fascinated Americans. The rise of Japan as a world power after its stunning defeat of Russia in 1905 had elevated its status in the American mind. The acclaim for Hayakawa, then, oddly suggested a strange mixture of xenophobia and xenophilia. Moreover, Hayakawa's success was also a result of savvy promotional techniques that exploited such contradictions in American culture. Walking a fine line between nativism and *Japonisme*, the Jesse L. Lasky Feature Play Company orchestrated a careful and quite deliberate strategy as it made *The Cheat* and other films starring Hayakawa. Daisuke Miyao, in his book-length study of the Japanese matinee idol, observed:

> Lasky's strategy was to locate Hayakawa in the movable middle-ground position in the racial and cultural hierarchy between white American and nonwhite other. On the one hand, Hayakawa's (and his characters') status had to be raised and distinguished racially or culturally from other nonwhite actors (and their characters) in order for the American middle-class audiences to sympathize with, identify with, or even desire Hayakawa more easily. On the other hand, Hayakawa's status had to be clearly differentiated from white Americans in terms of race. Any sexual relationship between Hayakawa's characters . . . and

> white women must be avoided in order not to cause any anxiety around miscegenation.[9]

Most improbably, a Japanese star had been born, in the midst of rising calls that "Japs must go!"

Following in Hayakawa's footsteps, George Kuwa and Kamiyama Sojin entered the Hollywood scene soon thereafter. Not nearly as successful as Hayakawa, these two actors nonetheless appeared in more than a hundred films, playing mostly evil and villainous Asian roles. Unfortunately, the reels of *The House Without a Key* and *The Chinese Parrot* have been lost, so we do not have a reliable means to assess the quality of their performances as the Chinese detective. But we do know that these two silent films constituted a rocky start for Charlie Chan. In fact, they almost killed off Chan's Hollywood career. In 1929, when Fox adapted *Behind That Curtain*, Biggers's third novel, it virtually wrote Charlie Chan out of the script! Billed last and played by a bald, British-accented E. L. Park, Chan appears for no more than a minute in an hour-long film. His supposed talkie debut, then, can hardly be called a Charlie Chan flick.

Despite Chan's near-disappearance from the screen, the tradition of depicting Asians as bogeymen and villainous predators who challenged the very essence of Caucasian purity was so well established that, Chan or not, it had become a fixture of American film culture. In fact, beginning with two short reels by Thomas Edison, *Chinese Laundry Scene* (1895) and *Dancing Chinamen-Marionettes* (1898), the foreign, exotic quality of the Chinese had become, as Graham Hodges puts it, "a staple of American filmmaking."[10] From narrative themes and set décor to costumes, a faux-Chinese ambience permeated Hollywood films, bringing to the mass audience once-forbidden pleasures through the display and consumption of exotic objects.[11] In this regard, Hollywood Orientalism was a variation, albeit far more accessible and affordable, of the Chinatown bus tour, which had just become fashionable in such cities as New York and San Francisco. In this curious form of "rubbernecking," a tourist could visit Chinatown on a bus that had ascending rows of seats like in a theater, equipped with a "megaphone man" who would ad-lib comments on the passing scenes of exotica.[12]

Hollywood's fascination with Chinese culture culminated in 1927 with the grand opening of the spectacularly ornate Grauman's Chinese Theatre. Financed jointly by Sidney Grauman, Mary Pickford, and Douglas Fairbanks, the $2 million theater was a Mount Olympus in the land of orange groves. At the groundbreaking ceremony, the sponsors invited Anna May Wong to shovel the first spadeful of dirt. In her Chinese silk robe, Wong looked rather like something out of a Hans Christian Andersen fairy tale. Ever since her debut in 1919, she had almost instantly metamorphosed from a Chinese laundryman's daughter to a Hollywood star, and she was indisputably the most important female Chinese symbol of the era. Not long after the Grauman's ceremony, she would make a cameo appearance in *The Chinese Parrot,* obviously to add some authentic Chinese flavor to a film about a Chinaman.

On May 18, 1927, Grauman's Chinese Theatre opened its doors. Soaring 90 feet, it boasted two gigantic coral-red columns supporting a jade-green roof. Between the columns flew a thirty-foot-long stone dragon. Many artifacts, including temple bells, pagodas, and stone "heaven dogs," had been imported from China and installed by Chinese artisans under the supervision of Chinese film director and poet Moon Quon. Inside the 2,258-seat theater, silver dragons spread across a ceiling sixty feet in diameter, circumscribed by gold medallions. With a pagoda as the box office, the theater also featured ushers dressed in Chinese costumes. An alluring wax statue of Anna May Wong would later grace the lobby. By all accounts, Grauman's Chinese Theatre was, in the words of Hodges, "a monument to Orientalism."[13]

Entering Hollywood in the midst of its Chinese craze, Charlie Chan, as a charming, exotic Chinaman, held enormous promise for filmmakers, even though reactions to the first three Chan numbers had been lackluster. What they needed to do was to find a good yellow face—or, better yet, a yellowface actor. As it turned out, the person who would save Charlie Chan from literally "falling out of the picture" and would propel the aphorism-spouting detective to stardom was an immigrant hailing not from Canton but from the snowy forests of Scandinavia: the Chinaman Warner Oland.

21

Yellowface

Warner Oland and Anna May Wong on the set of *Old San Francisco*, 1927 *(Courtesy of Wisconsin Center for Film and Theater Research, Madison)*

How could blacking up and then wiping off burnt cork be a rite of passage from immigrant to American?
—*Michael Rogin,* Blackface, White Noise[1]

Before he became Charlie Chan, Warner Oland, the Swedish silent film actor, already had made a name for himself by playing an orthodox Jew—and no ordinary orthodox Jew. It was Cantor Rabinowitz in the first talkie ever made in Hollywood, *The Jazz Singer* (1927).

Produced by Warner Bros. with its Vitaphone sound-on-disc system, *The Jazz Singer* featured Broadway's leading blackface entertainer, Al Jolson. The plot involves a Jewish boy named Jakie Rabinowitz, who is taken by jazz singing. Jakie's father, however, is a cantor who has always cherished the dream that Jakie would one day take his place in the synagogue. Furious with his son's distasteful obsession with Negro music, Cantor Rabinowitz physically punishes Jakie. After running away and being reborn as Jack Robin, Jakie makes a splash on Broadway as a blackface jazz singer. When he returns in glory to sing Irving Berlin's "Blue Skies" to his mother, his father comes home; in the middle of Jakie's crooning, he screams, "Stop!" The son is thrown out of the house until the father's death brings him home and back to the synagogue. To fulfill his father's last wish, Jakie takes the cantor's place and sings the Kol Nidre for his synagogue on the eve of Yom Kippur. The film ends with Jakie, in a wool cap and covered with burnt cork, performing a Negro number, "My Mammy," in front of his proud mother and an admiring Broadway audience.

Both Jolson's blackface and Oland's "Jewface" in the movie have provided ample fodder for analysis by cultural historians, who trace racial ventriloquism back to minstrelsy, the first and most important popular form of mass culture in nineteenth-century America. Whether in the form of comic skit, variety act, dance, or music, minstrel shows, as they were called, were vaudeville entertainment of racial parody performed mostly by cross-dressing white actors. Around the turn of the twentieth century, minstrelsy gave rise to a new form of popular entertainment: blackface. Even though whites in blackface and blacks in blackface had always been a key feature of minstrelsy, the new popularity of faces painted with burnt cork attained a new vogue at the height of the Eastern European immigration wave. As Michael Rogin argues in *Blackface, White Noise*, blackface in the early decades of the twentieth century gave whites an opportunity to act out and solidify their whiteness by playing and parodying blacks. James Baldwin puts it poignantly:

> No one was white before he/she came to America. It took generations and a vast amount of coercion before this became a white country. . . . There is an Irish community. . . . There is a German community. . . . There is a Jewish community. . . . There are English communities. There are French communities. Jews came here from countries where they were not white, and they came here in part because they were not white. . . . Everyone who got here, and paid the price of the ticket, the price was to become "white."

To turn European greenhorns in essence into white Americans, the melting pot, as Rogin points out, used racial masquerade to promote identity exchange but also to exclude unwanted racial groups.[2]

It is no surprise, then, that Hollywood's first blockbuster picture, *The Birth of a Nation,* featured blackface, as did Hollywood's first sound film, *The Jazz Singer.* If American literature established its national identity in the epic struggle between Indians and whites (consider Mary Rowlandson's captivity narrative and James Fenimore Cooper's *The Last of the Mohicans,* to name just a few), American film, as Rogin suggests, "was born from white depictions of blacks."[3]

In the workings of such a melting pot—or, rather, melting plot—yellowface, like blackface, redface, and Jewface, also played an important role. In *The Jazz Singer,* Cantor Rabinowitz's paternal "Stop!" marks a critical moment not only in the movie but also in the history of American motion pictures. "Stop!" is the last spoken word in *The Jazz Singer,* for thereafter the film reverts to the silent, pre-talkie mode. Oland's patriarchal Jew might have had the power to stop speech in the film, but the silent movies, with their pantomime gestures and intertitles, would soon die an unceremonious death, paving the way for the golden age of talkies in which the likes of Oland's Charlie Chan would charm viewers directly with their racial ventriloquism. The transition from silent movies to talkies was a radical break, but Oland's swapping between Jewface and yellowface, between a patriarchal Jew and an exotic Chinaman, whether evil or benign, was almost seamless.

The eminently versatile Warner Oland was born Johan Verner Ölund on October 3, 1879, in the rural village of Bjurholm, Sweden. His parents, Jonas Ölund and Maria Jojana Forsberg, were Lutheran shopkeepers with a modest income. At the impressionable age of thirteen, Oland emigrated with his parents to the United States. The family lived first in Worcester, Massachusetts, and then in New Britain, Connecticut, both areas with large Swedish populations. Having dropped the umlaut and Anglicized their name, the Olands were eager to immerse themselves in the American way of life, taking evening classes and learning English.

From the beginning, the young Swede wanted to be an actor. After graduating from drama school in Boston, he went to work on Broadway. In 1906, he toured with the Shakespearean company of actress Alla Nazimova and amassed considerable wealth from his success on stage. But after producing his own plays at the Hudson Theatre in New York, he lost the money, forcing him to drift into films.

Oland made his motion-picture debut playing John Bunyan in *The Pilgrim's Progress* in 1910, but due to his vaguely Asiatic features, he subsequently played many Oriental roles as well as the occasional Caucasian "heavy." "I owe my Chinese appearance to the Mongol invasion," Oland once said, referring to the fact that he had inherited a dollop of Asian blood from his Russian mother.[4] Throughout his career playing Asians, Oland never needed elaborate makeup. All he had to do was put a little goatee on his chin, push the ends of his mustache downward, and brush his eyebrows upward.

Prior to his role as Charlie Chan, Oland played an Oriental villain in half a dozen mostly silent films, including Wu Fang in *The Lightning Raider* (1918), Li Hsun in *Mandarin Gold* (1919), Okada in *The Pride of Palomar* (1922), Fu Shing in *The Fighting American* (1924), and Shanghai Dan in *Curly Top* (1924). All this culminated in his starring roles in the talkies: *The Mysterious Dr. Fu-Manchu* (1929) and *The Return of Dr. Fu-Manchu* (1930). By the late 1920s, Oland was indisputably Hollywood's top man for an on-screen Oriental.[5]

In 1930, following the second Paramount Fu Manchu picture, Fox hired Oland to play the role that would eventually make him famous. The idea of casting Oland as Chan might have originally come from Earl Biggers. After three unsuccessful attempts to film Biggers's novels, producers had been looking for an ideal lead man. In a letter to his publisher on January 7, 1931, Biggers wrote:

> I have completely lost touch with Fox, and haven't yet felt well enough to get involved in their troubles. I note with amusement that Warner Oland is playing Charlie. When I suggested him in October, Al Lewis, head of production on the Fox lot, roared at me: "A ham actor. I wouldn't have him on the lot." Well, I guess they changed their minds. Since he is the man that all the *Post* letter writers are pining to see in the role, I am glad that he is to try it at last. But hope to heaven he understands what sort of character Charlie is—not a sinister Fu Manchu.[6]

Biggers's worry was not unwarranted. The smiley, soft-spoken Charlie Chan was indeed a far cry from the satanic, green-eyed Fu Manchu. But Oland, the consummate professional, adapted well. To prepare himself for the role, Oland studied the Chinese language and read up on Chinese art and philosophy. In some of the later films, he was even able to deliver lines in his adopted "ancient language," albeit sounding a bit singsong.

In fact, Oland had become so steeped in the character that he often would assume the identity of Charlie Chan in real life, so much so that he could speak unscripted in Chan diction. Over a lunch of mandarin chicken and yellow tomato juice in the Fox commissary, Oland once commented to a reporter on his characteristic reticence to give interviews: "Don't talk too much. Words like sunbeams. The more they are condensed the more they burn." Moving on to other topics, such as his marriage to Edith Shearn, Oland spoke about himself in the third person as if he were Charlie Chan observing the life of Warner Oland:

> It is a marriage which is enduring because it is joined by the treasures of the mind which neither rust nor corrupt. They are as much married in their tastes and interests as in their affections. . . . He has habit, for instance, of putting lighted cigarettes—at all times he resembles a lighted chimney rather than a portly gentleman of some 200 pounds—on desks, tables, ancient books, choice prints. Accidents occur. I would like to tell him that he should pay attention to detail. Insignificant molehill sometimes more worthy of notice than conspicuous mountain.[7]

In preparing for his yellowface performance, Oland found comfort in the bottle. Unlike Charlie Chan, a teetotaler who takes an occasional sarsaparilla (an herbal, nonalcoholic drink), Oland had a serious drinking problem. At the beginning, having a nip, so to speak, before the shooting of a film actually improved Oland's characterization of Chan. It put a perennial grin on his face, making him look even more like the congenial Chan; it also slowed his speech, befitting a character whose fumbling for English words became a cinematic asset.

Watching *Charlie Chan Carries On* in the Fox production room on February 11, 1931, Biggers was very pleased with the film adaptation, as he told a friend the next day:

> I can give you the happy news that at last, after all these weary years, they have got Charlie right on the screen. Warner Oland is perfect in the part, he dresses it correctly and looks it beautifully, and he acts it charmingly and graciously, so that the spectators are bound to like him. That's a big step forward, of course.

> The boys who made the pictures were loud in their tales of how, at the preview in Riverside, two thousand people ate it up, sitting on the edge of their seats and gasping with excitement, hanging on Charlie's every word and laughing at most of them.[8]

The reviews affirmed Biggers's reaction. Even though Oland received only third billing and Chan did not appear until midway through the picture, the *New York Times* approved Oland's portrayal of a Chinese who was not a stereotypical villain or dimwit but a hero: "Mr. Oland's conception of Chan's manner of speaking is quite acceptable, and he relies on very little change in his appearance to play his part." The reviewer was especially taken with Chan's pearls of wisdom that dotted the film, "Only a very brave mouse will make its nest in a cat's ear," "He who feeds the chicken deserves the egg," and "Only a very sly man can shoot off a cannon quietly." The reviewer further enthused that the audience was so charmed by these Chanisms that "one could have listened to Charlie Chan for an hour longer."[9] Another review in *Film Daily* praised Oland's rendering of Chan: "The adaptation of this Earl Derr Biggers novel proves to be a natural for the screen and Warner Oland a perfect selection for the part of Chan. . . . Charlie is more than a detective. He is a witty philosopher and in this characterization Oland is at his best. Well cast and excellently directed by Hamilton MacFadden."[10]

"This picture," Biggers predicted, "is sure box-office, and that means there will be more Chan pictures." And he was right.[11]

Following the success of *Charlie Chan Carries On*, Fox bought the rights to *The Black Camel* in 1931 and adapted the novel for the screen, making Oland's Chan the central character. The company was so committed to the Chinese sleuth that it took the production on location to Honolulu, a far more costly operation than studio programming. It was there, on the glittering beaches of Oahu, that the real and the reel Charlie Chans would meet.

22

Between the Real and the Reel

Chang Apana and Warner Oland, Honolulu, 1931

(Courtesy of Everett Collection)

To know forgery, one must have original.
—Charlie Chan

In May 1931, a small, wrinkled old man visited the production set of a film on Oahu's Kailua Beach. He wore a white cotton shirt under a gray suit and tie. In his breast pocket was a black neckerchief with a kukui-nut slide. The wind was blowing very hard in this part of the island, less frequented by tourists. He held a cowboy hat in his hand. According to a *New York Times* reporter on the scene, the man, "whose features only on close inspection betrayed his Oriental origin," was none other than Chang Apana, who had been invited to watch the filming of the adaptation of *The Black Camel.* The film crew, which had extended this courtesy to the real-life detective, encouraged him to attend the shooting as often as he liked.

In fact, Apana missed very few days of filming. As the reporter later described in the *Times*, Apana "derived great amusement from the words put into his mouth by the author. He roared when Chan, played by Warner Oland, countered the remark, 'Inspector, you should have a lie detector,' with 'Lie detector? Ah, I see! You mean wife. I got one.' Fortunately it was only a rehearsal, and his laugh did not register on the film."[1]

Despite what the reporter said in print, I find it sad that we have no recording of Apana's roaring laughter on tape. I honestly would have hoped to hear the wordless laughter of the man who inspired the Chan icon. In a 1982 interview, Apana's nephew, Walter Chang, underscored his uncle's love of cinema and described how much Apana loved going to movies. Since he could not read English, Apana would have to take Walter to silent films so that the young man could translate the title cards for him: "He like the movies, Oh, the movies, that's why I try to tell you. We go movies. Every time when *pau* school, you know. He used to go work in the morning shift. Two o'clock he gets through the police department. I go down the police station wait for him, then we go the Empire Theater. . . . Why I go, because I have to explain to him. English, he don't know how to read and write. . . . We go to silent, silent kind."[2] Not surprisingly, Apana especially enjoyed watching those movies about his fictional double: "Oh, yeah, he see," Walter explained. "He see the picture. Oh yeah, he like that. He always laugh."[3]

ACCORDING TO HISTORIAN Robert C. Schmitt, the first motion picture actually arrived in pre-territory Hawaii on February 4, 1897. It was a seven-reel Edison Veriscope, consisting of *A Family Scene,*

A Watermelon Contest, Arrival of the Empire State Express, The Ferryboat Chicago Arriving at the Slip in New York, The Great McKinley Parade, The Spanish Bullfight, and *New York Fire Department on Active Duty.* At prices ranging from 25 cents to a dollar, the show, a most curious form of newfangled entertainment in an island culture steeped in its own mythological traditions, drew a small crowd at the Hawaiian Opera House but received rave reviews in local newspapers. In the next few years, especially after Hawaii became a territory, movies were presented sporadically on the islands. As the film industry matured, Hawaiians, like people on the mainland, caught the moviegoing fever. By 1909, only twelve years after the crude Edison show, there were as many as eleven movie houses in Honolulu, including Apana's favorite, the 930-seat Empire Theater near the Honolulu Police Headquarters.[4]

Audiences in the days of silent pictures were often noisy and sometimes unruly. On the night of February 10, 1905, a riot by nearly five hundred Chinese broke out in the Chinese Theater on Liliha Street during a kinetoscope malfunction. "There was first a rush to smash the machine," reads a front-page article published the next day, "wild disorder . . . the familiar Chinese cry to rush the police. . . . Then the mob attempted to wreck the box office." Police eventually restored order.[5]

Given the natural beauty of the islands, it should be no surprise that movies on Hawaiian themes appeared as early as 1898. In June that year, Burton Holmes, a famous traveler, photographer, and filmmaker who coined the word *travelogue,* took the first movies known to have been filmed in Hawaii. Notable later movies included Triangle's *Aloha Oe* (1915), Fox's *The Island of Desire* (1917), and Lasky's *The Bottle Imp* (1917). The latter starred Sessue Hayakawa as a Hawaiian sporting a Japanese grass-coat and Lehua Waipahu, a descendant of Queen Liliuokalani, as a local maid. All these movies were presented in the islands.[6] After Charlie Chan's film debut in 1926, the series immediately became a local favorite.

Among the forty-seven Chan film titles, *The Black Camel* has the distinction of being the only one actually filmed in the islands. Published as a novel in 1929, just a few months before the Great Crash, *The Black Camel* was Biggers's fourth Charlie Chan book but only the second set in Hawaii. The plot involves the murder of Shelah Fane, a Hollywood star with a dark secret in her past. After arriving on the island with a film crew, she is soon found stabbed to death at her beach house; hence the book title. "Black camel" is a Chinese metaphor for death. Several suspects mill around in the background: an ex-husband who still carries a torch for Fane, a jilted millionaire lover, a sleek and manipulative fortune-teller, and a disgruntled costar. In the course of the investigation, as Chan puts it, "Deceit sprouted everywhere and thrived like a weed." But Chan knows that "a gem is not polished without rubbing nor a man perfected without trials." Eventually he discovers a link between the Fane murder and another unsolved mystery in Hollywood, and he catches the killer by recovering the broken tip of a brooch pin in her shoe.

Despite making this movie during the depths of the Depression, Fox did not cut back on expenses. Besides paying Warner Oland $12,500 for the lead role, the company hired Bela Lugosi, who had just finished his role in the sensational *Dracula*, to play the slippery psychic Tarneverro. The decision to allow location shooting rather than to palm off Santa Monica as a makeshift Honolulu—especially at a time when most movie studios were strapped for cash—reflected Fox's determination to make the film into a blockbuster.

On the last day of shooting, Warner Oland and Chang Apana appeared in a photograph together. In it, the two detectives—one real-life and the other on-screen—stand against a backdrop of tropical flora, with Oland's strong arm wrapping around Apana's lean shoulder. At the bottom of a copy of the photo that once was kept in the Apana family, Oland inscribed, "To my dear friend, Charlie Chang, 'The bravest of all,' with best of luck from the new 'Charlie Chan,' Warner Oland."[7]

Two months after the departure of the Fox crew, Biggers arrived yet again on the island on July 2, 1931, for a monthlong summer vacation, and he renewed his friendship with Apana. Since their previous meeting, much had taken place. Biggers had suffered two heart attacks and had lost a great deal of money in the 1929 Great Crash. In June 1929, caught up in the frenzy of the first half of the year, Biggers bought, on the recommendation of Laurance Chambers, 100 shares of common stock of Meyer-Kiser Bank, an Indianapolis-based company that had close financial ties with Bobbs-Merrill. In May 1931, just two months prior to his departure for Hawaii, Biggers received the distressing news that Meyer-Kiser had closed its doors, one of the 3,600 bank failures across the country within two years after Black Tuesday. Fortunately, the new Chan books paid off and soon made up for Biggers's financial losses: *Charlie Chan Carries On*, published in the fall of 1930, sold 35,400 copies in four months, and the royalty statement shows that Bobbs-Merrill paid Biggers $17,140 in 1930 alone.

By contrast, Apana, now over sixty, was still making $250 a month as a detective. As Charlie Chan puts it in *The House Without a Key*, "I am policeman on small remuneration."[8] Apana never received any royalty for his Charlie Chan inspiration, and, according to Walter Chang, he never asked for any. "You know how much Apana get?" Walter said angrily in the interview. "Not even nickel! How you like that, not even five cents." At one point, Biggers tried to get Fox to hire Apana for a movie role for $500, but Apana turned it down. As Chang explained, "They offer him a job to go up the states and to play the picture. He say I cannot speak English, why I go. You know what I mean, I'm not an actor. I don't know how to speak English."[9]

During this meeting in 1931, Apana took Biggers for a long car ride during which they visited the scenes of Apana's greatest triumphs as a detective. In Chinatown, Apana pointed out the places where he used to leap from roof to roof like a human fly, busting opium dens and gambling parlors and chasing down criminals. "He went into them in great detail," Biggers recollected a year later. "He had more than bravery, this detective. He had brains. There was a robbery that he solved by finding a silk thread on a certain bedroom floor. A murder that was run down within twenty-four hours, because the Filipino who did it got mud from a certain section of the town on his shoes, hid them, and bought a new pair. I didn't get all this, but 'I say to him, why you wear new shoes this morning?' was the big dramatic climax."

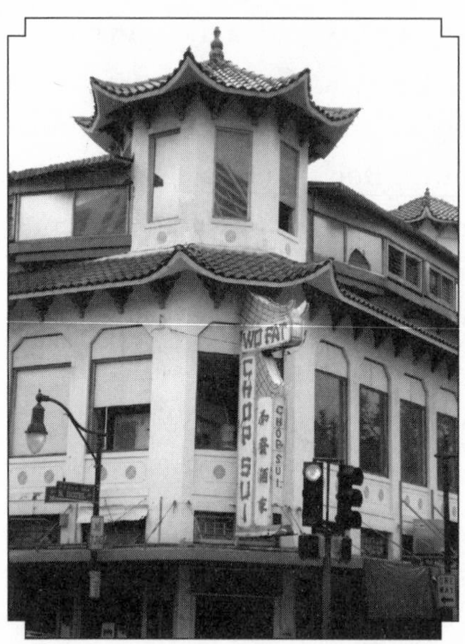

Wo Fat Restaurant, Chinatown, Honolulu *(Photo by author)*

Apana also showed Biggers his favorite restaurants, Wing Sing Wo and Wo Fat, both on Hotel Street. The former was run by folks from Apana's hometown. The latter, a chop-suey dive, would become famous one day, thanks to the popularity of the TV series *Hawaii Five-O.**

On August 1, 1931, the day of Biggers's departure, Apana arrived at the dock to see his friend off. In the midst of aloha music and hula dancing, Apana hung a crimson lei around Biggers's neck and waved good-bye in his broken English: "Old man now. Maybe I no be here when you come back. Aloha!"[10]

Sounding like a Chanism, the last words uttered by the humble detective to the celebrated mystery writer proved to be prophetic.

* When Leonard Freeman was in Honolulu in the late 1960s to work on the scripts for *Hawaii Five-O,* he often ate at Wo Fat, which would become the name of the Chinese villain in the television series.

23

Rape in Paradise

CHANG APANA, CIRCA 1932 *(Courtesy of Honolulu Police Department)*

The case that had everything.
—Time *magazine*

WHEN CHANG APANA stepped out of his home in Kaimuki on the morning of January 8, 1932, little did he know that he would be a direct eyewitness to one of the most sensational and disturbing cases in American courtroom history. Closing the door behind him, he spent a moment standing on the front lanai, taking in a fresh ocean breeze mixed with the fragrance of mai-say-lan in the garden. Just as he was about to walk down the steps and head out toward the police station, he spotted two cars racing past his home on Waialae Avenue. A white woman was erratically driving the first car, a blue Buick sedan, with two male passengers. The speeding vehicle was followed closely by a police car, inside which Apana saw two of his colleagues, Detective George Harbottle and Officer Thomas Kekua. From the high speed of the chase, Apana immediately recognized trouble. Soon the two cars, trailing a plume of dust, shot out of view. A few moments later, he heard three sharp cracks of a pistol, followed by the roar of engines.

That car chase, which had begun at the busy intersection of Waialae Avenue and Isenberg Road, had barreled through the sleepy neighborhood of Kaimuki before ending up ten miles later on a serpentine trail by the ocean near Hanauma Bay. When the police finally forced the blue Buick off the road and approached the vehicle with guns drawn, they discovered in the back of the car a body wrapped in bedsheets and soaked with water and blood. "I then noticed," as Detective Harbottle later wrote in his report, "a human leg sticking out of the white bundle, and I placed the occupants of the car under arrest."[1]

Yet the story does not begin, as few do, with a terrifying police chase and an arrest. Rather, we need to backtrack a few months to a late summer day—September 12, 1931, to be precise. On this muggy Saturday evening, just six weeks after Apana and Biggers waved farewell at the Honolulu docks (and exactly one week before the Japanese invasion of Manchuria), a young haole couple was entertaining some friends at their Manoa home. Nipping at the jar of bootleg *okolehao* (a potent Hawaiian moonshine), they listened to the Boys from Dixie and the Melody Sisters on the radio. The husband, Thomas Massie, a native of a small town in Kentucky, was a U.S. Navy officer stationed in Pearl Harbor. His wife, Thalia, age twenty, came from a family of wealth and influence, at least in name. Her father, Granville Roland "Roly" Fortescue, was a cousin of President Theodore Roosevelt. During the Spanish-American War, in the same year that Hawaii was annexed, young Teddy and Roly had actually fought side by side at the Battle of San Juan Hill in Cuba. Thalia's mother, Grace Hubbard Fortescue, née Bell, was a niece of Alexander Graham Bell, inventor of the telephone, and a granddaughter of Gardiner Greene Hubbard, first president of the Bell Telephone Company. She seemed, as they said, properly bred, but despite this illustrious background, Thalia's parents lacked in money what they had in pedigree. Grace tried hard to maintain the appearance of good breeding, though she would have to resort on occasion to giving bridge lessons to make ends meet.

The marriage of Thomas and Thalia was not a happy one. She was bored and was rumored to be going out with other officers. Thomas had threatened her with divorce. On this September night, the couple fought again. The domestic discord continued even after they and their friends left the house and arrived at the Ala Wai Inn, a Japanese teahouse and dance hall in Waikiki. At about midnight, Thalia left the dance floor and walked out of the inn alone. The next time Thomas spoke to her, almost two hours later by phone, Thalia cried out: "Something awful has happened. Come home."

The dutiful husband hurried home, where he was shocked by the sight of his wife: clad only in her nightgown, her jaw broken, and blood dripping from her upper lip. Wrought with emotion, Thalia described, tearfully, how she had been kidnapped by a gang of "Hawaiians." After leaving the inn, she said, she had been walking along Kalakaua Avenue toward the ocean for some air when a car pulled up beside her. Five Hawaiian boys forced her into their vehicle and drove her to an isolated area off Ala Moana Road. They then dragged her into the bushes, punched her, and raped her six or seven times. As Thomas would later confide to a jury in graphic detail, his wife, as she had relayed the horrific ordeal to him, was "in a total state of collapse and broken down from sodomy."[2]

Based on clues from another incident reported to the police that night—a shoving match between a Hawaiian woman and a local boy following a near car accident—the police soon rounded up five suspects, all youngsters of either Hawaiian or Asian descent: Ben Ahakuelo, Henry Chang, Horace Ida, Joseph Kahahawai, and David Takai. It was as if Fu Manchu had materialized, now in the guise of these five young men who came off to the public as the worst kind of sexual predators. Reality had fully collided with fantasy, as if all the sexual nightmares of a Caucasian minority had now come home to roost. When the news, like a thunderclap, reached the street the next morning, it sent shock waves through the whole territory. In the words of historian David Stannard, who has written the best book on the Massie Case, "this promised to be Hawaii's most explosive criminal case ever—the first one in history involving the rape, by Hawaiians, of a white woman, and a navy officer's wife at that."[3] The tabloids were eager to expand readership, and newspaper headlines screamed: "Gang Assaults Young Wife." The articles contained inflammatory details about how "a young woman of the highest character . . . a white woman of refinement and culture" had been attacked by a gang of "fiends." Rumors ran rampant throughout the ranks at Pearl Harbor, with claims that the "thugs" had violated a fellow officer's "kid bride" in every sordid way. Rumor, like fire, can spread quickly and lethally, and this particular conflagration showed no sign of being brought under control. One sailor later described what he had heard at the base: "There are only three orifices on the human body, and they kicked her and broke her pelvis and they bit the nipple practically off one of her breasts. They broke her jaw in such a manner that one of her teeth had to be taken out. They broke her nose. Blackened both of her eyes, of course. On her face was a perfect imprint of a rubber heel, where they stomped on her."[4]

Whether or not he truly believed these sensational accusations, Admiral Yates Stirling, the commandant of the Fourteenth Naval District, reacted to the news with rage and disgust. His first inclination, he said, was to "seize the brutes and string them up on trees." Stirling's reference to lynching was, as Stannard puts it, "no surprise to those who knew him." Though born in California, he had grown up in the South and had seen how whites had dealt vigilante justice to black suspects without a trial. In the early part of his military career, Stirling had "[fought] revolutionaries in the Philippines and Chinese warlords on the Yangtze River." To say that he did not like Asians is hardly an understatement. In his memoir, Stirling bragged about the indiscriminate killings and scorched-earth campaigns he had carried out in the Far East: "We burned the villages; in fact, every house for two miles from either bank was destroyed by us. We killed their livestock: cattle, pigs, chickens, and their valuable work animals, the carabaos [water buffalo], It seemed ruthless; yet it was after all war, and war is brutal." As the top U.S. Navy commander in the Pacific, he believed that Hawaii's polyglot population was a threat to America's security in the region. As Gavan Daws puts it, Stirling had nothing but scorn for what he called "enthusiastic priests of the melting-pot cult." Now that a carload of dark-skinned criminals had brutally attacked a white woman, much less the daughter of a prominent Eastern family, Stirling was determined to see justice served, one way or another.[5]

Thinking along the same lines was the most influential businessman in the islands, Walter Dillingham, then dubbed the J. P. Morgan of Hawaii. Born in Honolulu and educated, like Biggers, at Harvard, he was the head of the Dillingham Corporation, which had a virtual monopoly over construction, shipping, and land development in Oahu. Dillingham was also outspoken in his contempt for nonwhites. For many years, he had served as the vice chairman of the American Defense Society, a nativist organization founded in 1915 with members such as the eugenicist Madison Grant. In addition, the U.S. Navy was the biggest client of Dillingham's company, and Admiral Stirling was his personal friend. Therefore, Dillingham had also made up his mind that those "beasts," as he called them, would get what they deserved.[6]

At first, it appeared as if Stirling and Dillingham would have nothing to worry about. Lawrence Judd, the governor of Hawaii, was more than willing to take orders from the top military man and the top businessman. Throughout the territory years, a handful of sugar factors, known as the Big Five, would take turns and select their own representatives for the governor's position. In 1929, they chose Lawrence Judd, the grandson of Dr. Gerrit Judd, to be the governor and, make no mistake about it, to protect the interests of big business.

The other key figure involved in the Massie Case, who would also be eager to please people like Stirling and Dillingham, was Captain John McIntosh, chief of the Detective Division of the Honolulu Police Department. In fact, McIntosh was always frank to admit how he had attained his current position. "I was put there," as he had once told an interviewer, "by the business interests and the politicians." As the captain, McIntosh was known not only for his harsh treatment of nonwhite subordinates but also for his blatantly racist treatment of officers. In high-profile cases, according to Stannard, he often "removed nonwhite detectives from an investigation they had begun and replaced them with handpicked haoles." The Massie Case would prove no exception. By Sunday morning, none of the nonwhite detectives who had worked the case, except for John Jardine (Portuguese were not considered haole at the time), were allowed to handle the investigation.[7] Seeking to affirm his position and bring a speedy end to a grisly case, McIntosh had from the very beginning convinced himself that the five suspects in custody were guilty. He was so eager to convict them that he even tried to plant evidence: He drove the suspects' impounded car to the alleged crime scene after a rain and left behind tire marks in the west ground. The police photographer, sensing a frame-up, refused to take pictures.

From the start, the case was a travesty of justice, reflecting the entrenched corruption and racial prejudice that defined the territorial government. Judge Alva Steadman, in whom the haole elites had complete confidence, was assigned to the case. Three years earlier, Steadman had served as the judge in the sensational criminal trial of Myles Fukunaga, a nineteen-year-old Japanese youth with mental problems who had kidnapped and killed the ten-year-old son of a Hawaiian Trust Company executive. Fukunaga's motive was simple:

Hawaiian Trust was about to evict his parents from their Honolulu rental home, and he wanted revenge. But he also wanted a $10,000 ransom to help his parents out of the jam. In his ransom note, the deranged Fukunaga quoted from Shakespeare's *Macbeth*: "Life's but a walking shadow, a poor player/that struts and frets his hour upon the stage/ and then is heard no more. . . ." In a secret spot behind the Seaside Hotel in Waikiki, Fukunaga beat the young boy with a steel chisel and choked him to death. In the ensuing trial, which lasted two days, Fukunaga's lawyers offered no defense and called no witnesses. Such a sham was territorial justice at the time that the jury included the victim's bodyguard and gravedigger as well as members of the search party. After the guilty verdict, and despite the defendant's obvious insanity, Steadman sentenced him to death by hanging. It took only six weeks from arrest to execution, and Dillingham singled out Steadman as "a man's man in every way."[8]

Three years later, it seemed that all the cards were stacking against the five suspects. All except one: the facts. There were many questions that would cast serious doubts over Thalia's allegations. First and foremost, two doctors who examined her separately could not find any physical evidence of rape. Nor could the police find any trace of semen on Thalia's clothes or those of the suspects. Equally troubling was the fact that Thalia's accounts of the assault were remarkably inconsistent; it seemed that she was adding new details about that night as more information was conveniently revealed to her by the police. Especially damaging to her credibility was the fact that all five suspects had solid alibis during those hours; it was simply impossible for them to have had the time to commit the crime.

The suspects, whose plight had evoked great sympathy among the island's Asians and Hawaiians, were given an excellent team of lawyers dispatched by Princess Abigail Kawananakoa, the last living symbol of Hawaii's deposed monarchy. Out of desperation, the mother of Ben Ahakuelo, one of the two Hawaiian boys, had called the princess for help. The princess, a benevolent woman who genuinely cared for her people, asked well-known attorney William Heen to represent the defendants. Half Chinese and half Hawaiian, Heen was one of the most influential legal figures in the islands. A graduate of Berkeley's Hastings Law School, Heen had been the first non-haole to be appointed a circuit court judge. Even after his resignation in 1919, islanders called him Judge Heen for the rest of his life.[9]

For those anguished months in the fall of 1931, it was as if annexation had yet to happen, and the lives of these five young men symbolically came to represent the innocence of the island people now compromised by all the sinister forces of the haole occupiers. Opening on November 16, the trial was a spectacle no Hawaiian could forget. Heen and his team pounced on the facts and peeled the hard rind of falsehood off the prosecution's case, piece by piece. The trial went on for two weeks. In the ensuing ninety-seven-hour marathon deliberation, the jury—consisting of two Chinese, two Japanese, one Hawaiian, and seven whites—was deadlocked. Even after Judge Steadman had repeatedly rejected their "deadlocked" decisions and sent them back to the jury room hoping to force a guilty verdict, the twelve-member jury remained evenly divided: six for conviction, six for no conviction. As it was later revealed, the votes did not break down along racial lines. One white juror had voted not guilty from the first to the last ballot; and the jurors who pushed hardest for conviction were Chinese, Japanese, and Hawaiian.[10] Reluctantly, on December 6, Judge Steadman declared a mistrial, which caused a sensation greater than the alleged crime itself.

In Admiral Stirling's mind, such an outcome was an insult to law, to "the white man's most sacred tenets." To Dillingham, this was exactly what he had dreaded for so many years—irresponsible nonwhites running amok after being given the right to vote. Such a fear had driven him to join organizations like the American Defense Society in the first place. The verdict, or the lack thereof, was simply unacceptable to these two men and other haoles. They waged a war on the territory, especially against its nonwhite population, on multiple fronts.

Shortly after the trial ended, Admiral Stirling cabled Secretary of the Navy Charles Francis Adams. He described the brutality of the rape; the incompetence of the police department, with its "vast majority of Hawaiians and mixed bloods"; the inexperience of the prosecutors; and the racial bias of the jury. Then Stirling added something that soon would be picked up by newspapers across the nation: in Honolulu, he stated, there had been forty rape cases reported in the previous year, and in several of the cases the convicted criminals were released on parole after only four months of imprisonment.[11] Stirling's report about forty rapes was a barefaced lie, but it was as if a bombshell had been dropped, not only on the Department of the Navy but also in the mainland media. While the islands were more than five thousand miles from the American South, many of the territory's white settlers, no doubt threatened by their minority status, had racial attitudes strikingly similar to those in Dixie, though scented by a gentle tropical fragrance that could quickly grow rancid in time of crisis. The image of dark-skinned rapists running loose in the streets and assaulting white women tapped deeply into the worst fears of miscegenation. In response, Chief of Naval Operations Admiral William Pratt informed Stirling that he would stop sending fleets to Honolulu for two months, "unless justice is done at the coming retrial and the police and hoodlum conditions are thoroughly cleaned by local authorities."[12] The *New York Times* printed Stirling's report verbatim; *Time* magazine, under the heading of "Races: Lust in Paradise," reported that "Yellow man's lust for white women had broken bounds"; the headlines of the *Oakland Tribune* screamed, "Racial War Fear Grips Island City"; and William Randolph Hearst's chain of newspapers and tabloids began running lurid cartoons of "milk-skinned maidens being carried off to tropical lairs by brown brigands, bare-chested and slant-eyed."[13]

The U.S. Navy officers and sailors stationed at Pearl Harbor contributed mightily in escalating the level of tension. One day after the trial ended, the Honolulu police responded to at least eight riot calls, all between military men and nonwhite civilians. The worst incident took place when four carloads of sailors kidnapped Horace Ida, one of the five accused, and took him all the way up to the high cliff at the Nu'uanu Pali. Trying to coerce a confession out of Ida, they stripped him, beat him with leather belts and metal buckles, kicked him, and hit his head with a gun butt. Only after Horace "feigned unconsciousness" did they stop and throw his body into the bushes. The brutality fell just a notch short of fulfilling Admiral Stirling's prophecy that he would not be surprised to hear any day that one or more of the five accused "had been found swinging from trees by the neck up Nu'uanu Valley or at the Pali."[14]

It turned out that the admiral was correct in his prediction. Grace Fortescue, Thalia's mother, had arrived earlier in Honolulu to provide moral support for her daughter. Utterly disgusted by the outcome of the trial, she believed that unless she did something to ascertain a guilty verdict in the retrial, the five accused would probably walk free again and, under Hawaii's law, for good. Not wanting to take chances with the judicial system that had already failed her once, she devised a scheme.

On January 8, 1932, with the help of Thomas Massie and two other U.S. Navy officers, Fortescue lured Joseph Kahahawai into a car and drove him to her rented bungalow in Manoa. At the house, they waved guns at Kahahawai and demanded a confession to the rape. At some point, a gun went off and Kahahawai lay dead. Leaving one person behind to clean up the evidence at the house, Fortescue and her cohorts left to dump the body into the blowhole at Hanauma Bay. Detective George Harbottle spotted their car on Waialae Avenue; Kahahawai's cousin had already reported the kidnapping to the HPD and provided a description of the car. What ensued was a ten-mile car chase, part of which Chang Apana saw from the front steps of his Kaimuki house. The four were arrested on charges of murder.

At this point, the case that began as a young white woman's sensational allegation against five nonwhite men finally hit the central nerve of the entire nation. It put American culture to an ultimate test by exposing the glaring disparity between the rule of law and the rule of the mob—in this case, the lynch mob.

Lynching, one of the cruelest manifestations of racial hatred, persisted like a cancer in America for nearly a full century after Emancipation. According to records held at Tuskegee Institute, there were more than 3,400 black victims of lynching between 1880 and 1951. Kentucky, the home state of Thomas Massie, had one of the worst lynching records in the country. Between Massie's birth in 1905 and his departure for the U.S. Naval Academy in 1925, more than eight hundred blacks were known to have been lynched in ten Southern states, including Kentucky. In the words of David Stannard, that was a rate "of roughly one per week, year in and year out."[15] An anti-lynching bill was introduced in Congress in 1922; it was passed by the House of Representatives but blocked in the Senate.

Growing up in Maryland, south of the Mason-Dixon Line, Admiral Stirling empathized with Massie. He also knew how Massie, a fellow Southerner, must have felt, seeing those "niggers" walking free on the street after what they had done to his wife. The problem for Stirling now was how to protect Massie, his mother-in-law, and his navy comrades, who had defended the white man's honor. Hearing about the arrests of Massie and others, Stirling, over the objections of the territorial attorney general and the county prosecutor, kept the four suspects out of jail by taking them to one of his navy ships on the base. He also threatened Governor Lawrence Judd, hardly a proponent of Asian or Hawaiian rights, with a military takeover of the territorial government. What had merely been a sensational trial threatened to become a national scandal, since Stirling was eager to thwart the islands' democratic process.

It seemed that the United States, still mired in the Great Depression, actually stood behind Admiral Stirling—or at least that's what the popular media indicated. The *New York Sunday News* and the *New York Mirror* were the first two papers to hit the streets after the Massie family arrests. Under the headlines of "Honor Killing in Honolulu Threatens Race War," "Melting Pot of Peril," and "Guard Honor Slayers from Hawaiian Lynch Mob," the tabloids printed pictures and stories that suggested "the age old race war between the Occident and the Orient . . . threatens to envelop the Hawaiian Islands in a sea of blood." Very soon, major newspapers, including the *New York Post, Chicago Tribune*, and *San Francisco Chronicle*, began running editorials clamoring for the removal of Governor Judd and the declaration of martial law in the Hawaii Territory. They referred to the murder as either a "lynching" or an "honor killing." The forty or so newspapers owned by Hearst, which claimed about one-fourth of all the readership in the country, would print similar editorials written by the newspaper magnate himself. As if borrowing a page from Jim Crow, Hearst employed the most brazen racial language to whet his readers' prejudice:

> The situation in Hawaii is deplorable. It is becoming or has become an unsafe place for white women. . . . The whole island should be promptly put under martial law and the perpetrators of outrages upon women promptly tried by court martial and executed. Until such drastic measures are taken, Hawaii is not a safe place for decent white women and not a very good place for self-respecting civilized men.[16]

Back in Honolulu, Thomas Massie and the others were kept on the USS *Alton,* a decommissioned ship that had been used as a guesthouse for visiting VIPs. As the leading lady in the Gang of Four, Grace Fortescue occupied a cozy penthouse with "polished wood and gleaming metal," while enjoying a splendid view of the city through the portholes. "With staterooms for cells," writes Stannard, "the accused murderers of Joseph Kahahawai had available to them books, cards, and music . . . electric fans, call bells and all the conveniences of a modern hotel. The onboard officers' mess would provide their meals." A deluge of flowers and lavish bouquets—almost as if a head of state or the last queen of Hawaii had died—began to arrive as soon as the news about the arrests reached the mainland. Thousands of well-wishers sent cablegrams, along with floral arrangements that would soon fill up the ship.[17]

Aboard her floating penthouse, Fortescue consented to an interview with Russell Owen, a Pulitzer Prize–winning journalist working for the *New York Times.* Fortescue and her codefendants, as Owen observed, did not show "any trepidation or a feeling that they had done something for which they should be ashamed or sorry." She had, as she told him, "slept better since Friday, the 8th—the day of the murder—than for a long time."[18] What Owen would later omit in his published piece was even more revealing. To the question of "why she felt what had happened was justified," Fortescue replied that "she came from the South and that in the South they had their own ways of dealing with 'niggers.' " She seemed, as Owen indicated, unable to understand that "Hawaiians are not related to the Negroes."[19]

Fortescue was not alone in confusing Hawaiians with "Negroes." In 1928, four years earlier, a soldier on shore leave had shot and killed a Honolulu policeman named William Kama, who coincidentally was a close family friend to Kahahawai. Kama and his fellow officer, Sam Kunane, both Hawaiian, were trying to break up a fight between a few soldiers and local men when one of the soldiers, Chester Nagle, "pulled out a pistol and shot Kama in the head." Nagle then turned the gun on Kunane and shot him in the chest. At the court-martial, Nagle provided a very simple justification for the killing. When he shot Kama and Kunane, he said, he did not think they were police officers, because he had never heard of such a thing as a "colored policeman." Nagle's attorney also tried to defend him by insisting that Nagle did nothing more than shoot "two black men" who had approached him in a menacing manner. Eventually the military jury found Nagle guilty of manslaughter, but his sentence was reduced after he had been shipped out of the islands.[20]

As much as they believed that they had done nothing wrong by lynching a "nigger" rapist, Fortescue and her codefendants had to worry about the forthcoming trial in a civilian court—the same court that had already allowed the "thugs" to walk free. They would need to find, as they had been advised, the best defense attorney in the country.

Hailed as America's first celebrity attorney, Clarence Darrow was to the courtroom, as Stannard puts it, what Babe Ruth was to the baseball field.[21] Born in Farmington, Ohio, in 1857, Darrow was the son of Amirus Darrow, an ardent abolitionist, and Emily Eddy Darrow, an advocate of female suffrage and women's rights. Admitted to the bar at the age of twenty-one, Darrow began his legal practice in Youngstown, Ohio. He became known as the "Attorney for the Damned" for his successful defenses in a number of high-profile cases in which the defendants seemed all but certain of going to the gallows. In 1924, Darrow saved Leopold and Loeb—a Jewish duo of convicted murderers from good families in Chicago—from the hangman's noose by convincing the jury that the teenage killers were not completely responsible for their actions. In 1925, Darrow was the defense lawyer in the famous Scopes (Monkey) Trial, which involved the legality of teaching the theory of evolution in state-funded schools in Tennessee. The same year, he represented Ossian Sweet, a black doctor who had killed a white man when an angry mob had tried to drive the Sweet family out of their newly purchased home in Detroit. Without notes, Darrow delivered a seven-hour closing argument that ranged from a recounting of the barbaric history of slavery to a defense of a man's fundamental right to protect his home and family.[22] His rousing speech even moved the judge to tears, and the all-white jury acquitted Sweet. As Darrow admitted in his memoir, *The Story of My Life*, which had just appeared in early 1932, the secret of his success was his ability to connect with the jury and make them see what he wanted them to see. "I never liked technicalities," he wrote in the book. "I believe that few cases are ever won that way; I preferred to take outstanding facts and do the best I could with what was obvious to all."[23]

Given his reputation as the champion of the underdog or victimized, Darrow, by accepting the case of Grace Fortescue and her cohorts, would be on the wrong side of the fence. He would now have to defend four whites who had murdered a nonwhite victim. However, strapped for cash, Darrow found the retainer fee of $40,000 simply too enticing to pass up, so on March 24, 1932, he and his legal team arrived in Honolulu to prepare for the case.

When the trial opened on April 4, the courtroom was packed with local VIPs and journalists from the world's news organizations. Hawaii had just joined the worldwide network of wireless radio four months earlier, and direct radiophone service between Honolulu and the outside world had begun in early March. Darrow once said, "The practice of law has always appealed to the spectacular in life."[24] The timely arrival of wireless technology certainly enhanced the spectacle of the trial, and a worldwide audience did, so to speak, get its money's worth by tuning in to the daily updates from the remotest inhabitable islands in the middle of the Pacific. Radio stations across the mainland, according to Stannard, broadcast staged reenactments of the courtroom drama day in and day out during the monthlong trial.[25]

For America, especially after the defeat of the antilynching bill and with the resurgence of racial violence in the 1920s, the outcome of the trial would have explosive implications. Darrow was obviously aware of that, and, great lawyer that he was, he tried to tap into the spirit of the age, something that he called the "unwritten law." "While it could not be found in the statutes," Darrow said, "it was indelibly written in the feelings and thoughts of people in general." And in 1932, the unwritten law subscribed to by most Americans was the belief that "a man has the right to kill another man who has assaulted his wife . . . especially when the rape victim was white and the rapist was not." It was this law, not the statutory one, to which Darrow was appealing when he argued the Massie Case in front of the twelve jurors: seven white men, three Chinese, and two Hawaiians. Darrow strategically presented Thomas Massie as the one who had fired the shot that killed Joseph Kahahawai, even though there was no conclusive evidence. He skillfully characterized the killing as a case of a Southern (white) gentleman defending his wife's honor at a moment of rage. In his four-hour closing argument, which was carried live on radio across the United States, Darrow made a passionate appeal to the jury by invoking the power of the unwritten law. He argued that within each good person there is, "somewhere deep in the feelings and instincts . . . a yearning for justice, an idea of what is right and wrong, of what is fair between man and man, that came before the first law was written and will abide after the last one is dead." Following such a deep-seated, time-honored sense of justice, how could anyone sleep, Darrow histrionically asked, "hearing the words of Massie, picturing the tear-stained face of Massie's wife?"[26]

In closing arguments, prosecutor John Kelley identified the obvious flaw in the so-called unwritten law—its racial inequality. Yes, Mr. Darrow had spoken of mother-love and husband's honor, Kelley said. "Well, there is another mother in this courtroom. Has Mrs. Fortescue lost her daughter? Has Massie lost his wife?" Then, as described by Stannard in his brilliant book, Kelley looked toward where Joseph Kahahawai's parents were sitting and rested his case by asking, "Where is Kahahawai?"[27]

After two days of deliberation, the jury on April 29 delivered a verdict that stunned nations on three continents: all four defendants guilty of manslaughter. As soon as the first verdict on Thomas Massie had been read, Thalia first let out a scream and then uttered a piercing wail, causing others to be unable to hear the rest of the verdict. Darrow, the most venerated lawyer of his generation, sank into his chair, muttering: "I couldn't believe it. I couldn't think or understand how anybody could be that cruel."[28] The personal disbelief was squarely matched by the outrage expressed in the mainstream media. "I am astounded! Shocked!" said Floyd Gibbons in his Hearst column the next morning. "The Fortescue-Massie case verdict is legal mockery. . . . Are we no longer Americans? No longer free and white? Are all the mainland millions of us in a class with those seven white men of the Massie jury who let five yellow and brown men swing a verdict directly against the sympathies of the whole civilized world?" Then Gibbons went on to call for "white American rule in Hawaii."[29]

In the meantime, more than a hundred senators and representatives began pressuring Governor Judd to pardon the four convicted killers. They sent a threatening cable to Judd, expressing their "deep concern for the welfare of Hawaii" and stating that only "prompt and unconditional pardon of Lieutenant Massie and his associates" would ensure the continuation of that concern. In other words, pardon or else. Eventually, Judd even received a call from President Herbert Hoover. Even though the content of that phone conversation was never revealed, we can make a reasonable guess from the subsequent turn of events.[30]

On May 4, the judge sentenced each of the killers to ten years of imprisonment with hard labor. Within an hour, however, the four were sipping champagne at the Governor's Mansion across the street from the courthouse—Judd had commuted their sentence to one hour in custody of the High Sheriff of the Territory.

In retrospect, when Clarence Darrow was wrapping up his closing argument with a climactic rhetorical question, he looked into the eyes of the five nonwhite jurors and instinctively knew that he had just lost the last case of his career. As he would later recall, "When I gazed into those dark faces, I could see the deep mysteries of the Orient were there. My ideas and words were not registering." Sharing Darrow's conflation of Chinese and Hawaiians, Grace Fortescue made a similar observation of that dramatic moment: "The stoical Oriental faces betrayed no emotion."[31] The courtroom maestro, who had made a career out of making heartfelt appeals to jurors, had been tripped up by what he regarded as an insurmountable racial barrier. Maybe he was correct in blaming his defeat, however temporary, on the racial feelings of the jurors, but how could they think or feel otherwise when justice was in such lamentably short supply?

Seen from another perspective, however, it would be wrong to interpret the verdict as a mere expression of racism. The seven Caucasian jurors, each one of whom had the power to cause a jury deadlock, had certainly not cast their votes based on racial prejudice. As the *Chicago Tribune* put it in a front-page story the day after the verdict,

"Racial lines were obliterated by the jury's verdict, and the Hawaiian race cannot be in any way held responsible for this decision."[32] In fact, the seven white jurors had plenty of good or convenient reasons to acquit their fellow Caucasians: four of them worked for Big Five corporations; two were Walter Dillingham's employees.[33] The same *Chicago Tribune* story pointed out: "The greatest business houses in the Territory were represented on that jury." In addition to concerns with their own job security, the seven white jurors, as well as the five nonwhites, were also fully aware of the other possible consequence of their decision: martial law in Hawaii, or a military takeover of the civilian government. But in the end, each one decided to follow his or her conscience and obey the rule of law rather than choose the convenient path that had been followed by countless all-white juries across the nation in similar cases. As one of the white jurors put it after the trial, "Kahahawai was killed . . . and we could not allow ourselves to be swayed by emotions. Law and order must prevail."[34] Even though the governor's decision to commute the sentence had rendered the Massie Case yet another ugly manifestation of racism, the guilty verdict by a mixed-race jury seemed to indicate that, in the early 1930s, the racist foundation of American culture was showing signs of cracking, at least in Hawaii.

Months later, at the request of prosecutor John Kelley, Governor Judd hired the Pinkerton Detective Agency, the nation's leading private-investigation firm, to conduct an independent probe of the Massie Case. On October 3, 1932, after a thorough, three-month examination, the agency's report concluded: "It is impossible to escape the conviction that the kidnapping and assault was *not* caused by those accused. . . . We found nothing in the record of this case, nor have we through our own efforts been able to find what in our estimation would be sufficient corroboration of the statements of Mrs. Massie to establish the occurrence of rape upon her."[35] In other words, the rape had never occurred. Still, Joseph Kahahawai was dead, and many lives were ruined and careers shattered. Hawaii, now haunted by the specter of military rule and humiliated by the interference of a federal government five thousand miles to the east, would struggle in the wake of this racial tragedy for many years. Chang Apana, who had fought all his life for the rule of law, would have only months to live—certainly not long enough to see the day when the scales of justice could finally be fairly balanced.*

* On January 8, 1934, two years to the day after the death of Joseph Kahahawai, Thalia Massie filed for divorce on the grounds of extreme mental cruelty. In the remaining decades of her troubled life, she tried to commit suicide at least twice and eventually died of a barbiturate overdose on July 3, 1963, in an apartment near her mother in Palm Beach. Her ex-husband, Thomas Massie, was institutionalized at St. Elizabeth Hospital, near Washington, DC, in 1940. He was subsequently released and then he retired from the U.S. Navy with a permanent physical disability. After a quiet civilian life, he died on January 8, 1987, fifty-five years, again to the day, after the murder of Kahahawai. Only Grace Fortescue thrived, living comfortably off an inheritance from her father. At eighty-seven, she was once spotted parasailing in Acapulco. She died in 1979, at the age of ninety-five, sixteen years after the death of her troubled daughter.

24

The Black Camel

Chang Apana and Chief Charles Weeber, 1932

(Courtesy of Hawaii State Archives)

Death is the black camel that kneels unbid at every gate.

—Charlie Chan

Even if Chang Apana, then in his early sixties, had wanted to get involved in the Massie investigation, Captain John McIntosh's standard departmental policy of removing nonwhite detectives from important cases would have prevented him from doing so. This was in stark contrast to the Charlie Chan novels and films, in which the police chief invariably entrusts Detective Chan with a major case involving the murder of a prominent white person.

Although he had only been a spectator on that morning of January 8, 1932, Apana, like almost everyone else in Hawaii, was affected by the ongoing drama and disastrous fallout of the Massie Case. As soon as the first trial had ended in a hung jury, leading local white citizens reviled the Honolulu Police Department for its mishandling of the case and its perceived inability to protect whites from the dangers posed by "dirty" browns. They called for a major overhaul of the department. Within days, Walter Dillingham formed an emergency committee of the Honolulu Chamber of Commerce charged with the task of cleaning up the HPD. On January 22, 1932, a bill passed in the territorial legislature led to the creation of the five-member Police Commission, empowered to appoint a new police chief and to enact rules and regulations for the conduct of the HPD and its business in the City and the County of Honolulu. On January 27, the commission appointed Charles F. Weeber—Dillingham's personal secretary for the previous eleven years—as the chief of police and gave him the full authority to revamp the department.[1]

Even though he had no experience in police matters, Chief Weeber took bold steps and adopted new policies and procedures that had been totally alien under the old sheriff. Leon Straus, a police veteran, wrote about the HPD:

> To a number of officers that had entered the service prior to 1932, the "New Look" did not have much of a future. But within a relatively short time, it was quite evident that the so-called "New Look" was going to be a permanent fixture, and

> the die-hards found a strange world of modern concepts and techniques had been introduced and were gaining public favor and support. As might be expected, a goodly number of this group decided against remaining in the service, and retired on pension, transferred to other jobs, or resigned.[2]

Apana was offered a pension to retire, but he felt insulted. "What for do I want a pension?" he replied. "What would I do if I was not a policeman?"[3] On May 2, three days after the Fortescue guilty verdict and two days before the sentencing and commuting, Apana was injured in a car accident. He suffered a fractured collarbone and was taken to Queen's Hospital.[4] The injury forced Apana to reconsider the pension offer.

On May 15, eight police veterans, including Apana, retired as Chief Weeber's reorganization took effect. Local newspapers reported Apana's pension to be $123.75 a month, which was the maximum allowed by law (50 percent of his regular salary) but at the lower end of the average amount received by his fellow retirees.[5] To remedy this injustice and to recognize his extraordinary service, three prominent haole businessmen offered to make up the difference between Apana's active-duty pay and his pension for as long as he would live. The Chinese community in Honolulu presented him with a medal, reflecting his devotion to the force.[6]

News of Apana's retirement rankled Earl Biggers. He was concerned not that justice had abandoned either his hero, Apana, or the murdered Kahahawai, but that his readers might lose interest now that the real detective had gone off into the sunset. On May 20, he sent a request to his publisher: "Please call to your publicity man's attention the fact that Charlie has not by any means retired from the Honolulu force . . . he's just on a long—and in view of recent events it may prove a very long—leave of absence. What a bit of luck for me I wasn't nearly through a novel about the beauties of Hawaii when that mess broke!"[7]

The "novel" Biggers mentioned in the letter was his sixth Charlie Chan book, *Keeper of the Keys*. The *Saturday Evening Post* had just paid Biggers $40,000 for serial rights, an extraordinary figure during the Great Depression and about thirteen times Apana's annual pension. About to be published by Bobbs-Merrill in June, the novel actually was less about the sandy beaches of Hawaii than the snowy sierras in Northern California. In the book, Charlie Chan has just finished a big case in San Francisco. In honor of its proud son, the Chan Family Society has invited him to a banquet in Chinatown. It seems that the Honolulu detective is standing at the very pinnacle of fame—no wonder Biggers feared that news of Apana's retirement would diminish interest—when he receives a mysterious missive from a Dudley Ward, asking Chan to travel to his summer house in Tahoe. Riding on train tracks that were laid down by his countrymen more than half a century earlier, Chan contemplates the early history of Chinese immigration, the transpacific wave that washed him ashore on the island of Oahu many years ago. Finally arriving at the snow-capped resort on limpid Lake Tahoe, Chan realizes that he seems to be attending a convention of one woman's four jilted ex-husbands. A sharp report from an upstairs room soon leads the odd party to the dead body of the beautiful Ellen Landini, now "a fallen flower," to use Chan's prodigious metaphor, "that can no longer return to the branch."

In writing this book, Biggers extensively researched the history of Chinese in the American West. He drew upon the unenviable lives of Chinamen in mining, railroad construction, laundries, and other menial jobs, especially with the character Ah Sing, the novel's literal "keeper of the keys," who has long served the Ward family as a houseboy. His name obviously recalling Bret Harte's "heathen Chinee," who has "ways that are dark," Ah Sing remains under suspicion throughout Biggers's novel. In the end, however, Charlie Chan catches the killer and exonerates the keeper of the keys, so that Ah Sing, as he has long hoped, can return to China. "I envy you," Chan says. "You will walk again on the streets of the village where you were born. You will supervise the selection of your own burial place."[8] Such a long-awaited homecoming did not seem to lie in the future of Charlie Chan or of his real-life double, Chang Apana.

Unable to loll around at home, Apana soon went to work as a watchman at the Hawaiian Trust Company, for he had a large family to support. Oddly, he was now making more money than he ever could as a detective, and he was lucky to find a job at the height of the Depression, when the national unemployment rate spiraled out of control to 23 percent.[9] But the detective-turned-watchman soon received very sad news.

On April 5, 1933, two days before the ban was lifted on beer and light wines, signaling the end of Prohibition, Earl Derr Biggers passed away in Pasadena after suffering a massive stroke. He was a mere forty-eight. As his wife, Eleanor, described, "I was right beside him from Sunday until Wednesday afternoon and although he could not speak he did emerge from a coma several times on Tuesday and gave me that radiant smile we all knew so well. The end came gradually and quietly."[10]

Major newspapers and journals ran obituaries lamenting the passing of the celebrated, best-selling author. The *Los Angeles Times* wrote: "All America mourns the death of Earl Derr Biggers. Since his first great story, *Seven Keys to Baldpate,* he never fell below the standard which makes his books rank with the greatest of mystery stories. Biggers not only gave us fascinating mystery, but delightful humor."[11] The liberal *Nation* commended Biggers for aiding the cause of international understanding by creating a Chinese hero, which must have been a revolutionary concept in the age when most Asian characters, if they appeared at all in American fiction, resembled Fu Manchu. Other periodicals praised him for paying tribute to the Chinese role in building the cities, orangeries, and vineyards of the Pacific Coast. An editorial in the *Cleveland Plain Dealer* called Chan "the most appealing of any supersleuth since Sherlock Holmes."[12] The *Honolulu Star-Bulletin* called Biggers "one of Honolulu's most distinguished citizens," and the *Honolulu Advertiser* stated on its editorial page, "The death of Earl Derr Biggers is a distinct loss to American letters and to Hawaii in especial. . . . As the creator of Charlie Chan, delightful Chinese detective, he did much to spread Hawaii's fame to the world."[13] Of course, there had been no such tributes for twenty-year-old Joseph Kahahawai, who had been killed only two years earlier.

The Biggers funeral was held at Neighborhood Church in Pasadena. The pastor, Dr. Theodore G. Soares, told the mourning crowd about two telegrams of condolence that had arrived for Mrs. Biggers: one from a famous American personage whom Soares did not name, and the other from a bellboy at the Royal Hawaiian Hotel. "He was a very human man," said Soares of the deceased novelist, "and it is very great to be human."[14]

After cremation, Biggers's ashes were scattered over his beloved San Gabriel Mountains.

PERHAPS THE IDENTITIES—some might say "souls"—of Biggers and the Hawaiian detective he had immortalized were more linked than one might have imagined. In late 1933, Apana, according to Gilbert Martines, "developed an infection on his left leg," which was worsened by his diabetes. Even as the infection slowly spread, he "refused standard medical aid at first, and relied instead on remedies provided by a Chinese herbalist." But the infection grew worse. On December 2, the day the Mauna Loa volcano erupted, Apana was admitted to Queen's Hospital "with a very severe case of diabetic gangrene. Apana objected to his physician's suggestion that his left leg be amputated. He believed in the Chinese notion that if he lost a leg in this life, he would also be minus a leg in the afterlife"; hence, he would be an invalid for all eternity. Earlier in his career as the humane officer, he had had to work against the Chinese belief in reincarnation, but now, in the twilight of his life, he showed that he had never totally forsaken the folkways of his people. Five days later, over Apana's vehement objections, the doctor ordered the amputation. But it was too late; even blood donated by fellow police officers was not able to save his life.[15]

On December 8, 1933, as "Madame Pele" (the local epithet for the volcanic crater) spread ashes all over the islands and into the sea, Apana, the proud native son, died—only eight months after the death of the Ohio mystery writer who had turned him into a legend for the ages.

Apana's death, understandably, failed to garner the widespread attention of the American press that Biggers's death had received, but newspaper headlines flashed through Honolulu. One such was "Black Camel Kneels at Home of Chang Apana," referring to the Chinese saying made famous by Charlie Chan: "Death is the black camel that kneels unbid at every gate."[16] The molten lava spewing forth from the volcano was, as Martines puts it, "Madame Pele's way of shedding black tears of anguish over the passing of Apana."[17] In Chinese, it is called *tian ren gan ying*—the sympathy between heaven and human.

Several major mainland newspapers—including the *New York Times, Chicago Tribune, San Francisco Chronicle, Los Angeles Times,* and *New York Herald Tribune*—did carry respectful notices about the passing of the original Charlie Chan. Under the title "Chinese Detective, 'Charlie Chan,' Dead," the obituary in the *New York Times* called him "one of Honolulu's most picturesque characters." The *Los Angeles Times* stated: "[Apana's] greatest feats in detective work were in the old days of Chinese immigration when Hawaii was a hotbed of opium traffic. He was knifed and beaten in the line of duty, but never lost his courage. 'He was the gamest creature I ever knew,' was the comment of one of his brother officers."[18]

On Sunday, December 10, Apana's funeral service, attended by several hundred people, was held at the Nuuanu Mortuary in downtown Honolulu. Afterward, the coffin was carried to the hearse by six pallbearers, all members of the HPD. Leading the funeral procession were "four motorcycle police officers, four mounted policemen, and two squads of officials on foot." The Royal Hawaiian Band preceded the hearse, an honor reserved ordinarily for Hawaiian dignitaries. A handler led a white horse without a rider in the procession. It was supposedly the same mount used by the former detective while on active duty.[19] Apana was buried with dignity in the Chinese Cemetery in Manoa Valley, along with his sapphire wedding ring and his police badge, number 100.[20]

From his humble origins as a coolie laborer's son to his career as one of the most legendary detectives in the country, Chang Apana had certainly trekked a very long way in life. And the same can be said of Earl Derr Biggers, born in the nineteenth century in a small Ohio town. After struggling to graduate from an elite college, he had then become one of the best-selling authors in the world. Both of their careers spanned a critical period when America emerged as a world power, when Hawaii evolved from an independent kingdom to a U.S. territory. The most unlikely of comrades, they together had given birth to an unforgettable character who is strangely both American apple pie and Chinese chop suey. Despite their sudden and untimely deaths, the American folk hero Charlie Chan would live on, immortalized as a symbol of both racial bias and cultural fantasy.

25

Racial Parables

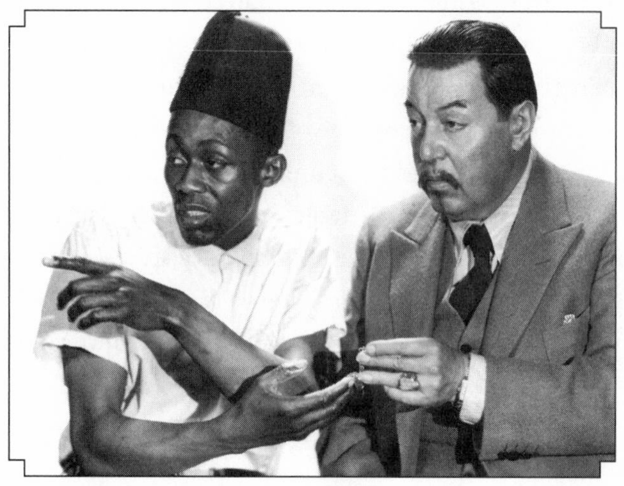

WARNER OLAND AND STEPIN FETCHIT IN *CHARLIE CHAN IN EGYPT*, 1935

(Courtesy of Everett Collection)

British tenacity with Chinese patience like royal flush in poker game—unbeatable.

—Charlie Chan

WITH THE DEATHS of Earl Biggers and Chang Apana, there were no more original Charlie Chan stories to adapt for the screen. Earlier in 1931, Fox had tried to create its own scripts based on the Chan character, but Biggers had adamantly objected to the idea, saying, "I wouldn't consent to that being done for any price whatever."[1] Now, with the passing of the author, Fox negotiated with

Eleanor Biggers and, in early 1934, bought the screen rights to the character.

At this time, William Fox's company was in serious financial trouble. In fact, it was no longer Fox's company, though it still bore his name. From the dingy Brooklyn nickelodeon he had bought in 1906, Fox had within two decades built one of the largest film empires in the world. In addition to distribution and production studios, the company had also created a chain numbering a thousand movie theaters by 1927. But a failed attempt to purchase MGM, a federal antitrust investigation, and the Great Crash did him in. In 1930, Fox was ousted from the company. Four years later, the Fox Film Corporation was still struggling, so it had high hopes for the Chan movies, as they were then, according to the *Los Angeles Times,* "the only successful feature series produced by Hollywood."[2]

The production team quickly set to work. They hired Philip MacDonald, a British mystery writer who was making a splash in America with his serial-killer novels, to write an original screenplay. They had the idea of launching the Chinese detective on a round-the-world trip of murder investigations. This scheme resulted in *Charlie Chan in London* (1934), followed the same year by *Charlie Chan in Paris,* both pictures inexpensive to make. As a gossip column in the *Los Angeles Times* reveals, "Being of simple story structure and dealing with elemental emotions, the films are quickly made, shot into the market and generally are well received at the box offices."[3]

Be that as it may, the third in the series, *Charlie Chan in Egypt* (1935), is perhaps one of the most controversial. In some ways, this film feels more like a racial parable than a detective mystery.[4] With a young Rita Cansino (soon to be Hayworth) as an exotic, beautiful Egyptian maid, the film presents a multiethnic cast of characters—a Chinese, a black, a Jew, and an Arab—who are pitted against a cabal of arrogant and greedy white men. The plot involves the discovery of the tomb of the ancient Egyptian high priest Ameti, a burial ground that was supposedly protected by the god Sahkmet. Sent by the French Archaeological Society to investigate the possible smuggling of tomb artifacts, Charlie Chan, played again by Warner Oland, arrives in Egypt by plane and then by a donkey, which he calls the "offspring of Satan" after the animal throws him to the ground. Professor Arnold, the lead archaeologist, has been mysteriously missing for more than a month, only to be found by Chan in a mummy case by using an X-ray machine. In the course of the investigation, Chan also solves a second murder, in which a vial of poison gas, hidden in a violin, is designed to break at the pitch of a certain note.

This slick and mysterious treachery pales, however, before the fantastic pairing of Chan with his black sidekick, Snowshoes, ingeniously and controversially played by Hollywood's most famous black high-jinkser, Stepin Fetchit. In the film, Fetchit portrays a fez-wearing, hookah-puffing, and easily frightened Negro lackey who has come to Egypt because a fortune-teller in Mississippi once told him that's where his ancestors came from. Foreshadowing the future duo of Sidney Toler's Charlie Chan and Mantan Moreland's Birmingham Brown, the interaction between the seemingly dimwitted Snowshoes and the supersharp Charlie, between "darkie" humor and "Chink" wisdom, actually adds, at least to many viewers, a distinct level of charm to a film that unfortunately has been reviled by subsequent critics on ideological grounds.

Civil rights advocates in the 1960s sought to redress the grievous stereotyping of Negroes in American movies, and they saw Fetchit as a prime example. Prior to the 1930s, the stereotypes of blacks in American films ranged from toms, coons, tragic mulattoes, mammies, and brutal bucks to field jesters. During the Great Depression, with the long breadlines and severe labor problems, a new on-screen stereotype of blacks emerged to meet the demands of the time: servants. From Fetchit's maligned handyman to Bill "Bojangles" Robinson's smooth-as-silk butler, Louise Beavers's jolly and submissive cook, and Paul Robeson's lordly Pullman-car porter, these black servants, in the words of film historian Donald Bogle, "provided a down-hearted Depression age with buoyancy and jocularity." With their degrading antics, ludicrous dialects, and incredible absurdities, the servants appeared to many at the time as "a marvelous relief from the harsh financial realities of the day. Not only their joy and zest but their loyalty, too, demonstrated that nothing in life was ever completely hopeless. The servants were always around when the boss needed them. They were always ready to lend a helping hand when times were tough."[5]

As the first distinctive black personality in American film history, Stepin Fetchit was the actor whose roles marked the transition from the old stereotypes to the new image. Born Lincoln Theodore Monroe Andrew Perry in Key West, Florida, in 1902, Fetchit adopted the stage name after he performed a vaudeville act called "Step and Fetch It." The name also fit well with the on-screen image he made famous: a plantation "darkie" who must step in (the Big House), fetch it, and then get out of the picture. When he joined Oland in the making of *Charlie Chan in Egypt,* Fetchit was at the height of his career. He had appeared in twenty-six films between 1929 and 1935 and sometimes was working in as many as four movies at a time. If Oland, a Scandinavian, was the top man for playing on-screen Orientals in the early 1930s, Fetchit was undoubtedly the best-known and most-successful black actor in Hollywood. At a time when contracts for black actors were rare, Fetchit was signed and re-signed by the Fox Film Corporation, which also did much to exploit and publicize Fetchit's flamboyant lifestyle: his six houses, sixteen Chinese servants, $2,000 cashmere suits, lavish parties, and twelve cars. Like a star athlete today, Fetchit was so popular in the 1930s that "Negro bootblacks and busboys were said to have imitated his notorious walk on the streets."[6]

In *Charlie Chan in Egypt,* Fetchit's character, Snowshoes, exploits almost all the clichés about a so-called nitwit black man: he was won by his white boss in a crap game; he sits around all day in an easy chair, puffing on a hookah; he brandishes a straight razor during a scuffle; he has come to Egypt supposedly to look up his "grandpappy"; and he harbors a naïve sentiment toward life on postbellum Southern plantations as he sweet-talks his black girlfriend into going back with him to Mississippi, where they wouldn't have to worry about getting jobs. Fetchit's characterization is so overblown, flashy, and exaggerated that, as Ken Hanke puts it, "the very stereotypical images they ostensibly represent become mocked by the format in which they are confined." Hanke, perhaps the most knowledgeable historian of Charlie Chan films, goes on to say, "One might go so far as to make the case that Stepin Fetchit was subversively antistereotypical."[7]

It would be hard to convince Fetchit's detractors that his roles were antistereotypical, just as it would be difficult to make a case for Charlie Chan in front of a jury that has already categorically denied any artistic or cultural merit of yellowface by white actors. Yet, to echo the sentiment expressed by Donald Bogle in his study of black film history, the essence of blackface or yellowface is not found in the racial stereotype itself but rather in "what certain talented actors have done with the stereotype," or what they have accomplished with even demeaning stereotyped roles.[8] What Fetchit accomplished with the Snowshoes character was, in a nutshell, a portrait of what he himself termed the "lazy man with a soul." Such a soulful person has, as Bogle puts it, become an integral part of the white household and involves himself in the affairs and troubles of his boss. He may still "be used for crude comic relief," but at heart he is "a harmless creature" who at crucial moments will come through.[9]

In *Charlie Chan in Egypt,* Snowshoes may be shoved around and yelled at by his white master, but it is he who is constantly relied upon; it is he who teams up with Chan, calls the police in time, and catches the guilty person in the act. His philosophical outlook on life, especially, is more in tune with Charlie Chan's Oriental wisdom than with his white master's greedy addictions. In fact, the whole film pitches colored—black, yellow, Arab—men against Anglo-European whites, with the former united by their interest in truth and justice and the latter condemned by their insatiable hunger for material wealth.[10] Chan is only interested in hunting down the wrongdoer; Snowshoes is completely nonchalant about the priceless unearthed treasures; and the Arab butler, Edfu Ahmad, is trying to protect his own cultural heritage. By contrast, the Anglo-Europeans, pursuing the "treasures of an ancient civilization primarily for material gain," have committed murder, larceny, and betrayal. At a telling moment in the film, Tom Evans, a headstrong, single-minded scholar, is able to translate the hieroglyphic symbols for "life" and "death" found inside the tomb, but he remains "insensitive to their meaning." Chan, however, immediately figures out their deeper, philosophical resonance by referring to the Confucian notion that between life and death is the reach of a man.[11] In the last scene of the film, Snowshoes, as the lazy man with a soul, completely shines through. When he asks Chan where he is going next, the latter dishes out a nice Chanism: "Journey of life like feather on stream—must continue with current." Pretending not to understand, Snowshoes replies blankly, "I guess you are right, but I'm going with you." Thus, Snowshoes, a seemingly dimwitted lackey, decides to follow a Chinaman's path of spiritual enrichment rather than the white men's expedition that has spawned nothing but death, sadness, and destruction.

Produced in 1935, *Charlie Chan in Egypt* was a racial parable that appeared in a fraught and incendiary age in which the world seemed to be careening again toward war and cataclysm. Two years earlier, Hitler had seized power in Germany, Mao Zedong and his Red Army had begun the Long March, and Stalin had started purging his political rivals after the assassination of S. M. Kirov. As those who are familiar with the 1930s know, the Nuremberg Laws, enacted on September 15, 1935, deprived German Jews of citizenship and the swastika became the official symbol of Nazi Germany. On October 3, led by its dictator, Benito Mussolini, Italy invaded Abyssinia, while the next year, the Spanish Civil War ignited the flames of discontent across Europe. Charged with racial and ethnic tensions, the world seemingly was waiting to explode, and Hollywood would not fail to notice. According to an article published on October 19, 1935, in the industry's flagship journal, *Motion Picture Herald*, "Hollywood is listening, even as the world listens to the newer rumblings of Mars on the Russo-Japanese border and on the waters at Malta and the Suez Canal."[12] If anything, setting Charlie Chan on a course of globetrotting was a sure sign that both the filmmakers and the audience were turning their attention to events of a grave political nature, not just a murder on Waikiki Beach or a jewelry theft in the Mojave Desert.

After London, Paris, and Egypt, Chan's next stop would be Shanghai. Born in Canton half a century earlier, Chan was now, as he put it, "most anxious to renew acquaintance with land of honorable ancestors."

PART FIVE

CHARLIE CHAN CARRIES ON

Charlie Chan's Bar, Sydney, Australia *(Photo by Susan M. Schultz)*

26

Charlie Chan in China

CHINESE MOVIE POSTER FOR *CHARLIE CHAN IN SHANGHAI*, 1936

(Courtesy of Wei Zhang)

I'm Anna May Wong
I come from Old Hong Kong
But now I'm a Hollywood Star
—Anonymous[1]

In the spring of 1936, the widowed Eleanor Biggers found herself traveling in Asia. On April 6, she sent a postcard from the Philippines to Laurance Chambers, her late husband's publisher and close friend. On the back of a card depicting the Shanghai Bund, she wrote, "In Manila, at the [undecipherable] Theatre, 'C.C.'s Secret' is playing this week and '7 Keys to Baldpate' announced for next. Huge posters of both adorn the building. Warner Oland is in Peiping, on vacation."[2]

Eleanor's postcard gives us a precious glimpse of the tremendous popularity of Charlie Chan in Asia, even as early as the 1930s. Especially in areas of large ethnic-Chinese populations, such as mainland China, Hong Kong, and Southeast Asia, the Chinese detective had amassed an enthusiastic following among movie fans who were supposedly his compatriots.

In the early twentieth century, urban Chinese were quickly drawn to the newest form of mass entertainment, *dianying* (film; literally, electrical shadows). According to government reports, by 1927 there were 106 movie theaters in China, with a total seating capacity of about 68,000. These were divided among eighteen large cities, chiefly treaty ports. Shanghai, taking the lion's share, had twenty-six cinemas and boasted the most lavish one of them all—the 1,420-seat Odeon, with modern-design floors and heavily upholstered balconies—a theater that rivaled if not outdid those great art-deco palaces in America in the 1920s and 1930s.[3]

Hailed as "the Paris of the Orient," Shanghai, in the decade before the 1937 Japanese invasion, enjoyed a flowering of modern urban culture unprecedented in Chinese history. With a population already surpassing three million in the early 1930s, the city was divided, like a highly intricate jigsaw puzzle, into foreign concessions [enclaves] and Chinese districts. At the heart of the so-called *shili yangchang* (ten-mile-long foreign zone) was the Bund, a strip of riverfront embankment famous for its majestic skyline. Department stores, movie theaters, coffeehouses, dance halls, and public gardens flourished both inside and outside the foreign zone. The latest models of Ford and Rolls-Royce whirred up and down the overcrowded streets, flaunting their breezily up-to-date modernity amid a sea of jinrickshas and wheelbarrows. In the words of British writer J. G. Ballard, who was born in Shanghai in 1930, the city was "a place of bizarre contrasts." Incongruously juxtaposed with graceful boulevards, elegant skyscrapers, and architecturally impressive art-deco apartment blocks were fetid back alleys, gambling dens, opium parlors, and a preponderance of prostitutes, ranging from the mink-coated to the scraggly and desperate. Ballard, the future dystopian novelist, was raised in the periphery of wealth, in a gated community of the foreign concessions. He recalled seeing, on the way to school in his chauffeured car, trucks touring the streets and removing the bodies of emaciated Chinese who had died during the night. "If Shanghai's neon lights were the world's brightest," Ballard concludes in his poignant autobiography, "its pavements were the hardest."[4]

In contrast to Americans, who had reacted largely with euphoria to the explosion of commodity culture in the 1920s, most Chinese came to regard these symbols of Western materialism and colonialism—skyscrapers, automobiles, department stores, even soap bars—with a mixed sense of wonder and oppression. Their response to Hollywood films was also quite mixed.

According to a 1927 report by the U.S. Department of Commerce, "The American motion picture enjoys far greater popularity among the Chinese than do the films of any other country outside of China. Aside from the greater lavishness of American pictures and their superior direction and technique, the Chinese also prefer the 'lived happily ever after' and 'triumph of right over wrong' ending which concludes most of our films, as compared with the more tragic finales of many European pictures."[5] A bit self-serving, the report nonetheless hints at the fact that the Chinese did not embrace Western culture without ambivalence or reservation. They were actually quite selective in their choice of movies, and the Chinese government, especially, practiced strict censorship over the distribution and screening of foreign motion pictures. After Chiang Kai-shek gained control of China in 1927, his Nationalist government established a review board that maintained an iron grip on the importation of foreign films. The board regularly banned foreign imports that, in its view, either portrayed Chinese in a negative manner or demonstrated any hostility toward Chinese. Famous English titles on the banned list included *The Thief of Bagdad*, *Shanghai Express*, and *The Bitter Tea of General Yen*. Interestingly, the board also blocked the distribution of movies for other reasons: *Frankenstein* and *Forgotten Commandment* because the board thought they carried an "aura of superstition," and *High Society* for having "pornographic content."[6]

The Charlie Chan series, however, easily passed muster with the board because these movies were regarded as the first American films with a positive, let alone brilliant and funny, Chinese character. Not only was Chan, in the eyes of the Chinese, a sea change from the sinister Fu Manchu stereotypes in earlier movies, but also, as a Chinese hero he appeared at a time when China was looked down upon by the Western powers. Even as the "made-in-USA" Chan was parading across the silver screen, charming millions of urban Chinese, the British, who policed the foreign zone in Shanghai, still had a sign hanging over the entrance to a park reading, "Neither Chinese Nor Dogs Allowed."

The Chinese government had long fought the battle over the images of Chinese in foreign media. Beaten and oppressed by Western imperial powers since the mid-nineteenth century, China felt racially stigmatized and was all too keenly aware of its inferior standing in the brutal world of international politics. Occasionally, however, through shrewd diplomacy, the Chinese could score a victory, as in the case of Fu Manchu. In the decades when Sax Rohmer was churning out his best-selling books about the insidious Chinaman, the Chinese government, though unable to influence the publication of these stories, was successful in blocking production of some of the later Fu Manchu films. In 1932, when MGM tried to make a new Fu Manchu number after four popular earlier films, the Chinese Embassy vehemently protested it. The United States, at that point alarmed by the rapid and ambitious expansion by Japan in the Far East, wanted to recruit China as an ally against the Japanese threat. As a result, the American government pressured MGM to pull the plug on the production.[7] In 1940, the Chinese also succeeded in obstructing the production of more Fu Manchu films by Republic Pictures, which in the previous year had brought out a fifteen-chapter movie serial, *Drums of Fu Manchu.*

With such a geopolitical context, Charlie Chan was accorded a near hero's welcome in China. According to Chinese film historian Wei Zhang, most of Warner Oland's sixteen Chan movies were aired in China, "to full houses and warm audience approval."[8] Even Lu Xun, perhaps China's greatest twentieth-century writer, a man well known for his bitter, razor-sharp essays, would not miss a single show of the hilarious Detective Chan. Xu Guangping, Lu Xun's longtime companion, recalled their frequent car rides, no matter what the distance, to cinemas in Shanghai to enjoy Oland's artful representation of a Chinaman.[9]

Charlie Chan's immense popularity in China set the stage for the warm reception of Warner Oland when he arrived for his first visit. On March 22, 1936, Oland was mobbed by journalists and cameras in Shanghai as he stepped off the steamship *Asian Empress.* The forgiving Chinese were ready to forget his appearance as Fu Manchu in three Paramount pictures and to embrace him enthusiastically as one of their own. "Holiday mood," says the Chinese detective in *Charlie Chan in Shanghai,* is "like fickle girl—privileged to change mind." So also was public sentiment. Not too long before, in 1930, at the showing of Harold Lloyd's *Welcome Danger,* Shanghai moviegoers had been outraged by its negative portrayal of Chinese, and their protest almost turned violent. And *Shanghai Express* (1932), starring none other than Oland as a mixed-blood Chinese villain, was also banned in China. Moreover, at the beginning of *Charlie Chan in Shanghai,* which had just been screened in the city, Charlie was seen singing a charming children's song about a Chinese princess, Ming Lo Fu, with an unfortunate reference to Emperor Fu Manchu. Despite the sweet charm of the ballad, the mention of Fu Manchu could have opened a can of worms and set off a chain of bad associations for the Chinese.

In the spring of 1936, however, the Chinese were ready to put aside all of that and celebrate the arrival of "Charlie Chan" as one of their own. Every major Shanghai newspaper and film studio sent reporters to interview the man dubbed "the great Chinese detective" in the headlines. Always a good sport and still quite fresh from his "reel" experience with Shanghai, Oland reciprocated the Chinese enthusiasm by staying in character and blurring the line, as usual, between fiction and reality. During a press conference at five o'clock on the day of his arrival, he answered reporters' questions while maintaining the Charlie Chan persona. In his familiar Chan costume, Oland declared, in a Swedish-accented Mandarin, "Visiting the land of my ancestors makes me so happy." At that moment, as Zhang puts it, "Warner Oland and Charlie Chan had merged into one, becoming in the eyes of those present, one and the same Chinese person."[10]

Such a warm reception stood in stark contrast to the snub accorded by the Chinese only a month earlier to Anna May Wong, who had made an appearance in *The Chinese Parrot* and had collaborated with Oland in several major China-themed films. One of the most enigmatic, glamorous, and sensational actresses, Wong had a shining but also difficult career in an industry beset by sexism and racism. Born in 1905 in Los Angeles's Chinatown, Anna May Wong (aka Wong Liu Tsong, yellow willow frost), was the second daughter of a Cantonese laundryman. Showing an early interest in Hollywood, she made her first cinematic appearance as a Chinese extra in 1919 in *The Red Lantern,* starring Alla Nazimova as a Eurasian woman who falls in love with an American missionary. Wong's beauty was so apparent that she soon caught the attention of Hollywood filmmakers, and her career quickly took off. Her most famous roles in the 1920s and early 1930s were in *Toll of the Sea, Piccadilly, The Thief of Bagdad, Old San Francisco, Daughter of the Dragon,* and *Shanghai Express.* In many of these, she shared equal billing with Douglas Fairbanks, Marlene Dietrich, and Warner Oland, among others. Walter Benjamin, one of Europe's most sophisticated intellectuals, after a brief encounter with Wong at a private party in Berlin, characterized her as "like the specks in a bowl of tea that unfold into blossoms replete with moon and devoid of scent." The flamboyant flaneur was thoroughly enraptured by Wong's stunning beauty.[11] According to Graham Hodges, Andy Warhol also paid tribute to her by "designing a camp collage of 'crazy golden slippers,'" a gesture of admiration for the Chinese actress. Another avant-garde artist, Ray Johnson, even "created an imaginary Anna May Wong Fan Club, fabricated meetings between fantasy enthusiasts, and fashioned lovely pieces of art devoted to Anna May."[12]

Wong would have become an even bigger star were it not for the racial mores in Hollywood that made it impossible for her to play certain roles. Interracial kissing, for instance, was an unspoken taboo in the early films, causing filmmakers to pass over Wong. Instead, white actresses were cast in roles that would have been perfect for her. Then, too, censorship reared its head, making the situation even worse for Wong. Fearful of government regulations and mindful of criticism by social conservatives who had been unhappy with the influence of movies, the film industry set up a self-censorship mechanism by founding the Motion Picture Producers and Distributors of America (MPPDA) in 1922 and hiring William Hays, former postmaster general of the United States and ex-chair of the Republican National Committee, as its head. Hays immediately began by banning scandalous actors, such as Roscoe "Fatty" Arbuckle, from the movies and instituted a morality clause for the industry. Over the years, Hays compiled a list of don'ts that were consolidated into the official censorship rules, the Motion Picture Production Code, published in 1930. Commonly known as the Hays Code, it spelled out what was acceptable and unacceptable content for motion pictures produced for public viewing in the United States. It imposed restrictions on such subject matter as sex, violence, religion, and race, and it banned any portrayal of miscegenation or interracial romance. Such prohibitions effectively condemned Wong to an almost permanent secondary role in romance films, always having to play tragic characters who are victims of abuse or die brokenhearted, with no "happily ever after." As she once put it, "I died so often. Pathetic dying seemed to be the best thing I did."[13]

Hollywood's most notorious snub of Wong occurred during the making of Pearl S. Buck's *The Good Earth.* At the apex of her reputation in 1935, Wong was nonetheless considered by MGM "too Asian" for the lead role of O-lan. A similar verdict befell other Asian actors who were deemed not to fit the producer's conception of "what Chinese people looked like." The film ended up using Asian extras only for "atmosphere." The lead roles went to Austrian actress Luise Rainer and American actor Paul Muni, making the award-winning movie a yellowface extravaganza and producing what one critic has called "MGM Chinese."[14]

Disgusted by MGM's racial policy, Wong decided to leave Hollywood for a while and visit the land of her parents for the first time. In January 1936, at a farewell party for her in Los Angeles, her longtime friend Warner Oland joked that it would be amusing for him to go to China with Wong, even though she had failed to secure the part of O-lan, which sounded like his own name. But he could not yet join her. "I am still Charlie Channing," said Oland. "This time in *The Circus*" (referring to the film *Charlie Chan at the Circus*).[15] Over the years, the two had collaborated in several films—notably, *Old San Francisco* (1927), *Daughter of the Dragon* (1931), and *Shanghai Express.* In *Old San Francisco,* which in hindsight seems like straightforward propaganda for Oriental exclusion, Oland played a Chinese villain masquerading as an Anglo capitalist, and Wong was his Eurasian concubine. In *Daughter of the Dragon,* derived from Sax Rohmer's novel *Daughter of Fu Manchu,* the Oland-Wong duo this time played a father-daughter relationship, prompting Oland, fresh from his Charlie Chan set at the Fox studio, to wisecrack: "Husband and wife? Father and daughter? This is getting pretty incestuous."[16] In *Shanghai Express,* Wong was a Chinese woman raped by Henry Chang, a Eurasian warlord played by Oland.

None of these films would endear Wong to the Chinese population she was soon to meet, even though Oland's roles in the same films were conveniently forgotten by the same constituency. Over the years, Wong had also starred or had cameo roles in several other movies that had raised the hackles of her critics in China. The first of such controversial roles was *The Thief of Bagdad* (1924), directed by Raoul Walsh. Starring Douglas Fairbanks as a carefree pickpocket enjoying a life of mischievous thievery and romantic love, the Arabian adventure was a feast for the eyes, with a spectacular display of production design and special effects. In the film, Wong is cast as a Mongol slave who betrays her mistress. What made Wong a sensation was also what scandalized her Chinese audience: her character was made to reveal ample sections of bare skin. In a crucial scene, as Fairbanks's character, bare-chested, holds a knife against the small of the scantily attired Mongol slave's back, "she pivots her body so that her face looks back with fear while the rest of her trembles with a mixture of terror and sensuality."[17] When the film was screened in China, many reviewers found her performance "degrading." Some ridiculed her as merely "a cat's paw, who plays minor roles." Her own father, a man devoted to Chinese traditions and values, felt disgraced by her role in the film.[18] *The Thief of Bagdad* subsequently was banned in China as a result of public outcry.

Wong's appearance in the second Charlie Chan film, *The Chinese Parrot*, similarly offended Chinese audiences. Starring Kamiyama Sojin, who as Chan does not even receive any feature billing, the movie casts Wong as a belly-dancing nautch girl, a role that drew scathing criticism in China. One reviewer stated that Wong was "losing face for China again." Another wrote: "In the movie, I saw Miss Wong dancing in a crowd of naked natives, violently twisting her bottom and her dance displayed no other movements." Her performance, the critics declared, was unacceptable to the Chinese audience.[19]

Such harsh criticism, though widespread, was hardly uniform. In

Chinese artistic circles, Wong had a coterie of influential friends who rallied to her side. They included Mei Lan Fang, Peking Opera's most famous twentieth-century singer (Wong's ostensible goal for this China trip was to learn stage techniques from Mei and, upon return, to build an English-speaking Chinese theater company to tour the globe); Wu Liangde, the editor of *Liangyou Huabao*, the Chinese *Cosmopolitan* of the day; and Hu Die, the so-called Empress of Movies in 1930s China. It is worth noting that, according to recent cultural historians, the kind of moralistic condemnation leveled at Wong and others came mostly from leftist hard-liners and Nationalist conservatives who frowned upon fantasies in movies and expressions of modern femininity. In fact, more open-minded intellectuals, artists, and other cultural elites, who had followed Wong's career for years, had great admiration for the world's most famous Chinese actress.[20]

This divergence of opinion set the stage for the dramatically contrasting receptions during Wong's China visit. When she arrived on February 9, 1936, aboard the SS *President Hoover,* thousands of fans flocked to the Shanghai dock and crowded along the Huangpu River to greet the illustrious star. Wellington Koo, soon to depart for his ambassadorial post in France, gave a lavish dinner reception in Wong's honor, a grand occasion attended by such Chinese elites as Lin Yutang, Mei Lan Fang, and others. Nonetheless, a month later in Hong Kong, a welcome scene turned vengeful, with an angry crowd shouting, "Down with Wong Liu Tsong—the stooge that disgraces China. Don't let her go ashore." Even her father, who had been staying for a while in his birthplace, a small village near Canton, was urged by the district delegation not to allow his daughter to come home to visit him. If she insisted on coming, they warned, "the entire [Wong] family might be expelled."[21]

Arriving in China a month after Wong did, and enthusiastically received by the Chinese as the honorable "Mr. Chan," Warner Oland crossed paths with his friend and costar in Hong Kong, toward the end of his trip. Wong treated Oland to a special Cantonese dim sum lunch. Over a tableful of delicacies, the two Hollywood stars com-

MOVIE POSTER FOR *CHARLIE CHAN SMASHES AN EVIL PLOT*, 1941

(Courtesy of Wei Zhang)

pared notes about their China trips. Despite the huge gap between their backgrounds—a Swede born in a small village tucked away in the snowy climes of northern Europe and a Chinese girl born in the steam and starch of her father's laundry in Los Angeles's Chinatown—they had one thing in common: they both had careers portraying Chinese on the silver screen, which had brought them fame as well as notoriety.

In a period when the Chinese film industry was still in its infancy, when many Chinese cinematographic productions tended to imitate Hollywood movies, it was only natural that the popularity of Charlie Chan would spawn made-in-China imitations. Almost immediately after Oland's visit, studios in Shanghai and Hong Kong began making a series of "homegrown" Charlie Chan films, including *The Disappearing Corpse, The Pearl Tunic*, and *The Radio Station Murders* in the 1930s, followed by *Charlie Chan Smashes an Evil Plot* and *Charlie Chan Matches Wits with the Prince of Darkness* in the subsequent decade.[22]

At the same time, all six of Earl Biggers's novels were translated into Chinese by Xiaoqing Cheng, one of the most gifted Chinese detective-fiction writers and translators of his day.

In the Chinese movies, most of which were directed by Xu Xinfu and starred Xu Xinyuan, the "Chinese" Chan was no longer a police officer but a private investigator like the American "private eyes" Sam Spade and Philip Marlowe. He was ably assisted not by his Number One or Number Two son, but instead by his daughter Manna—reminiscent of some of the later Sidney Toler Monogram Pictures films, in which Chan's daughter Iris would appear as one of his eager helpers. Unfortunately, most reels of these Chinese "knockoffs" have been lost. According to contemporary testimonies, Xu's Charlie Chan followed Oland's incarnation closely in almost all aspects: walk, talk, and dress.

Here we seem to have reached the final, if not slightly bizarre, frontier of yellowface, where a real Chinaman imitates a Swede's imitation of a Chinaman. Charlie Chan might have come home, but the exact location of home—in the age of the global circulation of images, meanings, and values—remains as elusive as clues to an unsolvable murder case.

27

Charlie Chan Soldiers On

Sidney Toler, circa 1910

(Courtesy of Poetry and Rare Books Library, University of Buffalo)

Carry on, Charlie.
—Inspector Duff of Scotland Yard[1]

The purple-blue blossoms of jacaranda signaled that spring was in full bloom in California that May of 1936. Warner Oland had returned from China just in time for the production of *Charlie Chan at the Race Track*, which began on May 18. At this point in his career, owing to the enormous success of the Chan series, Oland had accumulated considerable wealth. He and his wife now owned a ranch in the Carpinteria Valley near Santa Barbara; a farmhouse in Southboro, Massachusetts; a 7,000-acre ranch on the Mexican island of Palmita de la Virgen, and a cozy pied-à-terre in Beverly Hills. His initial salary for the Chan role a decade earlier had been $10,000 a picture, and that figure increased steadily over the years. After the merger of Fox and Twentieth Century Pictures in 1935, the new company, Twentieth Century-Fox Film Corporation, had agreed to pay Oland $20,000 for *Race Track*.

In the beginning, the producers had found it useful to give Oland a drink so that he would slur his dialogue, but now they recognized that his drinking problem had worsened, to the point that it hampered the production of the film. He would often disappear for days, only to be found somewhere in a useless alcoholic stupor. When he did show up, he would forget his lines or doze off. In the shooting of one scene in *Race Track*, Oland was supposed to play Chan watching a horse race, but he kept nodding off. Director H. Bruce Humberstone had to place a few extras around Oland to bolster him up. "I know you can't see anything," he told Oland. "But just turn your head with the sound."[2]

A nurse was even assigned to Oland to make sure he did not drink, but he managed to sneak booze into his lunch boxes or secrete it in a closet. Keye Luke, who played Charlie Chan's Number One son in the films, recalled the lunches he used to have with "Pop" at the production studio, where the latter would take out two thermos bottles. "For Number One son," Oland would say, "good split pea soup." Then, "looking over his shoulder to see if the coast was clear, he poured out a martini from the second thermos. 'For honorable father, tiger tea.' "[3]

The situation deteriorated so markedly that Oland's marriage collapsed in mid-1937, and he suffered a nervous breakdown, worsening his alcoholism. At the studio, he would repeatedly blow his lines and complain that the set was too drafty. The production team tried to change the number of the stage, but it did not fool Oland. At night, like a down-and-out character in a Pat Hobby story, he would wander off aimlessly into the streets and even forget who he was. On January 17, 1938, during the production of *Charlie Chan at the Ringside,* Oland walked off the set and simply disappeared. When he was found again, he made national headlines with a compromising photograph showing him sitting on the running board of his limousine and throwing away his shoes. Twentieth Century-Fox put Oland on suspension and threatened to sue him for the cost of the film, which had to be abandoned. After a month of hospitalization, he recovered slightly and appeared well enough for Darryl F. Zanuck, the president of the company, to sign a deal with him for three new Chan pictures at $30,000 apiece for the 1938–39 season. But Zanuck felt that Oland first needed a break, and that an ocean voyage might do him some good before resuming work. Therefore, in the spring of 1938, Oland sailed for Europe—more than anything to repair his nerves. Before departure, Oland told Keye Luke, "Honorable father have appointment to see blossoming trees in Florence," yet he was in fact bound for his native Sweden, which he had left as a boy of thirteen.[4]

While traveling in Europe during that politically toxic summer of 1938, Oland sent a postcard on July 10 to a friend in California. "Still climbing upwards. Two more days and I shall be home," he wrote. By "home" he meant his birthplace, a small Swedish village near the Gulf of Bothnia. No sooner had Oland arrived than he fell ill with bronchial pneumonia. On August 6, reposing in his mother's old bed, Warner Oland passed away, giving the lie to a Confucian aphorism that Oland had quoted in *Charlie Chan in Egypt,* "From life to death is reach of man." He was only fifty-seven years old.

In the obituary the next day, the *New York Times* paid homage to Oland's major achievement of impersonating a Chinese. Noting the crucial shift in Oland's career from evil Oriental characters to the honorable Detective Chan, the paper stated, "To a growing number of enthusiasts, he became closely identified with Earl Derr Biggers's philosophical super-sleuth. The hisses and grimaces of his long-nailed villainy were swiftly forgotten as Chan's traditional 'So sor-ry' and related politenesses, through Oland's reformed lips, became now box-office magic."[5] Other newspapers and journals, including the *Los Angeles Times, Honolulu Star-Bulletin*, and *Variety*, also carried the news of Oland's death.

At the Fox studio, preproduction of *Charlie Chan in Honolulu* had already started. The director, Sol Wurtzel, had cabled Oland to return at once. When word of his death reached Hollywood, Wurtzel called a halt for the day. But Oland's death, in the words of film historian Jon Tuska, "did not kill Charlie Chan."[6] The Chan series had become a huge moneymaker during the bleakest Depression years. With Oland, the studio had been making an average of three Chan films a year. Each was shot in four weeks, with an extra week for reshoots; it took only three month from the commencement of shooting to the release of the film. At a cost of about $250,000, each Chan number could gross more than $1 million in profit.[7] Charlie Chan, therefore, had no choice but to continue.

The company soon auditioned thirty-four actors, including J. Edward Bromberg and Noah Beery, Sr. On October 18, 1938, Fox announced its final choice of Sidney Toler, a Missouri native, as the new Chan. By this time, Toler had been knocking around Hollywood for about two decades, cameoing in movies that featured such stars as Marlene Dietrich, Claudette Colbert, and Clark Gable. Difficult as it was to replace Warner Oland, Toler brought updated interpretations of the Chan character in a world that soon would be thrown into the cauldron of war. Whereas Oland's Chan was polite and soft-spoken, Toler's character, in Ken Hanke's words, was "less humble" and "more irascible," carrying more acidity on the tip of his tongue.[8] Toler's makeup was also more pronounced, with his eyes pulled back to an exaggerated degree. To further improve the characterization, the producers resorted to the same trick they had used on Oland: letting Toler take a few "stiff belts" before the shooting so as to induce the friendly grin and slow his speech. It was as if dipsomania had become a prerequisite for playing Charlie Chan. As one of the crew members later recalled, "All those Chans were drunk while making those pictures. You'd have to be drunk just to talk that pidgin English."[9] It is worth noting, in all fairness, that the portrayers of Hawaii's most celebrated detective were hardly the only actors encouraged or even induced to use alcohol or drugs; the amphetamine-ridden, sedative-popping culture of Hollywood in this era caused the breakdown and emotional collapse of dozens of pressured and overworked stars—most notably, perhaps, Judy Garland.

Between 1938 and 1942, Toler made eleven Chan films, until the outbreak of war and a new set of federal regulations prompted Twentieth Century-Fox to discontinue the series. The Chan films owed a large percentage of their profits to the worldwide market, and the wars in Europe and Asia had truncated the foreign revenue. In addition, the federal government had filed an antitrust suit against film-producing companies that also owned theater chains. As a result, all the major companies, including Twentieth Century-Fox, began to cut back on their "B" movies, emphasizing instead their "A" products.[10]

When Toler heard the news of the series' cancellation, he immediately negotiated with Eleanor Biggers Cole, now remarried, and secured the rights to the character.[11] After looking for financial backers for more than a year, Toler resumed the series in May 1943 with Monogram Pictures, at the time still a low-budget studio.

One new addition to Monogram's Chan series was Mantan Moreland, who played Charlie's round-faced, wide-eyed, and superstitious chauffeur, Birmingham Brown. Along with Willie Best and Louis Armstrong, Moreland was widely regarded in black film history as one of "Stepin's Step-Chillun"—black actors who came of age in the wake of Stepin Fetchit's spectacular, though short-lived, career in Hollywood. With the diminution of the overseas market for Charlie Chan, Moreland's entrance, according to Ken Hanke, was Monogram's insurance policy, because "giving the talented black comic a major role in the films meant that they, like earlier Monogram horror films such as *King of the Zombies*, could be assured of a major release in Harlem and other primarily black areas on their strength as Mantan Moreland pictures." As Hanke further comments, "It was a shrewd move. With one swipe Monogram could garner both the Charlie Chan and the black audience."[12] Harking back to Fetchit's Snowshoes, Moreland's guest appearance with Chan also foreshadowed the future Hollywood practice of casting two racial-minority characters head-to-head, as we've seen more recently with Jackie Chan and Chris Tucker in the *Rush Hour* series. The double dosage of ethnic humor does, it would seem, kill two birds with one stone.

In some of the weaker Chan films, Moreland's cherubic Birmingham character, who is constantly "terr'fied of de ghosts," certainly brought some much-needed comic relief to the movies and the audience. In *The Scarlet Clue*, for instance, an otherwise-mediocre entry among the Chan films, the audience was treated to a hilarious nightclub routine performed flawlessly by Moreland and his offscreen partner, Ben Carter. Known as the "infinite conversation," the routine involved Moreland and Carter carrying on "an entire dialogue without ever finishing a sentence."[13]

After eleven new Chan films at Monogram, Sidney Toler died of cancer in February 1947. Even then, the Charlie Chan character persisted. He soon found another incarnation in Roland Winters, a professional actor who also moonlighted as a radio sports announcer. Born Roland Winternitz in Boston on November 22, 1904, Winters worked on a cargo ship when he was a teenager and later joined theater groups in his hometown. After a couple of bit parts in silent films, in 1931 he got a job announcing Braves and Red Sox baseball games on radio station WNAC, and he continued to work at the station until he was chosen as the new Charlie Chan.[14] Altogether, Winters would make six Chan numbers, beginning with *The Chinese Ring* in 1947 and ending with *The Sky Dragon* in 1949. Although his characterization, as Hanke points out, was closest to Biggers's original (he spoke some of Biggers's brightest original aphorisms from the novels), Winters was the least successful yellowfacer when compared with Oland and Toler. For one thing, his tall nose simply could not be made to look Chinese, and, at the age of forty-four, he also looked too young to resemble a seasoned Chinese sage.[15] Perhaps he was not enticed to take a nip of brandy while on the set, but for whatever reason, his Chan characterization was far less memorable.

While Mantan Moreland's comic antics continued to provide life support for the series, one unexpected bonus was the return of Keye Luke as Lee Chan, Charlie's Number One son. Like the fictional Charlie Chan, Keye Luke was born in Canton, China, in 1904 and had come to America when he was four months old. After growing up in Seattle and studying architecture at the University of Washington, he began his career painting murals at the shrine of Hollywood's Orientalism—Grauman's Chinese Theatre. Before becoming Warner Oland's Number One sidekick in 1935, Luke had played a few supporting roles in films, including Greta Garbo's *The Painted Veil* (1934). The collaboration between Oland and Luke was one of the most successful on-screen relationships in the Chan series. In their interaction one can feel a genuine affection and love, as we might expect between a father and a son. Lee's signature "Gee, Pop!" would become an heirloom handed down to his sibling after Luke dropped out of the series upon Oland's death in 1938. Luke also participated in the making of Peter Lorre's *Mr. Moto's Gamble,* which salvaged material from the unfinished *Charlie Chan at the Ringside.* Luke's resurrection in the last two Chan films, *The Feathered Serpent* and *The Sky Dragon,* though failing to breathe new life into a doomed series, at least gave it a nice closure. In the ensuing decades, Luke would make a name for himself as a Chinese actor both on-screen and off. He would play blind Master Po in David Carradine's *Kung Fu,* and he supplied the voice of Charlie Chan in the Hanna-Barbera animation series *The Amazing Chan and the Chan Clan* much later in the 1970s. Significantly, it was Keye Luke who would become the most vocal defender of Charlie Chan against his detractors: "There are a lot of things about the Chan character that these people don't understand," he once said in an interview. "They think it demeans the race. . . . Demeans! My God! You've got a Chinese hero!"[16]

The Charlie Chan series, which had had a strong run for two decades beginning in the late 1920s, finally concluded with the release of *The Sky Dragon* in May 1949. By this time, the chubby, wisecracking Chinese detective had already become a ubiquitous icon in American culture. The character had spawned radio dramas, comic strips, children's books, and even board games. As early as December 1932, the NBC Blue Network had premiered a Friday-night radio drama starring Walter Connolly as Charlie Chan, while Earl Biggers that same year had received offers from at least three radio networks for dramatization rights. The NBC series lasted only six months, but it was revived by the Mutual Network in October 1937 and by ABC in 1944. The last was a radio program called *The Adventures of Charlie Chan*, starring Ed Begley (who would later win the Academy Award for his supporting role in the 1962 film *Sweet Bird of Youth*) as Chan and Leon Janney as Number One son.[17] Walter Benjamin once said, "The radio listener welcomes the human voice into his house like a visitor." In the acoustic milieu of the pre-television age, the Chinaman's singsong voice would frequent American households like a charming visitor from an exotic, faraway land.

Chan's presence was hardly prescribed by only film and radio. From October 1938 to May 1942, the Charlie Chan comic strip, drawn by noted artist Alfred Andriola, appeared in Sunday newspapers across the nation. At the same time, publishers such as Whitman in Racine, Wisconsin, brought out comic books featuring the friendly detective. With their garish covers and fast-paced adventures, these books catered to curious children as well as adult aficionados. According to the noted mystery authority Otto Penzler, these tiny, fat, hardbound volumes, known as Big Little Books, "sometimes featured small drawings in the upper corners of the right-hand pages which could be flipped rapidly with the thumb to provide the illusion of figures moving a bit at a time, motion-picture-like."[18] To complete the picture, a board game called The Great Charlie Chan Detective Mystery Game (a forerunner to Milton Bradley's Clue) and a Charlie Chan Card Game were produced in 1937 and 1939, respectively.

This merchandise and paraphernalia extended Chan's life and influence beyond the novels and films, perpetuating his presence in the American imagination. Two decades after his debut as a minor character in 1925, Charlie Chan had become the nation's most recognizable Chinese folk hero. His career, however, was far from over. In the postwar years, Chan continued to enjoy some popularity, but, as we will see, his reputation would take strange turns, giving credence to a time-honored Chanism, "Wheel of fate has many spokes."

28

The Fu Manchurian Candidate

Warner Oland in *The Mysterious Dr. Fu-Manchu*, 1929

(Courtesy of Everett Collection)

I can see that Chinese cat standing there smiling like Fu Manchu.
—Ben Marco, in the film The Manchurian Candidate, *1962*

As the Charlie Chan finale, *The Sky Dragon*, toured theaters across the United States in the summer of 1949, Americans, already apprehensive about the mounting dangers of the cold war, were mourning the loss of China. After a four-year civil war, Mao Zedong's Red Army had soundly defeated the Nationalists, whom the United States had vigorously supported. On October 1, 1949, when Mao declared the founding of the People's Republic of China, it seemed as if the whole continent of Asia had just been swallowed up by a Red Sea. Within a year, the Korean War broke out, pitting the United States against the Communists from the North. At the same time, and as the 1950s progressed, millions of baby boomers, growing up in a decade of affluence and suburban sprawl, became familiar with a quaint Chinaman spouting aphorisms on the screen. Even though the Charlie Chan film series had concluded its production, Fox and major networks kept the reruns on TV and at movie theaters.

It was during this period that Charlie Chan's influence reached deeply into the American cultural psyche. His legacy as the first lovable Chinaman would also take an unexpected turn. Especially in the heyday of the cold war, his image became strangely and unfortunately intertwined with the fate of his evil twin, Dr. Fu Manchu. In the hard-boiled world of film noir, dubious characters with singsong Chinese names loomed ominously in the eerie background. *China* or *Chinatown* came to symbolize a villainous underworld, one that was synonymous with all that was rotten in midcentury urban America, the opposite of clean, white suburbia.

In this mix of symbols, Charlie Chan no longer simply represented the good cop in a whodunit mystery. The dark and evil atmosphere that the Charlie Chan movies invariably evoke—the mean alleys of Chinatown, foggy docks where fishy characters hover, slimy streets of Shanghai where criminals look like deadly cobras—all these exotic and often ersatz-Oriental milieus seemed to have stained the archetypal Chinaman, Charlie Chan. "The field," as Marshall McLuhan might put it, "has become the figure." Chan's stereotypical Chinese inscrutability had unwittingly made him what I would label a "Fu Manchurian Candidate."

I deliberately pun on *The Manchurian Candidate*, a 1962 film directed by John Frankenheimer, because it aptly captures the kind of Red-scare paranoia and xenophobia prevalent in the postwar period. Such sentiments, fanned by cold-war propaganda and McCarthyism, indeed tarnished the image of Charlie Chan and made him guilty by association. In some quarters of American culture today, "Charlie Chan" and "Fu Manchu" remain interchangeable epithets for the Chinaman, just as the Charlie Chan mustache and the Fu Manchu goatee are often as inseparable as peas and carrots—or, if you prefer, as ping and pong.

The Manchurian Candidate, starring Frank Sinatra, Janet Leigh, and Angela Lansbury, was a film adaptation of Richard Condon's eponymous 1959 best-seller. The movie reached cult status after Sinatra took it out of circulation in the wake of President Kennedy's assassination. Its plot involves Raymond Shaw, a decorated Korean War hero, who is brainwashed by Chinese Communists in Manchuria. During a combat mission, Shaw's platoon is ambushed and captured by the Red Army. Under the direction of evil doctor/spymaster Yen Lo, a Chinese psychiatric team brainwashes the POWs into believing that Shaw has saved their lives. Returning to the United States, Shaw receives a Presidential Medal of Honor for his alleged bravery, although he is in fact a sleeper agent still under the posthypnotic control of his handlers. With the queen of diamonds in a deck of playing cards as his subconscious trigger, Shaw is compelled to follow orders and commit murders and other subversive acts, which he cannot remember afterward.

The Chinese agent who controls Shaw's mind turns out to be a real "queen," Shaw's mother, who plots to overthrow the U.S. government by orchestrating and manipulating the presidential election. Her plan is foiled by Captain Bennett Marco, who was captured and brainwashed along with Shaw in Manchuria but has been having nightmarish flashbacks that give him a glimpse of the truth. With Marco's help, Shaw eventually is able to "deprogram" and free himself from his mental captor by fatally shooting his mother, her husband, and then himself.

Despite the popularity of the movie—it was so popular that it was remade in 2004 with Denzel Washington, Meryl Streep, and Liev Schreiber—only literary aficionados would know that the concept of having a brainwashed Communist mole inside the White House has its roots in Sax Rohmer's 1936 novel, *President Fu Manchu.*

It is hard to tell to what extent Richard Condon might have been self-consciously borrowing from Rohmer's book for his *Machurian Candidate,* but even a passing glance at the basic plots of the two novels reveals a striking resemblance. In *President Fu Manchu,* the insidious Chinaman attempts to conquer "the free world" by taking over the White House. For years, Fu Manchu has carefully and secretly groomed a presidential candidate who commands an irresistible appeal to the masses through his beautiful elocution. Fu has built a vast, catacomblike network named the Si-Fan, a secret society that "embraced in its invisible tentacles practically the whole of the colored races of the world." Through the Si-Fan, he bankrolls a bogus grassroots, patriotic movement, the League of Good Americans (called the "Loyal American Underground" in *The Manchurian Candidate*), to put his puppet in the White House.[1] But the most devious part of his design is to train, through posthypnotic suggestion, an amnesiac assassin who is programmed to kill upon hearing a trigger word from the controller.

What Raymond Shaw fails to accomplish in *The Manchurian Candidate*—he is supposed to shoot the presidential nominee at the party's convention six minutes into his acceptance speech, at the precise point where the speaker finishes a sentence ending with *liberty* (a cold-war buzzword)—the assassin in *President Fu Manchu* succeeds in doing. He kills the presidential nominee at a political convention in the middle of the latter's speech, right at the point where the speaker utters *Asia* (also a loaded word in the race war, as imagined by Rohmer). After the assassination, the deceased candidate's secretary, acting as Fu Manchu's mole, rises to the occasion and immediately becomes the obvious front-runner in the presidential campaign—something Shaw's "queen" mother has planned to do, thus instantly propelling her senator-husband, Johnny, into the national spotlight.[2]

What is most sensational about "the Fu Manchurian Candidate," as depicted by both Rohmer and Condon, is his supposed skill at brainwashing and mind control. It is said that Fu Manchu (an obvious prototype for Dr. Yen Lo) is a master of posthypnotic suggestion. Even an inadvertent look into Fu's jade-green eyes will immediately place you under the magic spell of the evil doctor, who can then creep up on you like a cat during your sleep and control your mind through dreams. After that, you will simply become his unwitting agent in your somnambulist state.

Such a mind-control technique might seem merely literary pulp, relegated to the confines of cheap paperback thrillers. The cold-war era, however, reified these nightmares and fears. In his introduction to the 2003 edition of *The Manchurian Candidate*, cultural historian Louis Menand puts Condon's 1959 book in excellent context:

> United Nations ground forces began military action in Korea on July 5, 1950. On July 9, an American soldier who had been captured two days before delivered a radio speech consisting of North Korean propaganda. Similar broadcasts by captured soldiers continued throughout the war. At the end of the war, the army estimated that one out of every seven American prisoners of war had collaborated with the enemy; twenty-one Americans refused to return to the United States; forty announced that they had become Communists; fourteen were court-martialed, and eleven convicted.[3]

In 1951, eight years before the appearance of Condon's novel, a journalist named Edward Hunter, who had served in the military during World War II, published *Brain-washing in Red China: The Calculated Destruction of Men's Minds*. Part ethnographic exotica and part anti-Communist propaganda, the book first introduced the Chinese term *xi nao* into the English vocabulary as "brainwashing." Based on his interviews with informants and hearsay from former POWs, Hunter made a sweeping claim:

> Brain-washing became the principal activity on the Chinese mainland when the Communists took over. Unrevealed tens of thousands of men, women, and children had their brains washed. They ranged from students to instructors and professors, from army officers and municipal officials to reporters and printers, and from criminals to church deacons. There were no exceptions as to profession or creed. Before anyone could be considered trustworthy, he was subjected to brain-washing in order to qualify for a job in the "new democracy." Only then did the authorities consider that he could be depended upon, as the official expression is worded, to "lean to one side" (Soviet Russia's) in all matters, and that he would react with instinctive obedience to every call made upon him by the Communist Party through whatever twists, turns, or leaps policy might take, no matter what the sacrifice. He must fight by all possible means and be ready, too, with the right answer for every contradiction and evasion in Party statements.[4]

Hunter asserted that the Chinese government also used the indoctrination procedures on POWs and any luckless foreigners who fell into their "talons" and tried to convert them to agents in its crusade against the free world.

Published in the midst of the Korean War, Hunter's book fed into the anti-Chinese hysteria. Two years after the armistice that ended the Korean War, the U.S. Army issued *POW: The Fight Continues after the Battle*, a deeply influential report on the Chinese treatment of American prisoners. Based on interviews with every surviving prisoner of war, the report revealed that many POWs had been brainwashed by Chinese Communists:

> The Chinese had carefully segregated the prisoners they had identified as incorrigibles, housing them in separate camps, and had subjected the prisoners they figured to be potential converts to five hours of indoctrination a day, in classes that

> combined propaganda by the instructors with "confessions" by the prisoners. In some cases, physical torture accompanied the indoctrination, but in general the Chinese used the traditional methods of psychological coercion: repetition and humiliation. The army discovered that a shocking number of prisoners had, to one degree or another, succumbed. Some were persuaded to accuse the United States, in radio broadcasts, of engaging in germ warfare—a charge that was untrue, but was widely believed in many countries.[5]

The army report, as Menand describes, "instigated a popular obsession with brainwashing" that lasted well into the late 1950s, if not beyond. "Stories about the experiences of American prisoners appeared in the *Saturday Evening Post*, *Life*, the *New York Times Magazine*, and *The New Yorker*. The term itself became a synonym for any sort of effective persuasion, and writers struggled with the question of whether things like advertising or psychiatric therapy might constitute subtle forms of brainwashing."[6]

Richard Condon, before publishing his 1959 best-seller, must have read some of these reports and articles. As a publicist for various Hollywood studios since 1936, he must also have been familiar with the fantastic tales of the insidious Dr. Fu Manchu, whose films raked in millions for the industry. The juxtaposition of these two sources—cold-war propaganda and racial fantasy—provided juicy material for Condon's suspenseful political thriller. The new anti-Communist hysteria now twinned with old anti-Chinese racism formed a combustible new weapon. A telling scene from the film even has Marco (Frank Sinatra) recollecting his nightmare about the Pavlovian Chinese brainwasher: "I can see that Chinese cat standing there smiling like Fu Manchu."

It was in this toxic political climate that the reruns of Charlie Chan, with their suggestively "Orientalese" titles—*Charlie Chan in Shanghai*, *The Chinese Cat*, *The Jade Mask*, *The Shanghai Cobra*—were aired. The honorable detective was now wisecracking in the poisoned air that every American was breathing. Alarmingly, it became good business to exploit these prevalent fears. In the decades to come, Hollywood continued to release films with faux- or proto-Mandarin titles, even though their plots had little to do with China or, for that matter, the Chinese: Rita Hayworth and Orson Welles's *Lady from Shanghai* (1948), Frank Borzage's *China Doll* (1958), Roman Polanski's *Chinatown* (1974), and Jane Fonda and Jack Lemmon's *The China Syndrome* (1979), to name just a few. Many of these films used the suggestion of "China" for no other purpose than to create a noirish atmosphere and evoke a feeling of paranoia.

The material is rich for analysis. In *Lady from Shanghai,* for instance, Rita Hayworth plays the seductive, bored Mrs. Rosalie Bannister opposite Orson Welles's Irish seaman character, Mike O'Hara. Hayworth, who made a brief appearance as a brunette maid in *Charlie Chan in Egypt,* had by now changed her last name from Cansino, used electrolysis to raise her hairline, and dyed her hair auburn. In the movie, the only reference that would justify the use of "Shanghai" in the title is an enigmatic conversation between Rosalie and Mike on a boat, where she confides to him that she once worked in Shanghai and that one would need more than luck in that Oriental den of iniquity. As she quotes the Chinese saying, "It is difficult for love to last long," Rosalie affects an air of the Shanghaiese, Oriental mystique. But the film's exploitation of the Chinese proverbial cliché was merely a weak imitation of Charlie Chan's marvelous aphoristic somersaults.

Never averse to exploring the darker crevices of the human imagination, Roman Polanski of course was aware of the sinister suggestiveness of Chinese names. In *Chinatown,* the title merely hovers in the background like a black cloud. As with Hayworth's *Lady from Shanghai,* the lead character—sharp-tongued, nosy private eye Jake Gittes (played by Jack Nicholson)—also boasts about having worked in Chinatown when he was in the police force. "It was bad luck to work there," he says, because you "can't always tell what's going on," and all you are doing is "putting Chinamen in jail for spitting on laundry." In this classic mystery work—laced with murder, conspiracy, corruption, incest, and adultery—Chinatown serves as the symbol for the crime-ridden dark side of the City of Angels. At the end of the film, after the brutal killing of Evelyn Mulwray (played by Faye Dunaway) on Alameda Boulevard, the camera zooms out to reveal a fading shot of the dreadful, cold, hard pavements of Chinatown. At this moment, Gittes's associate delivers the film's punch line, a hellish echo that penetrates the filthy, deadly night air: "Forget it, Jake. It's Chinatown." The "C word" here has yielded its full subliminal potency.

In *The China Syndrome*, the "C word" is used to significant effect again, this time in the realm of nuclear science. In 1971, the nuclear physicist Ralph Lapp, one of the participants in the Manhattan Project, had used the term *China Syndrome* to describe a hypothetical situation in which a nuclear meltdown at a U.S. power plant might cause radioactive material to burn a hole in the earth all the way to "the other side of the world." As a result, a generation of American children would come to associate the nuclear meltdown, a scene of Armageddon, with China. The 1979 film, with memorable performances by Jack Lemmon, Jane Fonda, and Michael Douglas, used the China image once again to represent a world where the most dangerous forces of nuclear physics could no longer be harnessed. In the film, Lemmon plays the nuclear-plant supervisor Jack Godell, who tries to expose a cover-up of safety violation and to stop a "China Syndrome" from becoming reality. With the eerie backdrop of the cold war and a nuclear disaster, the "C word," once having stood for a child's curiosity for the proverbial bottom of the world, now represents something totally nightmarish and unnerving.

In the neo-noir *China Moon*, starring Ed Harris and Madeleine Stowe, a story of seduction, murder, and deception in small-town America hinges on the signifying power of the title phrase—and this was released in 1994. "My grandmother used to call that a china moon," Harris's character says, as he and his lover row under a full moon on a lake where they will soon dump her husband's body, "like a big old plate of china. She said people would get affected by them, that they'd do strange things." Here the lowercase "c word," like the "China Syndrome," may not at first sound sinister, but as the story unfolds, the innocent reference to porcelain gives way to a far more powerful symbolism.

Charlie Chan—a double-C, like 007 the superspy—becomes, in effect, the supersign in this chain of symbolism: China, Chinatown, Chinaman, Chink, chop suey, chop chop, ching chong, and even the cynical, onomatopoeic ka-ching. To most audiences in the post–World War II years, Charlie Chan indeed came to represent China and the nefarious cultural meanings that were associated with Mao's Communist domain.

It would, of course, be an exaggeration, even folly, to claim that Charlie Chan was responsible for the prevalence of dark "C words" in postwar America. "World is large," Chan says, "me lowly Chinaman." But there is no denying that as the most prominent Chinese icon in those decades, Chan had unwittingly become a Fu Manchurian Candidate, a figure who tapped into the paranoia and hysteria unleashed by cold-war propaganda. It was this image of Charlie Chan that would, as we shall see, make him the prime target of Asian American criticism.

29

Will the Real Charlie Chan Please Stand Up?

WARNER OLAND AND HIS STAND-IN ON THE SET, EARLY 1930S

(Courtesy of Everett Collection)

I feel I must find the last surviving Charlie Chan of the movies and kill him.
I will use what I learned being his Number One Son against him.
Gee, pop, have I got a surprise for you!
—Frank Chin, "The Sons of Chan"

"Charlie Chan is dead," the writer Jessica Hagedorn dramatically proclaimed back in 1993. In the introduction to her groundbreaking anthology of contemporary Asian American fiction, Hagedorn declared, "Charlie Chan is our most famous fake 'Asian' pop icon . . . and a part of the demeaning legacy of stereotypes."[1] But the old Charlie Chan seemed to have died long before that.

In the late 1960s and early 1970s, a storm of protests by Asian Americans, in part inspired by the civil rights and Black Power movements, swept through the United States. The activists called for the end of the Vietnam War. They also called for the development of ethnic-studies programs in universities and reparations for Japanese internment during World War II. College campuses provided the most fertile ground for the movement. Students formed political alliances, published leftist journals, and held strikes at West Coast universities demanding curriculum reforms to include ethnic studies. The movement gave birth to the term *Asian American*. Indicating a new political and social consciousness, "Asian American" provided a clear break from the old labels of "Oriental" and "Asiatic," which carried a long association with racism and prejudice. As a character born at the exact moment when the 1924 Immigration Act codified "Asiatic" as a racial category, as a paunchy detective created by a white man and possessed of "Oriental" charm, Charlie Chan became a target of the activists' protests. Under pressure, major TV networks and local stations, which had been running Charlie Chan films for decades, decided to take him off the air. Thus began what Ken Hanke has dubbed "The Great Chan Ban."[2]

What the Asian Americans objected to may be summarized in a paragraph from the "Who is Charlie Chan?" entry in *Everything You Need to Know about Asian-American History* by Lan Cao and Himilce Novas: "In the eyes of many Asian Americans, Charlie Chan is in essence an effeminate, wimpy, nerdy, inscrutable Asian male, who helped plant the seed of the pervasive racist stereotype of Asian

Americans as the 'model minority.'"[3] Such a characterization, however, is a far cry from the Charlie Chan on the screen. It may be true, as I have described, that Chan is one of the many images of the "Chinaman" minted by whites in the past century, and many of these are negative, demeaning stereotypes. In the postwar period, especially, Chan's image was further tarnished by his metamorphosis into a Fu Manchurian Candidate—which may have been exacerbated by the sprawl of Red China. But to characterize Chan as "effeminate," "wimpy," and "nerdy" is well off the mark. In fact, blaming him for acting "inscrutable" is like accusing Jerry Seinfeld of being too funny or whining too much. It seems that just as Chan might have been used by some uninformed whites as an unflattering representative of a Chinaman, he has also been caricatured by Asian Americans, unaware of his historical reception in China itself, as merely a product of white racism.

Among Charlie Chan's chief opponents, Frank Chin is probably the most articulate and forceful. A self-styled "Chinatown Cowboy" and a first-rate writer of pugilist prose, Chin has, over the years, tried to hunt down Charlie Chan with a tenacity that may be matched only by the on-screen detective himself. In his essay "The Sons of Chan," Chin calls Charlie Chan "my movie father," for all the years he lived under the portly shadow of the iconic Chinaman. In his colorful Chinatown buck-caw-caw lingo, Chin revisits the origin of his "fake" ancestry and depicts the genesis of his movie father as a racial burlesque:

> So here, Earl Derr Biggers, the reincarnation of an antebellum southern cracker overseer sitting on the verandah, sippin his mint julep, listening to the happy darkies choppin cotton in the fields making racial harmony, was fixed in Hawaii, sitting on the lanai, sippin' his mai tai, whooping his ears out to hear the Kanakas harmonizing on a hit of the period as they chopped sugar. "Sing song, sing song, so Hop Toy/Allee same like China

> Boy,/But he sellee girl with joy/Pity poor Ming Toy!" And Earl Derr Biggers read about a Chinese detective named Chang Apana. He'd never heard of an "Oriental detective" before. A vision came to him. God kicked Earl Derr Biggers in the head and commanded him to give us Chinamans a son, in almost His image. And Charlie Chan was born. And, in a sense, so was I.[4]

Having condemned his movie father for his troubling genealogy, Chin goes on, in another essay, to compare Chan with the other Chinaman also born out of a white cradle, Fu Manchu. Chin claims that the two Chinese icons are "visions of the same mythic being, brewed up in the subconscious regions of the white Christian's racial wet dream." He is particularly critical of the way Asian masculinity is portrayed by Fu and Chan:

> Devil and angel, the Chinese is a sexual joke glorifying white power. Dr. Fu, a man wearing a long dress, batting his eyelashes, surrounded by muscular black servants in loin-cloths, and with his bad habit of caressingly touching white men on the leg, wrist, and face with his long fingernails, is not so much a threat as he is a frivolous offense to white manhood. Chan's gestures are the same, except he doesn't touch and, instead of being graceful like Fu in flowing robes, he is awkward in a baggy suit and clumsy.[5]

In Chin's analysis, what is most insidious about Chan is not so much his annoying, asexualized appearance as his being a symbol of acculturation, which Chin regards as a synonym for Christian conversion of the Chinese. Drawing upon the history of white, proselytizing missionary work in Chinatowns (not to mention Hawaii itself) in previous decades, Chin states that Christian conversion is cultural extinction, a form of behavior modification that foments an identity crisis. He describes it elegantly as a "self-destructive Ping-Pong game," which prompts a person to question his self-worth as a Chinese and yearn for the Christian, American way of life. Charlie Chan's cardinal sin, says Chin, is that he suffers from this same identity crisis and decides to pursue the path of the convert.

According to Chin, Chan's encounter with Ah Sing in the novel *Keeper of the Keys* is a sure sign that Chan is a straw man in the racial parable of conversion. Ah Sing, a variation of Bret Harte's "heathen Chinee" Ah Sin, as we saw earlier, represents a pagan Chinese who stubbornly stays pagan and rejects Americanization or Christian acculturation. As Chan admits in Biggers's novel, "[Ah Sing] is of my own origin, my own race, as you know. But when I look into his eyes I discover that a gulf like the heaving Pacific lies between us. Why? Because he, though among Caucasians many more years than I, still remains Chinese. As Chinese to-day as in the first moon of his existence. While I—I bear the brand—the label—Americanized." Calling Chan's confession "a schizoid internal dialogue," Chin goes on to tear apart the character: "The Charlie Chan movies were parables of racial order. In the cockeyed logic of that order, the greatest insult to Chinese America in these films, the casting of a white man in the role of Charlie Chan, was and still is no insult at all but part of the charm of the films and visual proof of our acceptance and assimilation by whites. They just eat us up."[6]

In Chin's razor-sharp analysis lies the core of Asian American criticism of the Charlie Chan character, a criticism that carries the weight of the Asian experience in contemporary America. Indeed, it would be hard to accept Chan as a likable character if you grew up listening to neighborhood kids chanting, "Ching Chong Chinaman sitting on a fence . . ." and having them taunt you with a Chanish "Confucius say. . . ." And it is certainly true that there are stereotypical aspects of Charlie Chan that smack of racial parody and mockery. After all, he is a product of his time, born in the nativist era of the 1920s and rising to stardom before the civil rights movement attempted to raise America's consciousness. But if every time we smelled the odor of racism in arts and literature we went out and rallied in the street, then we probably would have killed off everything from jazz to hip-hop, from George Carlin to Jerry Seinfeld. Out of the crucible we call art, there is rarely if ever what might be described as good, clean fun. Indeed, comedy can sting even more so. The yellowface of Charlie Chan, which Chin considers the most racist aspect of the character, actually finds strong historical parallels with Aunt Jemima, Uncle Tom, and Nigger Jim. Like these blackface figures, Charlie Chan epitomizes the creative genius of American culture and exemplifies what critic Stanley Crouch has called "the catalyst of the American experience"—cultural miscegenation.

Unfortunately, Charlie Chan has remained a thorn in the side of many Asian Americans today. Judging by their response whenever the iconic Chinaman pops up, it seems likely that some of the younger anti-Chan clan have not had the opportunity to take another look at the films for themselves—they have inherited their critical views from the older generation. In 2003, when the Fox Movie Channel announced that it was undertaking a Charlie Chan festival of restored prints (of the series produced from 1931 to 1942), the decision touched off a storm of protest. Three prominent organizations—NAPALC (National Asian Pacific American Legal Consortium), NAATA (National Asian American Telecommunications Association), and OCA (Organization of Chinese Americans)—coordinated a successful letter-writing campaign to have the films banned from the cable channel. Fox caved in to pressure and issued a statement explaining the cancellation of the series: "Fox Movie Channel has been made aware that the Charlie Chan films may contain situations and depictions that are sensitive to some viewers. Fox Movie Channel realizes that these historic films were produced at a time when racial sensitivities were not as they are today. As a result of the public response to the airing of these films, Fox Movie Channel will remove them from the schedule."[7]

In its campaign letters, NAATA called Chan "one of the most

offensive Asian caricatures of America's cinematic past." OCA's verdict on Chan was equally devastating:

> Charlie Chan is a painful reminder of Hollywood's racist refusal to hire minorities to play roles that were designed for them and a further reminder of the miscegenation laws that prevented interracial interaction even on screen. Asian Pacific Americans and many other minorities were not able to portray themselves on screen. Instead, they were inaccurately depicted by Caucasian actors, who wore face paint to act out stereotypical images of Asians as slanted eye, buck toothed, subservient, and non-English speaking.

Opposing such dismissive views are Charlie Chan fans, whose sheer number obviously convinced Fox to reconsider its earlier cancellation decision. Die-hard fans were outraged by the ban. Jerry Della Femina, the advertising guru, wrote, "Charlie always got his man. But then one day, Charlie Chan was murdered in cold blood. Killed by a whole generation that decided Charlie Chan movies were not politically correct."[8] Fox eventually decided not to do a whole festival but to broadcast three select films, followed by panel discussions led by Asian American representatives. Indeed, the debate continues.

In her op-ed piece published in the *New York Times* a few years before the Fox firestorm broke out, Long Island–born Chinese American writer Gish Jen also cited Charlie Chan as an example of what she called the "Asian Illusion" in America. She criticized the mainstream media for superimposing fanciful ideas onto real human beings and transforming everyday Asians into mysterious Orientals. "The aphorism-spouting Charlie Chan (played by Warner Oland, a white actor in yellowface) is godlike in his intelligence, the original Asian whiz kid," writes Jen. "You would not be surprised to hear he had won a Westinghouse prize in his youth. More message than human being, he recalls the ever-smiling black mammy that proliferated during Reconstruction: Don't worry, he seems to say, no one's going to go making any trouble."[9] Charlie Chan, in other words, is a "Yellow Uncle Tom" with brains. Jen's article provoked responses from Chan devotees whose letters continued to appear in the paper in subsequent months. "As a Caucasian who has seen just about every Charlie Chan movie there is," wrote one reader, "I must respond to the article by Gish Jen about stereotypes that perpetuate Charlie Chan as the Stepin Fetchit of Orientals. . . . Chan belongs in film history with Sam Spade and Philip Marlowe, not the land of coolies and Uncle Toms." Another letter pointed out that those films reflected "a far more pernicious bias against blacks," and that, in contrast, "at least Charlie Chan was a highly respected, wise and capable detective, dominating each of the films." Another Chan enthusiast concluded emphatically, "Long live Charlie Chan—detective, crimefighter and man."

That last statement speaks to the true longevity of Charlie Chan in American culture. Case in point: Just when Asian Americans began their criticism of Charlie Chan during the civil rights movement, there was a sudden outpouring of Charlie Chan–themed products on the mass market. First there was a handsome 1968 paperback, *Quotations from Charlie Chan*, edited by Harvey Chertok and Martha Torge, a collection of Chan's *bon mots* compiled in the manner of Chairman Mao's *Little Red Book of Sayings*, which was making the rounds among left-leaning peaceniks at the time. Another book of Chan's aphorisms soon followed. Entitled *The Wit and Wisdom of Charlie Chan*, it ironically quoted Frank Chin's stinging critique in its introduction: "In the tradition of two thousand films and stage productions . . . no Chinaman's ever played the role of Charlie Chan."[10] In November 1973, the *Charlie Chan Mystery Magazine* was born, with each of its four issues featuring a new Chan novelette by Robert Hart Davis. A year later, noted mystery writer Dennis Lynds came out with *The Return of Charlie Chan*, published by Bantam Books along with the paperback reprints of six Chan novels. And then there was the 1981 cinematic spoof, *Charlie Chan and the Curse of the Dragon Queen*, starring Peter Ustinov as an almost outlandishly stylized Charlie Chan. That same year, the film's novelization, authored by Michael Avallone, was published by Pinnacle Books.

The most phenomenally successful media product to resurrect Charlie Chan's image was the Saturday-morning cartoon series from William Hanna and Joseph Barbera, whose production studio dominated American television animation during the second half of the twentieth century. The Hanna-Barbera team had produced such classics as *The Flintstones*, *Scooby-Doo*, and *The Jetsons*. From 1972 to 1973, they created a sixteen-episode animation series, *The Amazing Chan and the Chan Clan*, aired by CBS on Saturday mornings. While the baby boomers had grown up on Charlie Chan's "Confucius say," Americans of this new generation, the Xers, had their breakfast milk and cereal accompanied by the adventurous Chan Clan, Chu Chu the dog, and Stanley Chan's "Wham bam, we're in a jam!" At an impressionable age, some of these tykes might even have learned to rhyme from the series: Chan, clan, van, plan; wham, bam, jam. Like the acoustic memory created by the radio dramas of their grandparents' generation, the voice of Keye Luke as Mr. Chan or the young Jodie Foster as Anne left a residual, if not indelible, mark on the minds of not a few Xers. As much as many well-meaning Asian Americans try to banish the character, Charlie Chan the Chinaman is here to stay. He is an American folk hero in the same tradition of Paul Bunyan (that scourge of environmentalism), or more complicated, nuanced characters such as Nigger Jim and Huck Finn, without whom American literature would be penurious.

Sometimes late at night, I turn on the TV and a Chinaman falls out. He is hilarious. They call him "Mr. Chan." Having grown up in China, where I have met thousands of Chans, I find him to be the strangest and most impressive Chan ever. He has amazing linguistic acrobatic skills on a par with anyone from Tin Pan Alley, dishing out colorful aphorisms at ease in his singsong pidgin:

Tongue often hang man quicker than rope.

Mind, like parachute, only function when open.

Man who flirt with dynamite sometime fly with angels.

Action speak louder than French.

He reminds me of Monkey King. In Chinese folk myth, Monkey King is an invincible trickster who hides his weapon in his ear. When necessary, he pulls out his weapon, a hair, and blows a puff of air. The hair instantly turns into a golden pole! Charlie Chan is that Monkey King, concealing his aphoristic barbs inside his tummy. But he is also the African American Signifying Monkey, or the Native American Coyote. He is a master of signifying, woofing, battling, or doing the dozens. His sayings may not be as nasty as the likes of "Yo mama is so stupid that she sold her car for gas money," but at times his sharp-tongued "Confucius say" imparts as much insult as wisdom.

When some people complain about Charlie Chan's deferential docility, especially in the presence of white men, they have simply underestimated the real strength of his character. Chan is a peculiar American brand of trickster prevalent in ethnic literature and incarnated by Mark Twain's Huck Finn and Herman Melville's Confidence Man (curiously named China Aster). It is a brand that also includes Jim Crow, the Bunker brothers, Al Jolson's Jazz Singer, and Stepin Fetchit and his numerous step-chillun. All these characters are indeed rooted in the toxic soil of racism, but racism has made their tongues only sharper, their art more lethally potent. Whether it's a jazzy tune coming from the lips of a blackface Jew or a yellow lie told by a ventriloquist Swede, the resilient artistic flower has blossomed *in spite of* as well as *because of* racism. This undeniable fact, insulting and sobering, has uniquely defined America.

As a man from China, I want to ask, "Will the real Charlie Chan please stand up?" So far, I have only seen his ghost most vividly appear in Wayne Wang's offbeat sleeper hit, *Chan Is Missing* (1982).

In this low-budget movie, an elderly Chinese American named Jo and his nephew Steve engage in a fruitless search through the streets of Chinatown for a Mr. Chan Hung. Chan has taken $2,000 from Jo and Steve to finalize a taxi-license deal, but he mysteriously disappears. A spoof on the Charlie Chan genre, the film shows a Chinatown mystery that has no solution. Unlike Charlie Chan and his sidekick, Jo and Steve sink deeper and deeper into the whereabouts of Chan and the puzzle of his real identity.

"This mystery is appropriately Chinese," Jo finally realizes. "What's not there seems to have just as much meaning as what is there. The murder article is not there. The photograph's not there. The other woman's not there. Chan Hung's not there. Nothing is what it seems to be. I guess I'm not Chinese enough. I can't accept a mystery without a solution."[11] Jo's admission to not being Chinese enough sounds to me like an echo of Charlie Chan's confession to his Americanization: "I bear the brand—the label—Americanized." Yet, unlike Frank Chin's unalloyed condemnation of acculturation, Wang's film offers a parable on the true identity of "Mr. Chan," or what it means to be a Chinese in America. As Presco, a young Filipino staff worker at Manilatown Senior Citizens Center, deadpans, "You guys are looking for Mr. Chan—why don't you look in the puddle?"[12]

In a puddle, after a storm, the mud settles to the bottom. And when you look into the puddle, you will see on the surface not just reflections of the blue sky and white clouds but also your own face. In our search for the truth about Charlie Chan, then, we don't need to look in faraway places such as China, where so many of the American brands we buy are manufactured. Instead, we need to look in that reflecting pool called America, where, as long as our eyes remain open, the images of ourselves will never cease.

As a man from China, a Chinese man come to America, I say: Chan is dead! Long live Charlie Chan!

Epilogue

Chang Apana's grave at the Chinese Cemetery, Manoa, Hawaii

(Photo by Susan M. Schultz)

Story are now completely extracted like aching tooth.
—Charlie Chan

Surprisingly, my first trip to Hawaii only came in January 2007. I had been invited by the English Department at the University of Hawaii–Manoa to attend a conference on translation, but my secret personal mission was to find the grave of Chang Apana, the real Charlie Chan.

Earlier that day, after delivering a presentation called "Chinese Whispers," I went to the Honolulu Police Department Museum to hear, so to speak, the whispers from the past, Chinese or otherwise. My conference host, Susan Schultz, drove me through downtown

Honolulu in the midst of what is known locally as "liquid sunshine"—a brisk shower of silky threads that shine in the sun. The police headquarters is a four-story concrete stronghold, looking like a big chunk of New York's United Nations Secretariat building lopped off, shipped around the globe, and placed in the middle of the Pacific. It is located at Beretania Street—Beretania being a Hawaiian rendering of the word *Britain* and named after British Consul Richard Charlton, who owned a plot of land in the area in the 1820s.

We parked the car and walked up to a front window that resembled a turnpike tollbooth. After telling the receptionist the purpose of our visit, we were each given a plastic badge and told to wait on a wooden bench by the window. I had never been inside an American police station, but I had watched enough episodes of *Law & Order* to know the basic protocols: hang onto your visitor's badge and wait till you are called.

The man who greeted us, when we eventually were led through the maze of hallways to the one-room museum, was a friendly, middle-aged African American police officer. He introduced himself as Eddie Croom, curator of the museum. From the film world of the 1930s when black sidekicks were invariably portrayed as inarticulate, superstitious, and easily frightened Negroes to the present moment when a distinguished black curator stood there to provide me with a glimpse of the history of my own race, America has progressed significantly, though even at the time of Chang Apana and Charlie Chan, Honolulu had already acquired the epithet of "the melting pot of the Pacific." It was always a city that brought all races together at the crossroads of the globe. Samuel King, Hawaii's legendary governor, once said, "The secret of Hawaii's racial harmony is that we're all in the minority." Even though King's remark sounds a bit too rosy, it does indeed contain a seed of truth that could not be denied as I searched for the story of Charlie Chan, real and fictional.

The room we entered looked like a brightly lit curio shop. In the middle were large, glass-fronted wall-to-wall cabinets with long display cases. Photographs, uniforms, helmets, badges, weapons, certificates, motorcycles, and other kinds of memorabilia seemed to choke the room. From images of the pre-Cook *kapu* system to posters for *Hawaii Five-O*, from the rifle that once had belonged to the infamous Koolau the Leper to the mug shots and arrest file of Grace Fortescue, this museum is a Hawaiian encyclopedia of crime and punishment brought to life.

"Officer Chang Apana," said the curator, wasting little time before turning to the subject of my interest, "joined the sheriff's office in 1898, just when the city was incorporated, a very exciting moment for Honolulu." While providing a brief summary of Apana's career, Officer Croom led us to a glass cabinet tucked discreetly in a corner of the room. Displayed inside were copies of vintage Charlie Chan books, old videotapes, and DVD films that had just been released by Twentieth Century-Fox—a sign that the museum had been following closely any new career moves of the character inspired by Apana. I saw photos and portraits of Apana as well as newspaper clippings I was anxious to read, but what particularly caught my attention was a brown-skin whip coiled like a snake ready to strike, a whip that the former *paniolo* had actually used to wage his historic, crime-fighting battle.

"When he retired in 1932," Officer Croom continued, "Apana was the longest-serving officer in the department. When he died a year later due to complications from leg amputation, his funeral procession rivaled the greatest royal processions of the era. In 2005, he was named one of the 100 most influential persons in the history of Hawaii."

Despite his familiarity with Apana's legend, the curator could not answer the question I had come there to ask: "Where is Apana buried now?" He told me that it was perhaps in the Chinese Cemetery in Manoa. He didn't know for sure.

Then I remembered Earl Biggers's description, in *The Black Camel*, of the Chinese Cemetery, "with its odd headstones scattered down the sloping hillside." Charlie Chan drives past this place in his battered Ford flivver on his way to work every day. Whether or not it is the right cemetery, Biggers obviously knew the significance of the final resting place to an immigrant like Apana and, by extension, Chan. In the novel, Chan has buried his mother in that cemetery, close to his Punchbowl Hill home, and his filial piety is an important part of his veracity as a fictional character of Chinese descent.

Saying our heartfelt thanks, we left the museum.

After a brief lunch at a local sandwich shop, Susan and I started driving toward the cemetery in the Upper Manoa Valley. Hailing from Virginia, Susan had lived and taught in Hawaii for almost two decades. Her red Dodge Neon seemed to know the local roads as well as a seasoned *paniolo*'s horse would know well-trodden trails.

Riding in the soft drizzle up and down the winding slopes of the Manoa Valley, we talked about the circuitous route by which I had arrived here in Honolulu. I told Susan how, at the age of eleven, I had secretly learned English by adjusting the dial of my grandfather's battered transistor radio just so, and then memorizing the exotic language of the Voice of America. I had to keep my discovery a secret because listening to those politically subversive foreign radio stations was illegal in those days. For some reason, looking for Chang Apana's traces made me remember those sweltering summers in Alabama and my bumbling restaurant efforts. I also recalled the immense challenges of getting a Ph.D. in a language that was, at least not yet, my own, and finally, the serendipity of stumbling upon my first Charlie Chan books at a Buffalo estate sale. In the doctoral dissertation I had finished at SUNY Buffalo, I devoted a chapter to Charlie Chan, comparing his pidgin speech to the kind of racial ventriloquism found in the works of Ezra Pound, Amy Lowell, and T. S. Eliot. My fascination with Charlie Chan didn't stop there. A few years later, I published a book of poetry called *CRIBS*. In it, I adopted a poetic diction that imitates Charlie Chan's pidgin, such as in this poem:

Think Haiku, Act Locu: An Experiment in Back-Translation

take it
with a grain of MSG

what's the memory size
of your abacus?

speak
in a chopsticked tongue

another day
another yen

the yin-yang
of base and superstructure

the great
Great Wall

be careful
not to get shanghaied

the Peking-duck congress
is just a bunch of lame mandarins

the two stick together
like ping and pong

he sold his birthright
for a bowl of hot & sour soup?

a writer is a man
of characters

a man is known
by his breast-strokes

sell haiku
buy locu

The rain had just stopped when we arrived at the cemetery. The entrance was a Chinese-style stone arcade, reminiscent of a *paifang*, the gate to a typical Chinese village. For many years, there was a tradition among overseas Chinese of shipping the bodies of their countrymen back to China for burial. As an old Chinese saying goes, "When a leaf falls to the ground, it returns to its roots." Those Chinese wishing to be buried in America would still prefer a resting place resembling the one in their home village. Hence the stone arcade, to create a sense of familiarity and homecoming.

It was, however, Sunday, and the cemetery office was closed. There was no map or directory to help us locate Apana's grave. We drove around in circles, passing thousands of tombstones standing mutely under a gray sky. Maybe because of the weather, but more likely the passage of time, most of the marble monuments had turned black, looking to me like a flock of black birds settled on a green meadow. Built on a slope, the cemetery faced a valley flecked with white bungalows that were almost as numerous as the graves. Under the shadows of a giant mountain, the worlds of the living and the dead now appeared in a quiet clash of black and white, as if trying to outmatch the other in number and anonymity.

Just as we were about to turn back, luck smiled on us; or, as Charlie Chan once put it, "One grain of luck sometimes worth more than whole rice field of wisdom." A sharp turn in the road, which we had not yet explored, led us right to a sign that read:

8. DETECTIVE CHARLIE CHAN (CHAN APANA).

A red arrow pointed toward a lot at the bottom of the hill. It seemed ironic that the sign misspelled Apana's name as "Chan Apana," as if reality was literally falling under the "spell" of fiction.

Our discovery was in the older section of the cemetery. We saw graves dating back to the late nineteenth century, making them the resting places for some of the earliest first-generation Chinese immigrants to come across the Pacific. The lot, no more than a single acre,

THE GRAVESTONE OF CHANG APANA *(Photo by Susan M. Schultz)*

contained several hundred stones but had no numbering system. The mysterious "8" then became even more of a mystery, like a broken 8-ball that could tell no fortune. We ran up and down the slope, trying different ways of counting to eight—the eighth grave in the direction of the arrow, the eighth row from the bottom of the slope, the eighth row from the top—all to no avail. The elusive "8," the luckiest number in Chinese numerology, suddenly felt like a trick to entice us, a Möbius strip that would lead us nowhere. It seemed that we needed the assistance of a sleuth like Charlie Chan.

The rain, which had sensibly paused for a while, now came down heavily. Running out of time, we decided to split up to canvass the area faster. Many of the stone inscriptions were in Chinese, and thus offered no clue to Susan, but it was she who found the grave. As I was circling around at the bottom of the slope, with raindrops trickling down my face and blurring my glasses, I heard Susan, from a few rows away, shout: "I found it!"

I quickly ran over, and there he was. It was a solitary grave, with two marble steps that had turned dark with age and moisture. The tombstone bore the English name "Chang Apana" at the top, while the

Chinese characters were etched below. A small bed of blooming lilies covered the back of the grave. The Chinese inscriptions provided information on Apana's hometown in southern China, even though he had been born in Hawaii. "Oo Sack Village, Gudu County, Chungshan District," read the inscription. His date of death was given as "December, 1934," though he had, in fact, died in December, 1933.

Despite the apparent death-date error, the gravestone yielded an important clue that I had thus far been unable to ascertain from other sources: his name in Chinese, 郑平 (Zheng Ping in Mandarin, or Chang Pung in the Cantonese pronunciation). For a long time, I had wondered what kind of name "Apana" was. Now I can be certain that "Apana" is a Polynesian variation of the Cantonese "Pung." The first *A* derives from the Chinese custom of adding "Ah" to a given name as a casual way of addressing someone, such as "Ah Sin" and "Ah Pung" (I'm called Ah Te in my family). The last *A* is a Polynesian addition, because in that language, as Herman Melville reminded us in his first book, *Typee*, all words end with a vowel.

In Chinese, 平 (Ping) means "peace, equilibrium," but it occurred to me, as I stood before his grave, that the man who bore the name of peace had not enjoyed much of it. On the contrary, violence—be it physical, emotional, or racial—had accompanied his journey through life. And yet, the man I would research turned out to be self-effacing and curiously taciturn; perhaps, then, the name fits the character after all.

The story of Chang Apana, as this book affirms, is much more than just one man's biography. Not only did his rough-and-tumble exploits inspire the creation of a memorable cultural icon, but the very creators of the Charlie Chan persona also led lives that were the stuff of legends. The stories of Earl Biggers, Warner Oland, Sidney Toler, and Anna May Wong, among others, were all part of the cultural mélange that Gertrude Stein called "The Making of Americans."

On our way back to the car, we saw a rainbow hanging in the sky. I observed that one iridescent end dipped into the emerald ocean while the other tumbled into the lush foliage of a remote Hawaiian mountain that had been washed as clean as it had been on the first day of the world.

Recalling what Earl Biggers once said, that "most people who have been to Hawaii long to return," I would now, "more ardently than most," want to return and explore further the legend of Charlie Chan.

APPENDIX I

A List of Charlie Chanisms

Action speak louder than French.

Advice after mistake is like medicine after dead man's funeral.

Always harder to keep murder secret than for egg to bounce on sidewalk.

At night all cats are black.

Biggest mistakes in history made by people who didn't think.

Big head is only a good place for very large headache.

Caution very good life insurance.

Dollars going into a gambling house are like criminals led to execution.

Door of opportunity swing both ways.

Even bagpipe will not speak when stomach is empty.

Even wise fly sometimes mistake spider web for old man's whiskers.

Every maybe has a wife called Maybe-Not.

Facts like photographic film—must be exposed before developing.

Falling hurts least those who fly low.

Favorite pastime of man is fooling himself.

A fool and his money never become old acquaintances.

The fool questions others, the wise man questions himself.

Front seldom tell truth. To know occupants of house, always look in back yard.

Guessing is cheap, but wrong guess expensive.

Hasty deduction, like ancient egg, look good from outside.
Hens sit often, but lay eggs.
He who rides on tiger cannot dismount.
An idle brain is the devil's workshop.
If befriend donkey, expect to be kicked.
If no one had praised the donkey's song, he would not still be singing.
Learn from hen—never boast about egg until after egg's birthday.
Man seldom scratches where he does not itch.
Man who flirt with dynamite sometime fly with angels.
Mind, like parachute, only function when open.
Murder like potato chip—cannot stop at just one.
No poison more deadly than ink.
Nut easy to crack often empty.
Optimist only sees doughnut, pessimist sees hole.
People who listen at keyholes rarely hear good of themselves.
Perfect case, like perfect doughnut, has hole.
Police do not read Emily Post.
Public opinion is often an envious dog barking at the heels of greatness.
Race not always won by man who start first.
The secret is to talk much, but say nothing.
Slippery man sometimes slip in own oil.
Smart fly keep out of gravy.
Some heads, like hard nuts, much better if well cracked.
Talk cannot cook rice.
Theory like mist on eyeglasses—obscures facts.
Time only wasted when sprinkling perfume on goat farm.
To know forgery, one must have original.
Tongue often hang man quicker than rope.
Too late to dig well when honorable house is on fire.
Trouble, like first love, teach many lessons.
Truth, like football—receive many kicks before reaching goal.
Very few after-dinner speeches are equipped with self-stoppers.

Way to find rabbit's residence is to turn rabbit loose and watch.

When money talk, few are deaf.

When searching for needle in haystack, haystack only sensible location.

The wise elephant does not seek to ape the butterfly.

Wrong pew, perhaps, but maybe correct church.

APPENDIX II

A List of Charlie Chan Films

Early Films

1. *The House Without a Key* (starring George Kuwa, 1926)
2. *The Chinese Parrot* (starring Kamiyama Sojin, 1927)
3. *Behind That Curtain* (starring E. L. Park, 1929)

Starring Warner Oland

4. *Charlie Chan Carries On* (1931)
5. *The Black Camel* (1931)
6. *Charlie Chan's Chance* (1932)
7. *Charlie Chan's Greatest Case* (1933)
8. *Charlie Chan's Courage* (1934)
9. *Charlie Chan in London* (1934)
10. *Charlie Chan in Paris* (1935)
11. *Charlie Chan in Egypt* (1935)
12. *Charlie Chan in Shanghai* (1935)
13. *Charlie Chan's Secret* (1936)
14. *Charlie Chan at the Circus* (1936)
15. *Charlie Chan at the Race Track* (1936)
16. *Charlie Chan at the Opera* (1936)
17. *Charlie Chan at the Olympics* (1937)
18. *Charlie Chan on Broadway* (1937)
19. *Charlie Chan at Monte Carlo* (1937)

Starring Sidney Toler

20. *Charlie Chan in Honolulu* (1938)
21. *Charlie Chan in Reno* (1939)
22. *Charlie Chan at Treasure Island* (1939)
23. *Charlie Chan in City in Darkness* (1939)
24. *Charlie Chan in Panama* (1940)
25. *Charlie Chan's Murder Cruise* (1940)
26. *Charlie Chan at the Wax Museum* (1940)
27. *Murder Over New York* (1940)
28. *Dead Men Tell* (1941)
29. *Charlie Chan in Rio* (1941)
30. *Castle in the Desert* (1942)
31. *Charlie Chan in the Secret Service* (1944)
32. *Charlie Chan in the Chinese Cat* (1944)
33. *Charlie Chan in Meeting at Midnight* (1944)
34. *The Jade Mask* (1945)
35. *The Scarlet Clue* (1945)
36. *The Shanghai Cobra* (1945)
37. *The Red Dragon* (1945)
38. *Dark Alibi* (1946)
39. *Shadows Over Chinatown* (1946)
40. *Dangerous Money* (1946)
41. *The Trap* (1946)

Starring Roland Winters

42. *The Chinese Ring* (1947)
43. *Docks of New Orleans* (1948)
44. *Shanghai Chest* (1948)
45. *The Golden Eye* (1948)
46. *The Feathered Serpent* (1948)
47. *The Sky Dragon* (1949)

Acknowledgments

Within the limited space of an acknowledgments page, I wish to express my enormous gratitude to Glenn Mott and Bob Weil, whose guidance and support were vital to this book. Ever since we first met on a muggy afternoon in Tuscaloosa, Alabama, in the summer of 1992, Glenn has been a friend in the truest sense of the word. An accomplished writer himself, Glenn has also been a guardian angel in my literary life, someone I can trust for honest opinions, editorial advice, and moral support. Without him, this book would not exist.

Having Bob Weil as my editor at Norton makes me feel like a fledgling actor working in a film directed by Alfred Hitchcock or Billy Wilder. Bob is a maestro who has a vision for books, a sharp eye for details, and an incredible devotion to his authors. His superb line-editing, unique in the publishing world today, possesses the touch of magic. He is simply the Maxwell Perkins of our time.

I also wish to thank Lucas Wittmann and Philip Marino at Norton for their excellent editorial guidance; Susan M. Schultz for that memorable drive in Honolulu, searching for the traces of Chang Apana; Officer Eddie Croom, curator of the Honolulu Police Department Museum, for his kind assistance with research; Nanette Napoleon, a devoted Hawaiian historian, for her generosity in sharing the fruits of her labor with me; and Gilbert Martines for his pioneering research on Chang Apana.

My friend Hank Lazer lent a helpful hand at a critical stage of my writing and offered some valuable advice. Katy Olson provided excellent editorial assistance. Mark Johnson generously read the manuscript with care and offered insightful remarks. Others who also helped in various ways include Mia You, Dave Roh, Rucker Alex, Michael Basinski, and Deborah Aaronson.

Kathleen Brandes, the final gatekeeper of my writing for this book, is simply the best copyeditor it has ever been my fortune to work with.

The following people at various institutions have also most ably and generously assisted me in accessing precious images and research materials: Cherry Williams, curator of the Lilly Library at Indiana University; Trinh Dang at Twentieth Century Fox Film Corporation; Cynthia Engle at the Bishop Museum in Honolulu; Alison Rigney at the Everett Collection in New York; Yessenia Santos at Simon & Schuster; Kawehi Yim at the Hawaiian Humane Society; George Lee at the *Honolulu Star-Bulletin*; and Dorinda Hartmann at the Wisconsin Center for Film and Theater Research.

The writing of this book coincided with the yearlong Fulbright residencies in Santa Barbara of Professor Dongfeng Wang and Professor Chunyan Chen, a great Chinese couple from Canton. Their visit brought China back to me, and their friendship nurtured my soul as much as their cooking nourished my body.

I have left for last my acknowledgment of the deepest bond, the two stars that, despite the distance, light up my lonely night sky: my children, Isabelle and Ira. Their absence from my daily life leaves a vacuum that can never be filled by phone calls, postcards, or even frequent visits. In some ways, it is for them that I sit down every day, open a vein, and write my heart out.

Notes

Prologue

1 "Disguised Apana Caught Gamblers," in *Pacific Commercial Advertiser,* July 13, 1904.

Chapter 1: Sandalwood Mountains

1 Gilbert Martines, "Modern History of Hawaii" (master's thesis, University of Hawaii, Manoa, 1990), p. 52.

2 Ibid., p. 39.

3 Isabella Lucy Bird, *Six Months in the Sandwich Islands: Among Hawaii's Palm Groves, Coral Reefs, and Volcanoes* (1881; reprint, Honolulu: Mutual Publishing, 1998), p. 17.

4 Mark Twain, *Letters from Hawaii,* ed. A. Grove Day (Honolulu: University of Hawaii Press, 1975), p. 28.

5 Kinau Wilder, *Wilders of Waikiki* (Honolulu: Topgallant Publishing Company, 1978), p. 4.

6 Jack London, "Koolau the Leper," in Jack London, *Stories of Hawaii,* ed. A. Grove Day (Honolulu: Mutual Publishing, 1986), p. 39.

7 Yunte Huang, *Transpacific Imaginations: History, Literature, Counterpoetics* (Cambridge: Harvard University Press, 2008), pp. 55–56.

8 Gavan Daws, *Shoal of Time: A History of the Hawaiian Islands* (Honolulu: University of Hawaii Press, 1974), pp. 49–50.

9 Michael Dougherty, *To Steal a Kingdom* (Waimanalo, HI: Island Style Press, 1992), p. 47.

10 Ibid.

11 Mark Merlin and Dan VanRavenswaay, "The History of Human Impact on the Genus *Santalum* in Hawaii," in *USDA Forest Service Gen. Tech. Rep.* (PSW-122, 1990), pp. 46–60.

12 Dougherty, p. 46.

13 Ibid., pp. 46–47.

14 Samuel M. Kamakau, *Ruling Chiefs of Hawaii* (Honolulu: Kamehameha Schools Press, 1961), p. 70.

15 Merlin and VanRavenswaay, p. 54.

16 Daws, p. 79.

17 James Cook, *Voyages of Discovery*. Compiled by John Barrow from authorized 18th-Century Admiralty Editions and Documents (Chicago: Academy Chicago Publishers, 1993), p. 405.

18 Tin-Yuke Char, *The Sandalwood Mountains: Readings and Stories of the Early Chinese in Hawaii* (Honolulu: University of Hawaii Press, 1975), pp. 36–37; Wai-Jane Char, "Chinese Merchant-Adventures and Sugar Masters in Hawaii: 1802–1852," in *Hawaiian Journal of History* 8 (1974), p. 4.

19 Wai-Jane Char, p. 4.

20 Daws, p. 44.

21 Bob Dye, *Merchant Prince of the Sandalwood Mountains: Afong and the Chinese in Hawaii* (Honolulu: University of Hawaii Press, 1997), p. 11.

22 Thomas G. Thrum, "Notes on the History of the Sugar Industry of the Hawaiian Islands," in *Hawaii Annual*, 1875, pp. 34–42.

23 Dye, pp. 11–12; Wai-Jane Char, p. 4.

24 Daws, p. 169.

25 Ibid., p. 173; Simon Winchester, *A Crack in the Edge of the World: America and the Great California Earthquake of 1906* (New York: HarperCollins, 2005), pp. 207–8.

26 Daws, pp. 178–79.

27 Tin-Yuke Char, pp. 57–58.

28 Daws, pp. 173–74.

29 "Report of President of Bureau of Immigration to Legislative Assembly," in *Bureau of Immigration Reports*, 1886, p. 23.

30 Twain, pp. 270–71.

31 Ibid., p. 258.

32 *Bureau of Immigration Report, 1882–1898,* 1: 266–77.

Chapter 2: Canton

1 W. Travis Hanes III and Frank Sanello, *The Opium Wars: The Addiction of One Empire and the Corruption of Another* (1975; reprint, New York: Barnes and Noble Publishing, 2002), p. 167.

2 Quoted in Ronald Takaki, *Strangers from a Different Shore: A History of Asian Americans* (New York: Penguin, 1990), p. 32.

3 Ibid.

4 Chung Kun Ai, *My Seventy Nine Years in Hawaii* (Hong Kong: Cosmorama Pictorial Publisher, 1960), p. 5.

5 Ibid, p. 6.

6 Hanes and Sanello, p. 34.

Chapter 3: *Paniolo*, the Hawaiian Cowboy

1 Takaki, pp. 71–72.

2 Ah Huna Tong, "Chang Apana Had Long and Enviable Record on Force," in *Honolulu Advertiser* (May 22, 1932).

3 "Many Present at Rites for Noted Sleuth," in *Honolulu Advertiser* (December 18, 1933).

4 Richard J. Cleveland, *A Narrative of Voyages and Commercial Enterprises* (Cambridge: John Owen, 1842), pp. 229–30.

5 Hawaiian Humane Society, *Poi Dogs and Popoki* (Honolulu: Hawaiian Humane Society, 1997), p. 18.

6 Joseph Brennan, *The Parker Ranch of Hawaii: The Saga of a Ranch and a Dynasty* (New York: John Day Company, 1974), pp. 21–31.

7 Ibid., p. 45.

8 Ibid., p. 32.

9 Ibid., pp. 35–36.

10 Ibid., p. 40.

11 Ibid., pp. 49–50.

12 Ibid., p. 48.

13 Ibid., p. 46.

14 Chester A. Doyle, "Charley Chan and Officer Apana," in *Honolulu Star-Bulletin* (December 1, 1935).

15 Helen K. Wilder, "About 'Charlie Chan' Apana," in *Honolulu Star-Bulletin* (January 3, 1936).

16 Brennan, p. 3.

17 Ibid., p. 57.

18 Martines, "Modern History of Hawaii," pp. 46, 43, 26.

Chapter 4: The Wilders of Waikiki

1 Kinau Wilder, pp. 1–2.

2 Dye, pp. 95–97; Elizabeth Leslie Wight, *The Memoirs of Elizabeth Kinau Wilder* (Honolulu: Paradise of the Pacific Press, 1909), p. 150.

3 Wight, p. 161.

4 Robert Louis Stevenson and Lloyd Osbourne, *The Wrecker* (London: Cassell & Company, 1892), pp. 9–10.

5 Kinau Wilder, p. 19.

6 Gilbert Martines, "In Search of Charlie Chan," in *Hawaii Herald* 4:2 (January 21, 1983), p. 1.

7 Martines, "Modern History of Hawaii," pp. 25, 44.

8 Wight, p. 150.

9 Earl Derr Biggers, *The Chinese Parrot* (New York: Grosset and Dunlap, 1926), p. 27.

10 Ibid., p. 14.

11 Helen Wilder, "About 'Charlie Chan' Apana."

12 Kinau Wilder, p. 99; Hawaiian Humane Society, p. 33.

13 Hawaiian Humane Society, p. 31–32.

Chapter 5: "Book 'em, Danno!"

1 Hawaiian Humane Society, p. 33.

2 Ai, pp. 45–46.

3 Biggers, *Chinese Parrot,* pp. 33–34.

4 Tong, "Chang Apana Had Long and Enviable Record on Force."

5 Hawaiian Humane Society, p. 28.

6 Martines, "Modern History of Hawaii," p. 29.

7 Ibid.

8 Daws, p. 286.

9 Ibid., p. 276.

10 Frederick Jackson Turner, *The Frontier in American History* (New York: Henry Holt, 1920), pp. 1–4.

11 Daws, pp. 287–90.

12 Albertine Loomis, "Summer of 1898," in *Hawaiian Journal of History* 13 (1979), p. 97.

13 Daws, p. 169.

14 Leon Straus, *The Honolulu Police Department: A Brief History* (Honolulu: The 200 Club, 1978), pp. 1–6.

15 George F. Nellist, ed., *The Story of Hawaii and Its Builders* (Honolulu: Honolulu Star-Bulletin, 1925), p. 305.

16 Straus, p. 22.

Chapter 6: Chinatown

1 Winchester, p. 331.

2 *Pacific Commercial Advertiser* (January 26, 1883).

3 Dye, p. 205.

4 Karen Sawislak, *Smoldering City: Chicagoans and the Great Fire, 1871–1874* (Chicago: University of Chicago Press, 1995), p. 48. Jason Puskar, "Underwriting the Accident: Narratives of American Chance, 1871–1935" (Ph.D. dissertation, Harvard University, 2004), p. 32.

5 Richard A. Greer, "'Sweet and Clean': The Chinatown Fire of 1886," in *Hawaiian Journal of History* 10 (1976), pp. 33–48.

6 Ibid., p. 45.

7 Ai, pp. 191–93.

8 Tin-Yuke Char, pp. 103–10.

9 Marie-Claire Bergere, *Sun Yat-sen*, trans. Janet Lloyd (Stanford, CA: Stanford University Press, 1998), pp. 25–26.

10 Yansheng Ma Lum and Raymond Mun Kong Lum, *Sun Yat-sen in Hawaii* (Honolulu: University of Hawaii Press, 1999), p. 5.

11 Ibid., p. 7.

Chapter 7: The See Yup Man

1 Bret Harte, "See Yup," in Bret Harte, *Stories in Light and Shadow* (London: C. Arthur Pearson, 1898), pp. 93–94.

2 Tin-Yuke Char, p. 151.

3 Martines, "Modern History of Hawaii," p. 40.

4 Roger Daniels, *Asian America: Chinese and Japanese in the United States since 1850* (Seattle: University of Washington Press, 1988), p. 68.

5 Tin-Yuke Char, pp. 140–41.

6 Dye, p. 199.

7 "Gamblers Escaped Through a Hidden Trapdoor," in *Pacific Commercial Advertiser* (May 20, 1904), p. 3.

8 Harte, "See Yup," p. 93.

9 Clarence E. Glick, *Sojourners and Settlers: Chinese Migrants in Hawaii* (Honolulu: University of Hawaii Press, 1980), p. 238.

10 "Disguised Apana Caught Gamblers," in *Pacific Commercial Advertiser* (July 13, 1904).

11 Martines, "Modern History of Hawaii," p. 37.

12 "Honolulu's Highways and Byways," in *Pacific Commercial Advertiser* (March 16, 1908).

13 Martines, "Modern History of Hawaii," p. 34.

Chapter 8: Desperadoes

1 Martines, "Modern History of Hawaii," p. 37.

2 "Tricks of Wiry Japs: No Joke to Try and Arrest Some of Them," in *Pacific Commercial Advertiser* (June 19, 1901).

3 "Officer Apana Sued for $2000," in *Pacific Commercial Advertiser* (July 6, 1905), p. 3.

4 John Jardine, *Detective Jardine: Crimes in Honolulu* (Honolulu: University of Hawaii Press, 1984), p. 40.

5 "Chang Apana Detective, In Fact and Fiction," in *Honolulu Police Journal* (October 1931), p. 34.

6 Daws, pp. 209–10.

7 A. Grove Day, ed., Introduction, in Jack London, *Stories of Hawaii*, pp. 10–11.

8 "Chang Apana Detective, In Fact and Fiction," pp. 34, 42.

Chapter 9: Double Murder

1 Earl Derr Biggers, *The House Without a Key* (Indianapolis: Bobbs-Merrill, 1925), p. 258.

2 "Chang Apana Detective, In Fact and Fiction," p. 34.

3 Martines, "Modern History of Hawaii," p. 33.

4 "Popular Girl Believed to Have Drowned," in *Honolulu Star-Bulletin* (July 3, 1919), p. 1.

5 "Chang Apana Detective, In Fact and Fiction," p. 42.

6 "Chinaman and Handsome Young Wife Murdered; Home Robbed," in *Honolulu Star-Bulletin* (May 1, 1913), pp. 1–2.

7 "Officers Trail Murderer and Loot to Lair," in *Honolulu Star-Bulletin* (May 2, 1913), pp. 1, 8; "Police Unravel Murder Mystery," in *Honolulu Star-Bulletin* (May 6, 1913), p. 4.

8 "Rodrigues Confesses to Double Murder," in *Honolulu Star-Bulletin* (May 7, 1913), pp. 1-3; Joseph Harrow, "Value of 'Unimportant' Evidence Shown in Murder Solution," in *Honolulu Police Journal* 1:2 (December 1931), pp. 6–7.

9 "Filipinos Are Arraigned; To Plead Monday," in *Honolulu Star-Bulletin* (May 22, 1913), p. 1; "Death the Punishment for Murder," in *Honolulu Star-Bulletin* (June 14, 1913), p. 1.

10 Joseph Theroux, "A Short History of Hawaiian Executions, 1826–1947," in *Hawaiian Journal of History* 25 (1991), pp. 147–55.

11 "Filipinos Expiate Murders," in *Honolulu Star-Bulletin* (July 8, 1913), p. 1.

12 Theroux, pp. 157–58.

13 Harrow, p. 48.

14 "Chinese Present Chief McDuffie with Badge," in *Honolulu Star-Bulletin* (July 30, 1913).

Chapter 10: The Other Canton

1 Carl Carmer, *Stars Fell on Alabama* (New York: Farrar and Rinehart, 1934), p. xiii.

2 James W. Loewen, *The Mississippi Chinese* (Cambridge: Harvard University Press, 1971).

3 Ted C. Fishman, *China, Inc.: How the Rise of the Next Superpower Challenges America and the World* (New York: Scribner, 2005), p. 137.

4 Barbara Gregorich, "Charlie Chan's Poppa: The Life of Earl Derr Biggers," in *Timeline: A Publication of the Ohio Historical Society* 16:1 (January–February 1999), pp. 2–3.

5 Ibid., p. 2.

6 Ibid., p. 4.

7 Earl Derr Biggers, unpaginated manuscript, Bobbs-Merrill Collection, Lilly Library, Indiana University; hereafter cited as Lilly Library.

8 Mark J. Price, "Mystery of Charlie Chan: Fictional Detective Follows Trail of Clues from Akron," in *Akron Beacon Journal* (May 5, 2008).

9 Ibid.

10 Sinclair Lewis, *Main Street* (first published 1920; reprint, New York: Penguin, 1995), p. 10.

Chapter 11: Lampoon

1 Gregorich, p. 5.

2 Ibid.

3 Ibid.

4 Henry Adams, *The Education of Henry Adams,* ed. Jean Gooder (New York: Penguin, 1995), p. 229.

Chapter 12: The Raconteur

1 Biggers, *House Without a Key,* p. 123.

2 Elrick B. Davis, letter to A. H. Hepburn, April 18, 1933, Lilly Library.

3 The content of this column was reproduced in the press release by Bobbs-Merrill on the eve of publication of Biggers's first novel, *Seven Keys to Baldpate,* in February 1913, Lilly Library.

4 Bobbs-Merrill biographical sketch of E. D. Biggers, unpaginated typescript, Lilly Library.

5 Gregorich, p. 6.

6 "Earl Derr Biggers Has Interview with World's Biggest Parrot," press release by the Publicity Department of Bobbs-Merrill, Lilly Library.

7 Gregorich, p. 6.

8 Earl Derr Biggers, *Seven Keys to Baldpate* (1913; reprint, Holicong, PA: Wildside Press, 2003), pp. 11–12.

9 "Earl Derr Biggers," in *Harvard College Class of 1907 Twenty-fifth Anniversary Report* (June 1932), p. 43.

10 "Earl Derr Biggers Has Interview."

11 Lilly Library, unpaginated manuscript.

12 Quoted in Gregorich, p. 6.

13 Ibid.

Chapter 13: The House Without a Key

1 Gregorich, p. 7.

2 "'Dope Traffic' Has Hawaii in Horrid Grip," in *Honolulu Advertiser* (May 4, 1924).

3 "Officers Seize Opium; Arrest Two Japanese," in *Pacific Commercial Advertiser* (March 9, 1920), p. 1. "Police Uncover Opium Store in Jap Garage," in *Pacific Commercial Advertiser* (April 7, 1920), section 2, p. 1. "U.S. Marshal Arrests Captain of Police; Charge Failure to Report Opium Haul," in *Pacific Commercial Advertiser* (March 23, 1920), section 2, p. 1.

4 Biggers, *House Without a Key*, p. 1.

5 Helen Walker, article about lecture given by Earl Derr Biggers in Pasadena, *Pasadena Star-News* (April 11, 1925). Biggers, *House Without a Key*, pp. 116–17.

6 E. D. Biggers, letter to Laurance Chambers, October 23, 1922, Lilly Library.

7 E. D. Biggers, letter to Laurance Chambers, December 18, 1922, Lilly Library.

8 E. D. Biggers, letter to Laurance Chambers, January 14, 1924, Lilly Library.

9 *Harvard College Class of 1907 Twenty-fifth Anniversary Report*, p. 43.

10 *Honolulu Star-Bulletin* (June 6, 1924), p. 6.

11 Earl Thompson, letter to J. David Reno, February 26, 1979, Honolulu Police Department Museum.

12 Gina Halkias-Seugling, Librarian, General Research Division, New York Public Library, e-mail to author, July 15, 2008.

Chapter 14: The Heathen Chinee

1 Biggers, *House Without a Key*, pp. 76–77.

2 Ibid., p. 82.

3 *Harvard College Class of 1907 Twenty-fifth Anniversary Report*, p. 43.

4 Daniels, p. 9; Takaki, p. 79.

5 Takaki, pp. 81–82.

6 Robert G. Lee, *Orientals: Asian Americans in Popular Culture* (Philadelphia: Temple University Press, 1999), p. 16.

7 Ibid., p. 37.

8 Milton Meltzer, *The Chinese Americans* (New York: Thomas Y. Crowell), pp. 4–6.

9 Takaki, pp. 84–86.

10 Meltzer, pp. 22–23, 1–2.

11 Takaki, p. 87.

12 Daniels, pp. 59–62; Winchester, p. 214.

13 Daniels, p. 39.

14 Ibid., pp. 34–39.

15 Takaki, pp. 101–2.

16 Ibid., p. 103.

17 Ibid., pp. 111–12.

18 Daniels, pp. 54–55.

19 Takaki, pp. 110–11.

20 F. Bret Harte, *The Heathen Chinee* (Chicago: Western News Company, 1870), pp. 1–9.

21 Gary Scharnhorst, "'Ways That Are Dark': Appropriations of Bret Harte's 'Plain Language from Truthful James,'" in *Nineteenth-Century Literature* 51: 3 (December 1996), pp. 377–99.

22 Robert Lee, p. 17.

23 Willoughby Speyers, letter to E. D. Biggers, February 4, 1931. E. D. Biggers, letter to Laurance Chambers, February 6, 1931. Laurance Chambers, letter to Biggers, February 9, 1931, Lilly Library.

24 E. D. Biggers, letter to Laurance Chambers, April 26, 1932, Lilly Library.

25 Robert Lee, p. 28.

26 Ibid., p. 42.

27 Ibid.

28 Hinton R. Helper, *The Land of Gold: Reality versus Fiction* (Baltimore: Henry Taylor, 1855), p. 88.

29 Robert Lee, pp. 41–42.

Chapter 15: Fu Manchu

1 Sax Rohmer, *The Insidious Dr. Fu-Manchu: Being a Somewhat Detailed Account of the Amazing Adventures of Nayland Smith and His Trailing of the Sinister Chinaman* (1913; reprint, San Jose, CA: New Millennium Library, 2001), p. 13.
2 Cay Van Ash and Elizabeth Sax Rohmer, *Master of Villainy: A Biography of Sax Rohmer* (Bowling Green, OH: Bowling Green University Popular Press, 1972), p. 63.
3 Ibid., p. 3.
4 Ibid., p. 4.
5 Ibid., p. 10.
6 Ibid., pp. 74–75.
7 Ibid., p. 75.
8 Ibid., pp. 75–77.
9 William Fu, *The Yellow Peril* (New York: Archon Books, 1982), p. 166.
10 John Michael, Introduction, in Sax Rohmer, *The Insidious Dr. Fu-Manchu*, p. iv.
11 Fu, p. 167.
12 Frank Chin, *Bulletproof Buddhists and Other Essays* (Honolulu: University of Hawaii Press, 1998), pp. 95–96.
13 Van Ash and Rohmer, p. 215.
14 Ibid., p. 288.
15 Ibid., pp. 72–73.
16 Ibid., p. 73.

Chapter 16: Charlie Chan, the Chinaman

1 David Robinson, *Hollywood in the Twenties* (New York: A. S. Barnes, 1968), pp. 9–14.
2 John Higham, *Strangers in the Land: Patterns of American Nativism 1860–1925* (New York: Atheneum, 1955), p. 4.
3 Ibid., pp. 271–72.
4 Ibid., p. 265.
5 Ibid., p. 291.
6 David Montgomery, *Fall of the House of Labor* (New York: Cambridge University Press, 1985), pp. 457–58.

7 Higham, p. 317.

8 Ibid., p. 270.

9 Ibid., p. 318.

10 Mae M. Ngai, "Illegal Aliens and Alien Citizens: United States Immigration Policy and Racial Formation, 1924–1945" (Ph.D. dissertation, Columbia University, 1998), p. 95.

11 Higham, p. 330.

12 Ibid., pp. 273, 313.

13 Biggers, *House Without a Key*, p. 119.

14 Ibid., pp. 175, 144.

15 Ibid., pp. 244–46.

16 Ibid., p. 84.

17 Ibid., p. 182.

18 Ibid., p. 208.

19 Agatha Christie, *The Murder of Roger Ackroyd* (1926; reprint, New York: Penguin, 2000), p. 25.

20 Ibid., p. 246.

21 Earl Derr Biggers, *The Black Camel* (New York: Grosset & Dunlap, 1929), pp. 104–5.

22 Earl Derr Biggers, *Keeper of the Keys* (1932; reprint, New York: Bantam Books, 1975), p. 137.

23 Francis Bacon, *The Advancement of Learning*, ed. G. W. Kitchin (New York: E. P. Dutton, 1934), p. 142.

Chapter 17: Kaimuki

1 Jardine, p. 40.

2 "Chang Apana Detective, In Fact and Fiction," p. 33.

3 Jardine, p. 40.

4 "Chang Apana Detective, In Fact and Fiction," p. 42.

5 Jardine, pp. 38–39.

6 "Lie Detector to Be Purchased If Trask Has Way," in *Honolulu Star-Bulletin* (March 1, 1924), p. 1.

7 Martines, "Modern History of Hawaii," pp. 33–34.

8 Jardine, p. 41.

9 Ibid., pp. 42–44.

10 Martines, "Modern History of Hawaii," p. 41.

11 Ibid., p. 43.
12 Ibid., pp. 43, 28, 45–46.
13 Ibid., p. 44.
14 John Takasaki, "Kaimuki," in *Hawaiian Journal of History* 10 (1976), pp. 64–73.
15 Martines, "Modern History of Hawaii," pp. 43–44.
16 Ibid., p. 44.
17 Ibid., p. 45.
18 Ibid., p. 44.
19 Ibid.
20 Ibid., pp. 41–42, 44–45.

Chapter 18: Pasadena

1 Ann Scheid, *Pasadena: Crown of the Valley* (Northridge, CA: Windsor Publications, 1986), p. 54.
2 Ibid., pp. 96, 143.
3 E. D. Biggers, letter to Laurance Chambers, November 21, 1924, Lilly Library.
4 Scheid, p. 128.
5 E. D. Biggers, letter to Laurance Chambers, October 21, 1925, Lilly Library.
6 Jon Tuska, *The Detective in Hollywood* (Garden City, NY: Doubleday, 1978), pp. 21–25.
7 Gregorich, p. 13.
8 E. D. Biggers, letter to Laurance Chambers, November 11, 1926, Lilly Library.
9 E. D. Biggers, letter to Laurance Chambers, December 10, 1930, Lilly Library.
10 Tuska, p. 110.
11 "The True Story of Charlie Chan As Confessed by His Creator, Earl Derr Biggers," in *Honolulu Advertiser* (September 11, 1932).
12 A copy of George Armitage's letter was enclosed in E. D. Biggers, letter to Laurance Chambers, January 7, 1931, Lilly Library.
13 Daws, pp. 331–33, 381–82.
14 Huang, *Transpacific Imaginations*, p. 19.

15 "Writer Boosts Hawaii in Tale," in *Honolulu Star-Bulletin* (February 9, 1925).

16 "Earl D. Biggers to Get Big Key," in *Honolulu Star-Bulletin* (April 15, 1925).

17 Doyle, "Charley Chan and Officer Apana."

18 "The Mainland Mail," in *Honolulu Star-Bulletin* (July 2, 1925).

19 "Earl D. Biggers to Get Big Key."

20 "Earl Derr Biggers Receives Key to the City of Honolulu," in *Honolulu Star-Bulletin* (June 19, 1925).

Chapter 19: A Meeting of East and West

1 Earl Derr Biggers, letter to Laurance Chambers, November 21, 1924, Lilly Library.

2 "Author Biggers Here to Dig Up New Mysteries," in *Honolulu Advertiser* (July 5, 1928).

3 David E. Stannard, *Honor Killing: Race, Rape, and Clarence Darrow's Spectacular Last Case* (New York: Penguin, 2005), p. 28.

4 Earl Derr Biggers, "Chang Apana Carries On," in *Fox Film Pressbook*, circa January 1932.

5 Ibid.

6 Biggers, *Black Camel*, pp. 25–28.

7 Biggers, "Chang Apana Carries On."

Chapter 20: Hollywood's Chinoiserie

1 Lucy Fischer, ed., *American Cinema of the 1920s: Themes and Variations* (New Brunswick, NJ: Rutgers University Press, 2009), p. 1.

2 Robert Sklar, *Movie-Made America: A Social History of American Movies* (New York: Random House, 1975), p. 86.

3 Biggers, *Black Camel*, p. 57.

4 E. D. Biggers, letter to Laurence Chambers, March 10, 1927, Lilly Library.

5 Robinson, p. 26.

6 Sessue Hayakawa, *Zen Showed Me the Way*, ed. Croswell Bowen (Indianapolis: Bobbs-Merrill 1960), pp. 97–98.

7 Daisuke Miyao, *Sessue Hayakawa: Silent Cinema and Transnational Stardom* (Durham, NC: Duke University Press, 2007), p. 1.
8 Richard Dyer, *Stars* (London: BFI, 1979), p. 30.
9 Miyao, p. 88.
10 Graham Hodges, *Anna May Wong: From Laundryman's Daughter to Hollywood Legend* (New York: Palgrave Macmillan, 2004), p. 20.
11 Michael Rogin, *Blackface, White Noise: Jewish Immigrants in the Hollywood Melting Pot* (Berkeley: University of California Press, 1996), p. 129.
12 Hodges, p. 20.
13 Ibid., p. 66.

Chapter 21: Yellowface

1 Rogin, p. 5.
2 Ibid., pp. 12–13.
3 Ibid., p. 15.
4 Ken Hanke, *Charlie Chan at the Movies: History, Filmography, and Criticism* (Jefferson, NC: McFarland, 1989), p. 1.
5 Ibid., p. 2.
6 E. D. Biggers, letter to Laurance Chambers, January 7, 1931, Lilly Library.
7 Quoted in Tuska, p. 117.
8 E. D. Biggers, letter to Laurance Chambers, February 12, 1931, Lilly Library.
9 Tuska, p. 109.
10 Quoted in Hanke, *Charlie Chan at the Movies*, p. 11.
11 Biggers, letter to Chambers, February 12, 1931.

Chapter 22: Between the Real and the Reel

1 "Charlie Chan At It Again," in *New York Times* (June 21, 1931).
2 Martines, "Modern History of Hawaii," pp. 28–30. *Pau* is a Hawaiian word meaning "over."
3 Ibid., p. 32.
4 Robert C. Schmitt, "Movies in Hawaii, 1897–1932," in *Hawaiian Journal of History* 1 (1967), pp. 73–74.

5 Ibid., p. 75.

6 Ibid., p. 77.

7 Martines, "Modern History of Hawaii," pp. 14–15.

8 Biggers, *House Without a Key*, p. 270.

9 Martines, "Modern History of Hawaii," p. 32.

10 Biggers, "Chang Apana Carries On."

Chapter 23: Rape in Paradise

1 Stannard, p. 246.

2 Ibid., p. 55.

3 Ibid., p. 92.

4 Peter Van Slingerland, *Something Terrible Has Happened* (New York: Harper & Row, 1966), p. 312.

5 Stannard, p. 104; Daws, p. 322.

6 Stannard, pp. 117, 143–44.

7 Ibid., pp. 88, 101.

8 Theroux, p. 150; Stannard, p. 161.

9 Stannard, p. 141.

10 Ibid., p. 218.

11 Cobey Black, *Hawaii Scandal* (Waipahu, HI: Island Heritage Publishing, 2002), p. 127.

12 Ibid., p. 128.

13 Ibid., p. 117.

14 Stannard, pp. 224–25.

15 Ibid., p. 154.

16 Ibid., pp. 264–67.

17 Ibid., p. 258.

18 Russell Owen, "First Interview with Mrs. Fortescue; Gives Her Reactions to Honolulu Tragedy," in *New York Times* (February 8, 1932).

19 Russell Owen, "Hot Lands and Cold," in Hanson W. Baldwin and Shepard Stone, ed., *We Saw It Happen: The News Behind the News That's Fit to Print* (New York: World Publishing Co., 1941), pp. 221–22.

20 Stannard, p. 100.

21 Ibid., p. 293.

22 Ibid., p. 295.

23 Clarence Darrow, *The Story of My Life* (New York: Scribner's, 1932), pp. 426–27.
24 Ibid., p. 428.
25 Stannard, p. 367.
26 Ibid., pp. 376, 371.
27 Ibid., p. 375.
28 Ibid., p. 380.
29 Floyd Gibbons, column in *San Francisco Examiner* (April 30, 1932).
30 Stannard, pp. 384–87.
31 Daws, p. 327.
32 *Chicago Tribune* (April 30, 1932).
33 Stannard, p. 327.
34 Ibid., p. 382.
35 Van Slingerland, pp. 325–26.

Chapter 24: The Black Camel

1 Stannard, p. 281.
2 Straus, p. 33.
3 "Chang Apana Detective, In Fact and Fiction," p. 33.
4 "Chang Apana Is Struck by Auto," in *Honolulu Star-Bulletin* (May 3, 1932).
5 "Apana Pension Total Will Be $123 a Month," in *Honolulu Star-Bulletin* (May 13, 1932).
6 Martines, "Modern History of Hawaii," p. 42.
7 E. D. Biggers, letter to Laurance Chambers, May 20, 1932, Lilly Library.
8 E. D. Biggers, *Keeper of the Keys*, p. 192.
9 Martines, "Modern History of Hawaii," p. 42.
10 Eleanor Biggers, letter to Laurance Chambers, April 9, 1933, Lilly Library.
11 Lee Shippey, "Earl Derr Biggers," in *Los Angeles Times* (April 7, 1933).
12 Gregorich, p. 18.
13 *Honolulu Star-Bulletin* (April 6, 1933); *Honolulu Advertiser* (April 7, 1933).
14 *Pasadena Post* (April 8, 1933).

15 Martines, "Modern History of Hawaii," p. 46.

16 Biggers, *Black Camel*, p. 59.

17 Martines, "In Search of Charlie Chan," p. 10.

18 "Chinese Detective, 'Charlie Chan,' Dead," in *New York Times* (December 10, 1933); "Detective Real-Life Chan Dies," in *Los Angeles Times* (December 10, 1933).

19 "Many Present at Rites for Noted Sleuth," in *Honolulu Advertiser* (December 18, 1933).

20 Martines, "Modern History of Hawaii," p. 48.

Chapter 25: Racial Parables

1 E. D. Biggers, letter to Laurance Chambers, September 23, 1931, Lilly Library.

2 Untitled news/gossip column, *Los Angeles Times* (November 25, 1934).

3 Ibid.

4 Tuska, p. 115.

5 Donald Bogle, *Toms, Coons, Mulattoes, Mammies, and Bucks: An Interpretive History of Blacks in American Films*, new 3d ed. (New York: Continuum, 1996), pp. 35–36.

6 Ibid., pp. 39–41.

7 Hanke, *Charlie Chan at the Movies*, p. 45.

8 Bogle, pp. xxii–xxiii.

9 Ibid., pp. 42–43.

10 Tuska, p. 115.

11 Ibid.

12 "Hollywood Starts War Cycle," in *Motion Picture Herald* (October 19, 1935), p. 18.

Chapter 26: Charlie Chan in China

1 This ballad was written by someone for Anna May Wong, who once sang it at a party hosted by Kamiyama Sojin. Quoted in Hodges, p. 65.

2 Eleanor Biggers, postcard to Laurance Chambers, April 4, 1936, Lilly Library.

3 Leo Lee, *Shanghai Modern: The Flowering of a New Urban Culture in China, 1930–1945* (Cambridge: Harvard University Press, 1999), p. 83.

4 J. G. Ballard, *A User's Guide to the Millennium* (New York: HarperCollins, 1996), pp. 286–87.

5 Leo Lee, p. 96.

6 Don Marion, "1930s Censorship of Western Films," in *The Chinese Mirror: A Journal of Chinese Film History*, http://www.chinesemirror.com/index/western_films_in_china (accessed March 2, 2009).

7 Van Ash and Rohmer, pp. 214–15.

8 Wei Zhang, *Qianchen Yingshi: Zhongguo zaoqi dianying de linglei saomiao* (Past movie matters: Other sketches of early Chinese films) (Shanghai: Shanghai Dictionary Publishing House, 2004), p. 232. See also Don Marion, "Charlie Chan in China," in *The Chinese Mirror*, http://www.chinesemirror.com/index/2008/05/charlie-chan-in.html#more (accessed March 2, 2009).

9 Guangping Xu, *Huiyi Luxun: Shinian xieshou gong jianwei* (Recollections of Luxun: A decade of being together, through thick and thin) (Shijiazhuang, China: Hebei Jiaoyu Publishing House, 2000), p. 79.

10 Zhang, p. 232.

11 Hodges, p. 77.

12 Ibid., p. 232.

13 Ibid., p. 71.

14 Victor Jew, "Metro Goldwyn Mayer and Glorious Descendant: The Contradictions of Chinese American Employment in the Hollywood Studio System during the 1930s" (paper presented to 2003 meeting of American Historical Association). Quoted in Hodges, p. 154.

15 Hodges, p. 157.

16 Ibid., p. 113.

17 Ibid., p. 49.

18 Ibid., pp. 50–51.

19 Ibid., p. 69.

20 Leo Lee, pp. 99–101; Hodges, p. 162.

21 Hodges, pp. 166–67.

22 Marion, "Charlie Chan in China."

Chapter 27: Charlie Chan Soldiers On

1 Earl Derr Biggers, *Charlie Chan Carries On* (first published 1930; reprint, New York: Pyramid Books, 1969), p. 150.

2 Tuska, p. 119.

3 Ibid., pp. 117–18.

4 Ibid., p. 125.

5 "Warner Oland, 57, Screen Star, Dies," in *New York Times* (August 7, 1938).

6 Tuska, p. 126.

7 Steve Rhodes, "Warner Oland," http://charliechanfamily.tripod.com/id85.html (accessed August 31, 2009).

8 Hanke, *Charlie Chan at the Movies*, pp. 110–11.

9 Tuska, p. 143.

10 Ibid., p. 148.

11 Ibid.

12 Hanke, *Charlie Chan at the Movies*, p. 170.

13 Ibid., p. 191.

14 Howard M. Berlin, *The Charlie Chan Film Encyclopedia* (Jefferson, NC: McFarland, 2000), p. 345.

15 Hanke, *Charlie Chan at the Movies*, p. 220.

16 Ibid., p. xv.

17 Otto Penzler, "Collecting Mystery Fiction," in *The Armchair Detective* 15:2 (1982), p. 120.

18 Ibid.

Chapter 28: The Fu Manchurian Candidate

1 Sax Rohmer, *President Fu Manchu* (Garden City, NY: Doubleday, 1936), p. 202.

2 Richard Condon, *The Manchurian Candidate* (first published 1959; reprint, New York: Thunder's Mouth Press, 2003), p. 306.

3 Louis Menand, Introduction, in Richard Condon, ibid., pp. x–xi.

4 Edward Hunter, *Brain-washing in Red China: The Calculated Destruction of Men's Minds* (New York: Vanguard Press, 1951), p. 4.

5 Menand, p. xi.

6 Ibid., pp. xi–xii.

Chapter 29: Will the Real Charlie Chan Please Stand Up?

1 Jessica Hagedorn, ed., *Charlie Chan Is Dead: An Anthology of Contemporary Asian American Fiction* (New York: Penguin, 1993), p. xxi.

2 Ken Hanke, "The Great Chan Ban," in *Scarlet Street* 50 (2004).

3 Lan Cao and Himilce Novas, *Everything You Need to Know about Asian-American History* (New York: Penguin, 1996), p. 60.

4 Frank Chin, *The Chinaman Pacific and Frisco R.R. Co.: Stories* (Minneapolis: Coffee House Press, 1988), p. 132.

5 Chin, *Bulletproof Buddhists and Other Essays*, pp. 95–96.

6 Ibid., p. 98.

7 Hanke, "The Great Chan Ban," p. 27.

8 Jerry Della Femina, "Charlie Chan and the Politically Correct Mafia," in *Jewish World Review* (April 30, 2004).

9 Gish Jen, "Challenging the Asian Illusion," in *New York Times* (August 11, 1991).

10 Anonymous, *The Wit and Wisdom of Charlie Chan* (Hollywood, CA: Chapbook, 1976).

11 Wayne Wang, *Chan Is Missing: A Film by Wayne Wang*, with introduction and screen notes by Diane Mei Lin Mark (Honolulu: Bamboo Ridge Press, 1984), p. 73.

12 Ibid., p. 34.

Selected Bibliography

Much of this book is based on original research gleaned from archival materials held at various libraries and institutions, including the Honolulu Police Department Museum, Lilly Library at Indiana University (Bloomington), Hawaii State Archive, Bishop Museum (Honolulu), Everett Collection, and Poetry and Rare Books Library of the University at Buffalo. In addition, for facts regarding the lives of Chang Apana and Earl Derr Biggers, I have relied on newspaper articles published in *Pacific Commercial Advertiser* (cited as PCA), *Honolulu Advertiser* (HA), *Honolulu Star-Bulletin* (HSB), *Pasadena Star-News, New York Times,* and *Honolulu Police Journal,* as listed below chronologically:

"Tricks of Wiry Japs: No Joke to Try and Arrest Some of Them." PCA (June 19, 1901).

"Gamblers Escaped Through a Hidden Trapdoor." PCA (May 20, 1904).

"Disguised Apana Caught Gamblers." PCA (July 13, 1904).

"Officer Apana Sued for $2000." PCA (July 6, 1905).

"Honolulu's Highways and Byways." PCA (March 16, 1908).

"Chinaman and Handsome Young Wife Murdered; Home Robbed." HSB (May 1, 1913).

"Officers Trail Murderer and Loot to Lair." HSB (May 2, 1913).

"Police Unravel Murder Mystery." HSB (May 6, 1913).

"Rodrigues Confesses to Double Murder." HSB (May 7, 1913).

"Filipinos Are Arraigned; To Plead Monday." HSB (May 22, 1913).

"Death the Punishment for Murder." HSB (June 14, 1913).

"Filipinos Expiate Murders." HSB (July 8, 1913).

"Chinese Present Chief McDuffie with Badge." HSB (July 30, 1913).

"Popular Girl Believed to Have Drowned." HSB (July 3, 1919).

"Officers Seize Opium; Arrest Two Japanese." PCA (March 9, 1920).

"U.S. Marshal Arrests Captain of Police; Charge Failure to Report Opium Haul." PCA (March 23, 1920).

"Police Uncover Opium Store in Jap Garage." PCA (April 7, 1920).

"Lie Detector to Be Purchased If Trask Has Way." HSB (March 1, 1924).

" 'Dope Traffic' Has Hawaii in Horrid Grip." HA (May 4, 1924).

"Brevities." HSB (June 6, 1924).

"Writer Boosts Hawaii in Tale." HSB (February 9, 1925).

Helen Walker, "Lecture by Earl Derr Biggers." *Pasadena Star-News* (April 11, 1925).

"Earl D. Biggers to Get Big Key." HSB (April 15, 1925).

"Earl Derr Biggers Receives Key to the City of Honolulu." HSB (June 19, 1925).

"The Mainland Mail." HSB (July 2, 1925).

"Author Biggers Here to Dig Up New Mysteries." HA (July 5, 1928).

"Charlie Chan At It Again." *New York Times* (June 21, 1931).

"Chang Apana Detective, In Fact and Fiction." *Honolulu Police Journal* (October 1931).

"Chang Apana Is Struck By Auto." HSB (May 3, 1932).

"Apana Pension Total Will Be $123 A Month." HSB (May 13, 1932).

Ah Huna Tong, "Chang Apana Had Long and Enviable Record on Force." HA (May 22, 1932).

"The True Story of Charlie Chan As Confessed by His Creator, Earl Derr Biggers." HA (September 11, 1932).

"Many Present at Rites for Noted Sleuth." HA (December 18, 1933).

Chester A. Doyle, "Charley Chan and Officer Apana." HSB (December 1, 1935).

Helen K. Wilder, "About 'Charlie Chan' Apana." HSB (January 3, 1936).

Books and Articles

Adams, Henry. *The Education of Henry Adams*, ed. Jean Gooder. New York: Penguin, 1995.

Ai, Chung Kun. *My Seventy Nine Years in Hawaii.* Hong Kong: Cosmorama Pictorial Publisher, 1960.

Bacon, Francis. *The Advancement of Learning*, ed. G. W. Kitchin. New York: E. P. Dutton, 1934.

Ballard, J. G. *A User's Guide to the Millennium.* New York: HarperCollins, 1996.

Bergere, Marie-Claire. *Sun Yat-sen*, trans. Janet Lloyd. Stanford, CA: Stanford University Press, 1998.

Berlin, Howard. *The Charlie Chan Film Encyclopedia.* Jefferson, NC: McFarland, 2000.

Biggers, Earl Derr. *Behind the Curtain.* First published 1928; reprint, New York: Grosset & Dunlap, 1940.

———. *The Black Camel.* New York: Grosset & Dunlap, 1929.

———. "Chang Apana Carries On." In *Fox Film Pressbook*, circa January 1932.

———. *Charlie Chan Carries On.* First published 1930; reprint, New York: Pyramid Books, 1969.

———. *The Chinese Parrot.* New York: Grosset & Dunlap, 1926.

———. *Harvard College Class of 1907 Twenty-fifth Anniversary Report*, 1932.

———. *The House Without a Key.* Indianapolis: Bobbs-Merrill, 1925.

———. *Keeper of the Keys.* First published 1932; reprint, New York: Bantam Books, 1975.

———. *Seven Keys to Baldpate.* First published 1913; reprint, Holicong, PA: Wildside Press, 2003.

Bird, Isabella Lucy. *Six Months in the Sandwich Islands: Among Hawaii's Palm Groves, Coral Reefs, and Volcanoes.* First published 1881; reprint, Honolulu: Mutual Publishing, 1998.

Black, Cobey. *Hawaii Scandal.* Waipahu, HI: Island Heritage Publishing, 2002.

Bogle, Donald. *Toms, Coons, Mulattoes, Mammies, and Bucks: An Interpretive History of Blacks in American Films.* New 3d ed. New York: Continuum, 1996.

Brennan, Joseph. *The Parker Ranch of Hawaii: The Saga of a Ranch and a Dynasty.* New York: John Day Company, 1974.

Brodersen, Momme. *Walter Benjamin: A Biography*, trans. Malcolm R. Green and Ingrida Ligers. New York: Verso, 1989.

Bureau of Immigration. "Report of President of Bureau of Immigration to Legislative Assembly." In *Bureau of Immigration Reports*, 1886.

Cao, Lan, and Himilce Novas. *Everything You Need to Know about Asian-American History*. New York: Penguin, 1996.

Carmer, Carl. *Stars Fell on Alabama*. New York: Farrar and Rinehart, 1934.

Char, Tin-Yuke. *The Sandalwood Mountains: Readings and Stories of the Early Chinese in Hawaii*. Honolulu: University of Hawaii Press, 1975.

Char, Wai-Jane. "Chinese Merchant-Adventures and Sugar Masters in Hawaii: 1802–1852." *Hawaiian Journal of History* 8 (1974).

Chin, Frank. *Bulletproof Buddhists and Other Essays*. Honolulu: University of Hawaii Press, 1998.

———. *The Chinaman Pacific and Frisco R.R. Co.: Stories*. Minneapolis: Coffee House Press, 1988.

———. "Come All Ye Asian American Writers of the Real and the Fake." In *The Big Aiiieeeee! An Anthology of Chinese American and Japanese American Literature*, ed. Jeffery Paul Chan et al. New York: Meridian, 1991.

Christie, Agatha. *The Murder of Roger Ackroyd*. First published 1926; reprint, New York: Penguin, 2000.

Cleveland, Richard J. *A Narrative of Voyages and Commercial Enterprises*. Cambridge, UK: John Owen, 1842.

Condon, Richard. *The Manchurian Candidate*. First published 1959; reprint, New York: Thunder's Mouth Press, 2003.

Cook, James. *Voyages of Discovery*. Compiled by John Barrow from authorized 18th-Century Admiralty Editions and documents. Chicago: Chicago Academy Publishers, 1993.

Daniels, Roger. *Asian America: Chinese and Japanese in the United States since 1850*. Seattle: University of Washington Press, 1988.

Darrow, Clarence. *The Story of My Life*. New York: Scribner's, 1932.

Daws, Gavan. *Shoal of Time: A History of the Hawaiian Islands*. Honolulu: University of Hawaii Press, 1974.

Dougherty, Michael. *To Steal a Kingdom*. Waimanalo, HI: Island Style Press, 1992.

Doyle, Arthur Conan. *Sherlock Holmes: The Complete Novels and Stories*. vols. I, II. New York: Bantam, 2003.

Dye, Bob. *Merchant Prince of the Sandalwood Mountains: Afong and the Chinese in Hawaii*. Honolulu: University of Hawaii Press, 1997.

Dyer, Richard. *Stars*. London: BFI, 1979.

Femina, Jerry Della. "Charlie Chan and the Politically Correct Mafia." *Jewish World Review* (April 30, 2004).

Fischer, Lucy, ed. *American Cinema of the 1920s: Themes and Variations.* New Brunswick, NJ: Rutgers University Press, 2009.

Fishman, Ted C. *China Inc.: How the Rise of the Next Superpower Challenges America and the World.* New York: Scribner, 2005.

Glick, Clarence E. *Sojourners and Settlers: Chinese Immigrants in Hawaii.* Honolulu: University of Hawaii Press, 1980.

Greer, Richard A. " 'Sweet and Clean': The Chinatown Fire of 1886." *Hawaiian Journal of History* 10 (1976).

Gregorich, Barbara, "Charlie Chan's Poppa: The Life of Earl Derr Biggers." *Timeline: A Publication of the Ohio Historical Society* (January–February, 1999).

Hagedorn, Jessica, ed. *Charlie Chan Is Dead: An Anthology of Contemporary Asian American Fiction.* New York: Penguin, 1993.

Hanes, W. Travis III, and Frank Sanello. *The Opium Wars: The Addiction of One Empire and the Corruption of Another.* First published 1975; reprint, New York: Barnes and Noble Publishing, 2002.

Hanke, Ken. *Charlie Chan at the Movies: History, Filmography, and Criticism.* Jefferson, NC: McFarland, 1989.

———. "The Great Chan Ban." *Scarlet Street* 50 (2004).

Harrow, Joseph. "Value of 'Unimportant' Evidence Shown in Murder Solution." *Honolulu Police Journal* 1:2 (December 1931).

Harte, F. Bret. *The Heathen Chinee.* Chicago: Western News Company, 1870.

———. *Stories in Light and Shadow.* London: C. Arthur Pearson, 1898.

Hawaiian Humane Society. *Poi Dogs and Popoki.* Honolulu: Hawaiian Humane Society, 1997.

Hayakawa, Sessue. *Zen Showed Me the Way*, ed. Croswell Bowen. Indianapolis: Bobbs-Merrill, 1960.

Helper, Hinton R. *The Land of Gold: Reality versus Fiction.* Baltimore: Henry Taylor, 1855.

Higham, John. *Strangers in the Land: Patterns of American Nativism 1860–1925.* New York: Atheneum, 1955.

Hodges, Graham Russell Gao. *Anna May Wong: From Laundryman's Daughter to Hollywood Legend.* New York: Palgrave Macmillan, 2004.

Huang, Yunte. *CRIBS.* Kaneohe, HI: Tinfish Press, 2005.

———. *Transpacific Displacement: Ethnography, Translation, and Intertextual*

Travel in Twentieth-Century American Literature. Berkeley: University of California Press, 2002.

———. *Transpacific Imaginations: History, Literature, Counterpoetics.* Cambridge: Harvard University Press, 2008.

Hunter, Edward. *Brain-washing in Red China: The Calculated Destruction of Men's Minds.* New York: Vanguard Press, 1951.

Jardine, John. *Detective Jardine: Crimes of Honolulu,* ed. Bob Krauss. Honolulu: University of Hawaii Press, 1984.

Jen, Gish. "Challenging the Asian Illusion." *New York Times* (August 11, 1991).

Jew, Victor. "Metro Goldwyn Mayer and Glorious Descendant: The Contradictions of Chinese American Employment in the Hollywood Studio System during the 1930s." Paper presented at the 2003 meeting of the American Historical Association.

Kamakau, Samuel M. *Ruling Chiefs of Hawaii.* Honolulu: Kamehameha Schools Press, 1961.

Lee, Leo Ou-fan. *Shanghai Modern: The Flowering of a New Urban Culture in China, 1930–1945.* Cambridge: Harvard University Press, 1999.

Lee, Robert G. *Orientals: Asian Americans in Popular Culture.* Philadelphia: Temple University Press, 1999.

Lewis, Sinclair. *Main Street.* First published 1920; reprint, New York: Penguin, 1995.

Loewen, James W. *The Mississippi Chinese.* Cambridge: Harvard University Press, 1971.

London, Jack. *Stories of Hawaii,* ed. A. Grove Day. Honolulu: Mutual Publishing, 1986.

Loomis, Albertine. "Summer of 1898." *Hawaiian Journal of History* 13 (1979).

Lum, Yansheng Ma, and Raymond Mun Kong Lum. *Sun Yat-sen in Hawaii.* Honolulu: University of Hawaii Press, 1999.

Martines, Gilbert. "In Search of Charlie Chan." *Hawaii Herald* 4:2 (January 21, 1983).

———. "Modern History of Hawaii." Master's thesis, University of Hawaii, Manoa, 1990.

Merlin, Mark, and Dan VanRavenswaay. "The History of Human Impact on the Genus *Santalum* in Hawaii." *USDA Forest Service Gen. Tech. Rep.* PSW-122, 1990.

Miyao, Daisuke. *Sessue Hayakawa: Silent Cinema and Transnational Stardom.* Durham: NC: Duke University Press, 2007.

Montgomery, David. *Fall of the House of Labor.* New York: Cambridge University Press, 1985.

Nellist, George F., ed. *The Story of Hawaii and Its Builders.* Honolulu: Honolulu Star-Bulletin, 1925.

Ngai, Mae M. "Illegal Aliens and Alien Citizens: United States Immigration Policy and Racial Formation, 1924–1945." Ph.D. dissertation, Columbia University, 1998.

Pace, Mildred Mastin. *Friend of Animals: The Story of Henry Bergh.* New York: Charles Scribner's Sons, 1942.

Penzler, Otto. "Collecting Mystery Fiction." *The Armchair Detective* 15:2 (1982).

Puskar, Jason. "Underwriting the Accident: Narratives of American Chance, 1871–1935." Ph.D. dissertation, Harvard University.

Price, Mark J. "Mystery of Charlie Chan: Fictional Detective Follows Trail of Clues from Akron." *Akron Beacon Journal* (May 5, 2008).

Robinson, David. *Hollywood in the Twenties.* New York: A. S. Barnes, 1968.

Rogin, Michael. *Blackface, White Noise: Jewish Immigrants in the Hollywood Melting Pot.* Berkeley: University of California Press, 1996.

Rohmer, Sax. *The Insidious Dr. Fu-Manchu: Being a Somewhat Detailed Account of the Amazing Adventures of Nayland Smith in His Trailing of the Sinister Chinaman.* First published 1913; reprint, San Jose, CA: New Millennium Library, 2001.

———. *President Fu Manchu.* Garden City, NY: Doubleday, 1936.

Rzepka, Charles J. "Race, Region, Rule: Genre and the Case of Charlie Chan." *PMLA* 122:5 (October 2007): 1463–81.

Sawislak, Karen. *Smoldering City: Chicagoans and the Great Fire, 1871–1874.* Chicago: University of Chicago Press, 1995.

Scharnhorst, Gary. " 'Ways That Are Dark': Appropriations of Bret Harte's 'Plain Language from Truthful James.' " *Nineteenth-Century Literature* 51:3 (December 1996): 377–99.

Scheid, Ann. *Pasadena: Crown of the Valley.* Northridge, CA: Windsor Publications, 1986.

Schmitt, Robert C. "Movies in Hawaii, 1897–1932." *Hawaiian Journal of History* 1 (1967).

Sklar, Robert. *Movie-Made America: A Social History of American Movies.* New York: Random House, 1975.

Stannard, David E. *Honor Killing: Race, Rape, and Clarence Darrow's Spectacular Last Case.* New York: Penguin, 2005.

Stevenson, Robert Louis, and Lloyd Osbourne. *The Wrecker.* London: Cassell & Company, 1892.

Straus, Leon. *The Honolulu Police Department: A Brief History.* Honolulu: The 200 Club, 1978.

Takaki, Ronald. *Strangers from a Different Shore: A History of Asian Americans.* New York: Penguin, 1990.

Takasaki, John. "Kaimuki." *Hawaiian Journal of History* 10 (1976).

Theroux, Joseph. "A Short History of Hawaiian Executions, 1826–1947." *Hawaiian Journal of History* 25 (1991).

Thrum, Thomas G. "Notes on the History of the Sugar Industry of the Hawaiian Islands." *Hawaiian Annual* (1875).

Toler, Sidney. *Stage Fright and Other Verses.* Portland: Smith and Sale, 1910.

Tuska, Jon. *The Detective in Hollywood.* Garden City, NY: Doubleday, 1978.

Twain, Mark. *Letters from Hawaii,* ed. A. Grove Day. Honolulu: University of Hawaii Press, 1975.

Van Ash, Cay, and Elizabeth Sax Rohmer. *Master of Villainy: A Biography of Sax Rohmer,* Ed., with foreword, notes, and bibliography, Robert E. Briney. Bowling Green, OH: Bowling Green University Popular Press, 1972.

Wang, Wayne. *Chan Is Missing: A Film by Wayne Wang.* Introduction and screen notes by Diane Mei Lin Mark. Honolulu: Bamboo Ridge Press, 1984.

Wight, Elizabeth Leslie. *The Memoirs of Elizabeth Kinau Wilder.* Honolulu: Paradise of the Pacific Press, 1909.

Wilder, Kinau. *Wilders of Waikiki.* Honolulu: Topgallant Publishing Company, 1978.

Winchester, Simon. *A Crack in the Edge of the World: America and the Great California Earthquake of 1906.* New York: HarperCollins, 2005.

Xu, Guangping. *Huiyi Luxun: Shinian xieshou gong jianwei* (Recollections of Luxun: A decade of being together, through thick and thin). Shijiazhuang, China: Hebei Jiaoyu Publishing House, 2000.

Zhang, Wei. *Qianchen Yingshi: Zhongguo zaoqi dianying de linglei saomiao* (Past movie matters: Other sketches of early Chinese films). Shanghai: Shanghai Dictionary Publishing House, 2004.

Index

Page numbers in *italics* refer to illustrations.

acculturation, assimilation, 281–82, 288
acoustic memory, 286
Adams, Henry, 100–101
Adorno, Theodor, 190
Ahakuelo, Ben, 214, 217
Ah Pung, 7–8, 17, 20–21, 25–27, 29–30; *see also* Apana, Chang
Ah Sin (in *The Heathen Chinee*), 128–29, 131, 137, 147, 154, 233, 282
Ah Sing (in *Keeper of the Keys*), 132, 233, 282
Ai, Chung Kung (A. I.), 23–25, 45, 59
Aiona, C. K., 27
Akron, Ohio, 89–90, 92
Alabama, 84–85, 292
Amazing Chan and the Chan Clan, The, 265, 286
American Defense Society, 149, 215, 218
Andriola, Alfred, 266
animal rights, 42–46
anti-Chinese sentiments, *see* exclusionism; racism
antilynching bill, 221, 225
Apana, Annie Lee Kwai (Mrs. Chang Apana), 63, 164–65
Apana, Cecilia, 62, 165
Apana, Chang:
- basis for Charlie Chan, xvi–xvii, xix, 3, 89, 162, 181, 185, 209
- birth, 7–8, 237
- death and funeral, 8, 42, 235–36, 291
- derivation of name, 296
- and Earl Biggers, 77, 184–86, 208–10
- filming of *The Black Camel,* 205–6
- grave and tombstone, 8, *289,* 294–96, *295*
- Humane Society officer, 26, 43, 44–48, 235
- marriages and family, 41, 62–63, *161,* 164–70, 207

Apana, Chang (*continued*)
as *paniolo,* 3, 35–36, 41–42, 164, 166, 291
Parker Ranch, 35–36
photographs, *5, 186, 205, 211, 230*
physical description, 36, 47, 69
and Warner Oland, 205–10, 208
and Wilder family, 41–42
see also Ah Pung
Apana, Chang, Honolulu police career:
awards and honors, 60, 291
bullwhip, xix, *1,* 3, 30, 36, 66, 185, 291
Chinatown beat, 55, 209–10
detective division, *73,* 162–63, 209
employment records, 8
gambling raids, 1–3, 65–67, 69–70, 162
Kalihi double murder, 76–79
"Kana Pung," 3, 47
leprosy deportation, 70–72
missing persons, 75
opium raids, 26, 65–66, 108, 169, 209
retirement, 232, 234
"See Yup man," 63–67, 185
Apana, Rose, 168–69
aphorisms, xv, 154, 264, 269, 275, 284, 285, 286–87; *see also* Chanisms
Armitage, George, 177–78
Army, U.S., Nagle court-martial, 223
Ash, Frances, 75
Asian American activism, 279–86
Asians:
Asian-themed films, 189–91, 194–97, 274–76
"Chinaman" in American culture, 120, 122, 145, 186, 270, 277, 280, 286–87
Chinese exoticism, 58, 132–35, 145, 195–96
coolie labor (contract laborers), 7–8, 17–20, 24, 29, 39, 130, 131, 153
depictions of Asian men, 135, 144, 279, 281, 287
as foreigners, 46–47, 85, 151, 152, 160
motion picture casting policy, 254, 264, 284
motion picture stars, 192–95, 196, 252–56
motion picture stereotypes, xix, 144, 186, 250, 269, 279–80, 282, 284–85
stereotypes, xvi–xvii, xviii, 250, 269, 277, 279–81, 282
as villains, 195, 201–2, 254–55, 269
white power and Asian stereotypes, 279–81
yellowface, 134, 197, 198–204, 242, 254, 258, 283–84
see also China; Chinese immigration; exclusionism; Orientalism; racial parody; racism
Asiatic, as racial category, 151
Aunt Jemima, xvi, 147, 283
Avallone, Michael, 286

Bacon, Francis, 158–59
Baldwin, James, 199–200
Ballard, J. G., 249
Bantam Books, 285
Battle of Manila, 50–51
Beavers, Louise, 240
Begley, Ed, 266

Behind That Curtain, 115, 176
Behind That Curtain (film), 195, 302
Bell, Alexander Graham, 213
Bell, Edward, 14–15
Benjamin, Walter, 253, 266
Benson Murder Case, The (Van Dine), 107, 173–74
Bergh, Henry, 42–43, 44
Biggers, Earl Derr:
  American cultural role, 296
  appeal of Hawaii, 182, 297
  Behind That Curtain, 115, 176
  birth and childhood, 86, 88–89, 91–92, 103, 237
  The Black Camel, 157–58, 185, 208, 291–92
  and Chang Apana, 77, 113, 114, 184–86, 208–10, 232–33
  Charlie Chan Carries On, 89, 202–4, 209
  The Chinese Parrot, 41–42, 46–47, 105, 173, 175, 176
  Chinese translation of novels, 258
  creation of Charlie Chan, 75, 89, 113, 114, 122, 176–77, 181, 185–86
  death, 234, 236
  early career, 102–6, 109
  Frank Chin on, 280–81
  at Harvard, 96–98, 101, 174
  in Hawaii, 109–12, 181–86, *181,* 186, 208–10
  Keeper of the Keys, 132, 158, 233, 282
  in Pasadena, *171,* 172–76
  photographs, *81, 102, 181, 186*
  Seven Keys to Baldpate, 105–7, 234
  Traveler column, 103–4
  see also House Without a Key, The
Biggers, Eleanor Ladd, 105, 106, 172, 176, 234, 239, 248, 263
Biggers, Robert J., 88
"Big Little Books," 266
Bird, Isabella, 8
Birth of a Nation, The (film), 142, 149, 200
Black Camel, The (Biggers), 157–58, 185, 208, 291–92
Black Camel, The (film), 143, 185, 204, 205–6, 207–8
blackface, 199–200, 242, 283, 287
Black Power movement, 279
Bobbs-Merrill Company, 103, 105, 172, 173, 179, 209, 233
Bogle, Donald, 240, 242
Boston, Mass., xix, 89, 102, 201
Boston Herald, 106–7
Boston Traveler, 103–5
Both, Jessie de, 183
Boxer Rebellion, 90, 140
brainwashing, 270–74
Brenchley (English tourist), 33
Brennan, Joseph, 28
Brown, Arthur Morgan, 53, 63
Brown, Birmingham (fictional character), xvi, 240, 263–65
Brown, Jacob, 53
bubonic plague, 56–58
Buffalo, N.Y., 86, 87, 91, 292
bullwhip, xix, *1,* 3, 30, 36, 66, 185, 291
Bund, the (Shanghai), 248–49
Bunker, Chang and Eng (Siamese Twins), 133–34, 287
Bunyan, Paul (fictional character), 286
Busch, Adolphus, 171

California, 17–18, 120–26
California Supreme Court, 125–26

Canary Murder Case, The (Van Dine), 174
cannibalism, 9, 20, 26
Canton, China, 10, 22–27, *22*, 32, 64–65, 122
Canton, Ohio, 86, 89, 91
Cao, Lan, 279–80
Carlin, George, 283
Carmer, Carl, 84–85
Carradine, David, xix, 265
Cass, John, 18
Casserly, Eugene, 131
cattle, cattle industry, 31–36, 43, 46
CBS television network, 286
Chambers, David Laurance, 105, 112, 113, 132, 209, 248
Chan, Charlie (Akron laundry owner), 89–90, 92
Chan, Charlie (fictional character):
  Asian American criticism of, 277, 279–86
  character traits, xvi–xvii, xix, 62, 118, 152, 153, 174, 270
  as "Chinaman," 146, 152–54, 160, 186, 286
  in Chinese films, 257
  cultural icon, xv, 3, 191, 266–67, 269, 277, 278, 285–87
  filmography, 302–3
  Kamiyama Sojin as, *187*, 191
  legacy of novels, 131, 174
  "letter" from, 177–78
  merchandising, 266–67, 285–86
  popularity in Asia, 248–52
  racial stereotyping, 277, 279–80, 282
  radio programs, 266
  Sidney Toler as, 263–64
  silent films, 191, 195
  television series, 286
  see also Biggers, Earl Derr; Oland, Warner
Chan, Jackie, xix, 264
Chandler, Raymond, 74, 154
Chang Jong Tong (Apana's father), 7–8, 17
Chang, Joe (Apana's nephew), 184, 185
Chang, Walter, 47–48, 161, 165, 206, 209
Chan Is Missing (film), 287–88
Chanisms:
  examples, 22, 102, 146, 205, 230, 267, 289, 299–301
  structure and use, 104, 155–60, 185, 204, 243, 286–87
Chaplin, Charlie, 193
Charlie Chan and the Curse of the Dragon Queen (film), 286
Charlie Chan at the Race Track (film), 259–60
Charlie Chan at the Ringside (film), 261, 265
Charlie Chan bar (Sydney), *245*
Charlie Chan Carries On (Biggers), 89, 202–4, 209
Charlie Chan Carries On (film), 131, 143, 202–4
Charlie Chan Film Festival, 283–84
Charlie Chan films:
  Chinese productions, 257–58
  Fox Film Corp. series, 262–66, 268, 274, 282
  Monogram Pictures series, 240, 263–65
  title list, 302–3
Charlie Chan in Egypt (film), *238*, 239–43, 261, 264, 275
Charlie Chan in Honolulu (film), 262

Charlie Chan in London (film), 239
Charlie Chan in Paris (film), 239
Charlie Chan in Shanghai (film), *247*, 251–52, 274
Charlie Chan Mystery Magazine, 285
Charlie Chan's Caravan / Charlie Chan Omnibus, 87
Charlie Chan Smashes an Evil Plot (film), *257*
Charlie Chan spin-offs, 285–86
Cheat, The (film), 193, 194
Cheng Xiaoqing, 258
Chertok, Harvey, 285
Chiang Kai-shek, 250
Chicago Tribune, 222, 227–28, 236
Chillingworth, Charles, 63, 69–70
Chin, Frank, xviii, 144, 278, 280–83, 285, 288
China:
  banned films, 250, 251, 255
  film industry in, 257–58
  geopolitical status, 250–51
  negative symbolism, 275–76, 277
  popularity of American films, 249–50
  racial stigmatization, 250
China Doll (film), 275
"Chinaman," 120, 122, 145, 186, 270, 277, 280, 286–87
Chinaman, John (in *The Land of Gold*), 134, 137, 147, 154
China Moon (film), 276–77
China Syndrome, The (film), 275, 276
Chinatown (film), 275–76
Chinatowns:
  Denver, 124
  Honolulu, 1–3, *28*, *37*, 53–66, *54*, *57*, *68*, 209–10
  missionary work in, 281
  negative stereotypes, 58, 269, 275–76
  New York City, 195–96
  San Francisco, 56, 124, 125, 195–96
Chinese Exclusion Act, 20, 51–52, 126–27; *see also* exclusionism
Chinese exoticism, 58, 132–35, 145, 195–96
Chinese immigration, 120–27
  California gold rush, 17–18, 120–22
  coolie labor (contract laborers), 7–8, 17–20, 24, 29, 39, 130, 131, 153
  halting of, 160
  in Hawaii, 14–17, 29, 62, 236
  transcontinental railroad, 122–24
  see also exclusionism; immigration
Chinese lanterns, 94–95
Chinese Laundry Scene (film), 195
Chinese Parrot, The (Biggers), 37, 41–42, 46–47, 105, 173, 175
Chinese Parrot, The (film), *187*, 191, 195, 196, 252, 255, 302
Chinese Ring, The (film), 264
"Ching Chong Chinaman," 117, 119
Ching dynasty, 26, 60
Christian conversion, 281–82
Christie, Agatha, 154, 156
Chun Shee (Apana's mother), 7
Civil Rights Act (1870), 126
civil rights movement, 85, 282, 285
Clark, James Beauchamp, 50

Cleveland, Richard J., 30
Cleveland Plain Dealer, 102–3, 234
Cohan, George M., 107
cold war, 268–69, 272–77
Collins, Wilkie, *The Moonstone,* 175
Condon, Richard, 270–74
Confucius, 158
"Confucius say," xx, 282, 286, 287
Connolly, Walter, 266
Cook, James, 9, 14, 20
Coolidge, Calvin, 150–51, 152
coolie labor (contract laborers), 7–8, 17–20, 24, 29, 39, 153
cowboys (*paniolos*), 3, 28, 30–36, 41, 164
Cox, Palmer, *Brownie* series, 88
Crocker, Charles, 122
Croom, Eddie, 290–91
Crouch, Stanley, xx, 283
Croy, Homer, 176
cultural miscegenation, xvi, xvii, xix–xx, 283
culture industry, 190
curios, 11, 132
"C" words and negative symbolism, 277

Dancing Chinamen-Marionettes (film), 195
Darrow, Clarence, 92, 224–27
Daughter of the Dragon, The (film), 143, 254
Davis, Robert Harte, 285
Davis, William, 12
Daws, Gavan, 15, 17, 18, 215
Delayed Birth Records (Hawaii), 8
Della Femina, Jerry, 284
Deng Xiaoping, 84
Department of Commerce, U.S., 249
detective fiction, xix, 154, 175, 258, 285
Dewey, George, 50
Diamond Head, 7, 8, 29, 39, 110, 111, 165
Dillingham, Walter, 215–16, 217, 218, 228, 231
dipsomania, 262–63
Dixon, Thomas, 142
Dole, Sanford, 45, 51
Dougherty, Michael, 11
Doyle, Arthur Conan, 119, 174
Doyle, Chester A., 35, 180
Drums of Fu Manchu (film), 251
Dye, Bob, 15–16
Dyer, Richard, 193

Eastland, James, 50*n*
eccentricities of writers, 105
Edison, Thomas, 195
Edison Veriscope, 206–7
Edward, Prince of Wales, 41
Eliot, Charles W., 96, 97
Eliot, T. S., 97, 98, 99, 174, 292
Emerson, Ralph Waldo, 121, 122
Empire Theater (Honolulu), 206
Eskbank House (Hawaii), 39–41
ethnic studies programs, 279
exclusionism:
  Chinese Exclusion Act, 20, 51–52, 126–27
  Cubic Air Ordinance, 125
  Fifteen Passenger Bill, 126
  foreign miners' license tax, 120–21, 125, 126

Immigration Act (Johnson-Reed Act; 1924), 147–52, 160, 279
Laundry Ordinance, 125
executions, 78–79, 217

Fairbanks, Douglas, 193, 196, 253, 255
Father Knows Best, xviii
Faulkner, William, 99
FBI (Federal Bureau of Investigation), 144
Feathered Serpent, The (film), 265
Fetchit, Stepin, xvi, *238,* 240–43, 263, 285, 287
Film Daily, 204
film noir, xviii, 269, 275, 276–77
Finn, Huckleberry (fictional character), 286, 287
Fitzgerald, F. Scott, 147, 174
Fong, Hiram, 50*n*
Fong Wah, 139–40
"foreign devils," 46–47
foreign miners' license tax, 120–21, 125, 126
Fortescue, Grace Hubbard, 213, 220, 222–24, 227, 229*n*, 291
Fortescue, Granville Roland "Roly," 212–13
Fort Shafter, 76, 77
Foster, Jodie, 286
Fox, William, 192, 239
Fox Film Corporation:
Charlie Chan films, 195, 202–4, 208–9, 241, 262–66, 268, 274, 282
history of, 131, 192, 238–39
and Stepin Fetchit, 241
see also Twentieth Century-Fox Film Corporation
Fox Movie Channel, 283–84
Frankenheimer, John, 269
Frankenstein (film), 144
Franklin, Benjamin, 158, 159
freak shows, 132–33
Freeman, Leonard, 210*n*
French, William, 16
"Frontier Thesis" (Turner), 49
Fukunaga, Myles, 216–17
Fu Manchu (fictional character):
Chinese reaction to, 250–51
comparison to Charlie Chan, 147, 269–70, 281
creation of, xviii, 136–45
film versions, *136,* 143, 201–2, 250–51, *268,* 274
see also Rohmer, Sax
Further Mysteries of Fu Manchu, The (film), 143

gambling, 2–3, 55, 56, 63–66, 68–70, 162, 165, 210
germ warfare, 274
Gibbons, Floyd, 226
Gilman House (Honolulu), *108*
ginseng, 10
Goethe, Johann Wolfgang von, 158
Golden Dragon Restaurant (Warren, Ohio), 93–95
gold rush, 17–18, 120–22
Goldwyn, Samuel, 192
Good Earth, The (film), 254
Grant, Madison, 148–49, 152, 215
Grauman's Chinese Theatre, *189,* 196, 265
Gray, Mrs. La Vancha Maria Chapin, 108, 110
Great Chicago Fire, 55–56
Great Crash (1929), 146, 208, 209, 239

Great Depression, 95, 113, 221, 233, 234, 240
Great War, the (World War I), 141, 142, 148
Gregorich, Barbara, 109
Griffith, D. W., 142, 149
guano, 39
Gung Wong, 175–76

Hagedorn, Jessica, xviii, 279
Hanauma Bay, 212, 220
Hand of Fu-Manchu, The (Rohmer), 142–43
Hanke, Ken, 242, 262, 263–64, 279
Hanna-Barbera television series, 265, 286
haole, definition, 32
Harte, F. Bret, 20, 61, 64, 117, 127–31, 132, 233, 282
Harvard University, 96–101, 174
Hawaii:
  annexation by United States, 20, 48–53, 166, 178, 213, 218
  appeal of, 182, 207, 297
  arrival of motion pictures, 206–7
  arrival of wireless technology, 225
  Big Five Corporations, 216, 228
  Chinese immigration, 14–17, 29, 62, 236
  contract-laborers (coolie labor), 7–8, 17–20, 24, 29, 39
  history, 9–20, 30–31, 48–53, 55–60
  Kingdom of Hawaii, 52
  Kona weather, 2, 40
  law enforcement, 52–53, 78–79
  map, *xiii*
  Menehune (little people), 166
  protection of children, 47–48
  Provisional Government, 38
  racial attitudes, 38, 78–79, 216, 217, 219, 290
  Republic of Hawaii, 49, 51
  response to Charlie Chan books, 179–80
  sandalwood trade, 11–13, 32
  statehood, 178–79
  sugar industry, 11, 15–17, 18–19, 20, 216
  territorial status, 178–79
  whaling industry, 17, 18, 34, 52
  see also Honolulu
Hawaiians confused with Negroes, 223, 227; *see also* lynching
Hawaiian Trust Company, 216, 234
Hawaii Board of Health, 57
Hawaii Five-O, 44–45, 75, 137, 210, 291
Hawaii Humane Society, 31, 36, 42–43, *44*, 48, 53
Hawaii National Guard, 51
Hawaii Planters' Society, 39
Hawaii Tourist Bureau, 177, 178, 180, 184, 186
Haworth Pictures Corporation, 193
Hayakawa, Sessue, 192–95, 207
Hayes, Rutherford B., 126
Hays, William, 193, 253
Hayworth, Rita, 239, 275
Hearst, William Randolph, 219, 222
Heathen Chinee, The (Harte), 20, *117,* 127–31, 132
Heen, William, 217–18
Helper, Hinton Rowan, 133, 134
Heraclitus, 158

Hermetic Order of the Golden Dawn, 138
Higham, John, 149–50, 152
Hoar, George Frisbie, 50, 127
Hodges, Graham, 195, 253
Hollywood, *189*, 191–92, 195–96, 265, 274–75; *see also* motion picture industry
Holmes, Burton, 207
Holmes, Sherlock (fictional character), 119, 144, 154, 234
"Hong Kong," 121–22, 134–35
Hong Kong, 248, 256, 257
Honolulu:
  bubonic plague, 56–58
  Chinatown, 1–3, *28*, *37*, 53–66, *54*, *57*, *68*, 209–10
  Chinatown fire, 55–58, *57*, *68*, 166
  Chinese Revolution, 58–60
  Chinese Theater riot, 207
  description, 8–9
  Gilman House, *108*
  Gray's Beach, 110
  growth of crime, 53, 109, 163–64
  Massie Case, 211–29, 231
  Punchbowl Hill, 29, 153, 177
  Wo Fat Restaurant, *210*
Honolulu Advertiser, 109–10, 113, 234–35
Honolulu Advertiser's Club, 183
Honolulu Chamber of Commerce, 231
Honolulu Police Department (HPD):
  Apana as role model, 163
  Apana funeral, 236–37
  building description, 290
  crime-busting squad, 74–75
  detective division, 72, *73*, 162–63, 209–10
  employment records, 8
  forensic methods, 163
  graft and corruption, 109–10, 169, 216
  history, 52–53
  Massie Case, 212–29, 231
  "New Look," 231–32
  racism, 216, 231
  shooting of Hawaiian officers, 223
  "whipping squad," 163–64
Honolulu Police Department Museum, 289–91
Honolulu Rapid Transit, 45
Honolulu Star Bulletin, 35, 75, 113–14, 179–80, 234, 262
hoodlum, derivation of term, 125
horses, 30–31, 43, 45
House Without a Key, The (Biggers):
  appearance of Charlie Chan, 118–20, 152–56, 157, 209
  concept and writing, 108, 110, 112–14, 119
  film version, 191, 195, 302
  plot and characters, 73–74, 110–11, 118–20, 152–56
  publishing, 119, *146*, 149, 152, 172, 176–77
  reception and popularity, 119, 152, 179–80, 182–83
Hsiao, Isabelle, 168, 170
Hsing Chung Hui (Revive China Society), 59, 60
Huang, Yunte, "Think Haiku, Act Locu," 293
Hu Die, 256
Humane Society (Hawaii), 31, 36, 42–43, *44*, 48, 53
Humberstone, H. Bruce, 260
Hunter, Edward, 272–73

Ida, Horace, 214, 219–20
immigration:
  anti-immigration sentiments, 55, 100–101, 120–27, 131, 134, 147–52, 160, 191
  community identity, 200
  Henry Adams on, 100–101
  national-origin quotas, 151
  restrictions on, 127, 150–51, 160
  U.S. policy, xvii–xviii, 62, 122, 125, 126–27
  see also Chinese immigration; exclusionism; nativism
Immigration Act (1924), 147–52, 160, 192, 279
indoctrination, *see* brainwashing
industrial capitalism, 150
"infinite conversation," 264
Insidious Dr. Fu-Manchu, The (Rohmer), 142
Iolani Palace, 51
Iolani School, 58
Irish workers, 122, 123, 130
isolationism, 150

James, Henry, 100
James, William, 96–97
Japan, 50, 160, 194, 251
Jardine, John, 70, 161, 162, 163–64, 216
Jarvis Island, 39
Jazz Age, 146–47
Jazz Singer, The, 143, 198–99, 200
Jen, Gish, 284–85
Jewface, 199, 200
"Jim Crow," 287
Johnson, Albert, 150
Johnson, Ray, 253
Johnson-Reed Act (1924), *see* Immigration Act (1924)
Jolson, Al, 143, 199, 287
Judd, Elizabeth Kinau, *see* Wilder, Elizabeth Kinau Judd
Judd, Gerrit P., 38
Judd, Lawrence, 215–16, 221, 222, 227, 228

Kahahawai, Joseph, 214, 220, 222, 225, 226, 228, 235
Kaimuki, Hawaii, 161, 166–70, 212
Kalakaua, King, 35, 48, 56
Kalalau Valley, 71–72
Kamehameha I, King, 12, 14–15, 30, 31, 32, 51, 182
Kamehameha III, King, 38, 52
Kamehameha V, King, 8, 34, 39
"Kana Pung," 3, 47
kapu system of law enforcement, 52, 291
Karloff, Boris, *136*, 143–44
Kawananakoa, Abigail, Princess, 183, 217
Kealakekua Bay, 9, 14, 31
Keeper of the Keys (Biggers), 132, 158, 233, 282
Kelai, George, 65, 68
Kellett, John, 74–76, 162, 169
Kelley, John, 226, 228
Kendrick, John, 11–12
Kennedy, John F., 270
Kentucky, 221
Kerouac, Jack, xix
King, Samuel, 290
King of the Zombies (film), 263
Kipling, Rudyard, 97, 138, 154, 181
koa wood, 179, 180
Kona weather, 2, 40
Koo, Wellington, 256
Koolau (leper), 9, 71–72, 291

Korean War, 269, 272–74
Ku Klux Klan, 85, 142, 147, 149–50
Kung Fu (television series), xix, 265
Kuomintang (Nationalist Party), 59
Kuwa, George, 191, 195, 302
Kwai, Kam, 75, 163, 169

Ladd, Eleanor, *see* Biggers, Eleanor Ladd
Lady from Shanghai (film), 275
Laemmle, Carl, 192
Land of Gold, The (Helper), 134, 137, 147, 154
Lapp, Ralph, 276
Lasky, Jesse L., 194, 207
laudanum, 18
Leave It to Beaver, xviii
Lee, Ang, xx
Lee, Bruce, xix
Lee, Fook, 108, 113, 114
Lee, Robert G., 134
Lee Kwai family, 62–63
leprosy, 20, 70–72, 179
Lewis, Al, 202
Lewis, Sinclair, 83, 87, 88, 94–95
Liangyou Huabao magazine, 256
Life magazine, 274
Liliuokalani, Queen, 49, 71, 207
Limehouse District (London), 139–40, 145
Lodge, Henry Cabot, 50, 106
London, Jack, 9, 53, 70, 71, 179
Lorre, Peter, 265
Los Angeles, 124, 275–76
Los Angeles Times, 234, 236, 239, 262
Low, Mary, 33
Lowell, Amy, 292
Lugosi, Bela, 208
Luke, Keye, 260, 261, 265, 286
Lum, Joaquin, 163
Lu Xun, 251
lynching, 220–23
Lynds, Dennis, 285

Macbeth (Shakespeare), 217
mah-jongg, 2, 162, 165
mai-say-lan tree, 167, 212
Manchu regime, 26, 47, 59–60
Manchurian Candidate, The (Condon), 270–74
Manchurian Candidate, The (film), 269–74
Manifest Destiny, 10, 49–50
Manila Bay, Battle of, 50–51
Manoa Valley, 8, 16
Manoa Valley Chinese Cemetery, 237, 289, 291–92, 294–97
Mao Zedong, 84, 243, 268–69, 277, 285
Marine Corps, U.S., Battle of Manila, 51
market days, 24–25
Marlowe, Philip (fictional character), xix, 154, 258, 285
martial law, 222, 228
Martines, Gilbert, 8, 41, 165, 235, 236
Maryland Hotel, 172–73
Mask of Fu Manchu, The (film), *136*, 143–44
Massie, Thalia (Mrs. Thomas Massie), 212–13, 217, 226, 228, 229*n*
Massie, Thomas, 212–13, 220–21, 222, 225–26, 227, 229*n*
Massie Case, 211–29, 231
mass media:
  Apana death, 236

mass media (*continued*)
Asian American criticism of, 284–85
Charlie Chan spin-offs, 285–86
Massie Case, 221–22, 225, 226
Orientalism, 284–85
Matson, Anna, 55–56
Mauna Kea, 28, 36
Mauna Loa, 33, 235–36
Mayer, Louis B., 192
McCarthyism, 194, 269
McDougall, John, 120
McDuffie, Arthur, 63, 74–77, 79, 109–10, 169
McGarrett, Steve (fictional character), 44–45, 75, 137
McIntosh, John Nelson, 162, 216, 231
McKinley, William, 48, 51, 91McLuhan, Marshall, 269
Meares, John, 14
Mei, Lan Fang, 256
melting pot concept, 148, 149, 151, 153, 200, 215, 290
Melville, Herman, 11, 17, 32, 287, 296
Menand, Louis, 272, 274
Metcalf, Simon, 14
Meyer-Kiser Bank shares, 209
MGM (Metro-Goldwyn-Mayer), 192, 239, 250–51, 254
MGM Chinese, 254
Middle Kingdom, 26
minstrelsy, 134–35, 199
miscegenation, xx, 126, 133, 195, 219, 254, 283, 284
missionaries, 9, 38, 52, 59, 281–82
Miyao, Daisuke, 194–95
Molokai, 70–71
mongrelization, 148, 150
Monkey King, 287
Monogram Pictures, 240, 258, 263–65
Montaigne, Michel de, 158
Moreland, Mantan, xvi, 240, 263–65
Motion Picture Herald, 243
motion picture industry:
antitrust case, 263
Asian stars, 192–95, 196, 252–56
Asian stereotypes, xix, 144, 186, 250, 269, 279–80, 282, 284–85
Asian-themed films, 189–91, 194–97, 274–76
casting policy, 254, 264, 284
censorship, Hays Code, 193–94, 253–54
Chinese film industry, 248–52, 257–58
films banned in China, 251–52
Hawaiian-themed films, 207–8
history, 190–92, 200–201
morality clause, 253
Negro stereotypes, 240–43
picture palaces, 189–91, 206, 248
racism, 240–43, 254, 264, 283, 284
Motion Picture Producers and Distributors of America (MPPDA), 193, 253
Motion Picture Production Code (Hays Code), 253–54
Mr. Moto's Gamble (film), 265
mules, 45, 46
Murder by Death (film), 155
murder cases, 76–79, 217
Mutual Network, 266
Mysteries of Dr. Fu Manchu, The (film), 143

Mysterious Dr. Fu-Manchu, The (film), 143, 201, *268*
Mystery of Dr. Fu-Manchu, The (Rohmer), 141–42

NAATA (National Asian American Telecommunications Association), 283–84
Nabokov, Vladimir, 105
NAPALC (National Asian Pacific American Legal Consortium), 283
Nation magazine, 234
nativism:
  annexation debate, 50
  organizations, 149
  racial overtones, 153, 215, 282
  resurgence, 148–52
  Saturday Evening Post articles, 148–49, 152
  xenophobia, 141–42, 147, 148, 150, 156, 194, 269
Navy, U.S., Massie Case, 212–29
Nazimova, Alla, 201, 252
NBC Blue Network, 266
Needham, Moses, 109–10
Negroes:
  confused with Hawaiians, 223, 227
  film industry stereotypes, 240–43
  see also lynching
New York Herald Tribune, 236
New York Mirror, 221
New York Post, 222
New York Public Library, 111, 113, 114, 137
New York Sunday News, 221
New York Times, 107, 204, 205–6, 219, 223, 236, 261, 284–85
New York Times Magazine, 274
New Yorker, The, 189, 274
Nigger Jim (fictional character), xvi, 147, 283, 286
Northport, Ala., 85
Novas, Himilce, 279–80
nuclear meltdown as China Syndrome, 276
numerology, 295
Nuremberg Laws (Germany), 243
Nu'uanu Pali, 214, 220

Oahu, 29, 53, 215
Oahu Country Club, 183–84
Oakland Tribune, 219
OCA (Organization of Chinese Americans), 283–84
occultism, 137–39
Odeon cinema (Shanghai), 248
okolehao (moonshine), 212
Oland, Warner:
  alcoholism, 203, 260–61
  and Anna May Wong, 254–55, 256–57
  and Chang Apana, 205–10, *205,* 208
  as Charlie Chan, *iv,* 131, 202–4, 208, 238, 251, 259–62, *278,* 302
  in China, 248, 251–52, 253, 256
  cultural role, 296
  death, 261–62
  early life and film career, 143, 198–99, 201–2, 241, 253, 254–55
  as Fu Manchu, 143, 251, *268*
  in *The Jazz Singer,* 198–200
  and Keye Luke, 261–62, 265
  marriage, 203
Old San Francisco (film), *198,* 254
Oo Sack Kee Loo club (Honolulu), 62

Oo Sack village, 23–24, 296
opium, 26, 65–66, 75, 108, 109, 169, 209, 236
Opium Wars, 22, 23, 140
Organization of Chinese Americans (OCA), 283–84
Orientalism:
  Chinese exoticism, xviii, 132–33
  clichés, 180, 269
  film noir, xviii, 269, 275, 276–77
  Hollywood versions, 195–96, 274–75
  mass media, 284–85
Ouija boards, 137, 138, 145
Owen, Russell, 223

Pacific Commercial Advertiser, 69, 70
Painted Veil, The (film), 265
paniolos (cowboys), 3, 28, 30–36, 41, 291, 292
Paramount Pictures, 143, 192, 202, 251
paranoia, 275, 277
Park, E. L., 195, 302
Parker, John Palmer, 32–36
Parker, Samuel, 35
Parker Ranch, 28, 34–36
Pasadena, 171–73
Pasadena Star News, 172, 173
Pathé Studios, 191
Peale Museum (Philadelphia), 132–33
Pearl Harbor, 212, 219
Pelham Manor, 112–13
Pennsylvania Gazette, 159
Penzler, Otto, 266
People's Republic of China, 269, 273–74
Perkins, Maxwell E., 174
Phelps, Michael, 144
Philippine Islands, 50–51
picture palaces, 189–91, 206, 248
pidgin English, 118, 121–22, 134–35, 154–56, 158, 160, 286–87, 292
"pig trade," 18–19
Pinkerton Detective Agency, 228
Pinnacle Books, 286
plantations, 16, 18, 20, 29, 38, 39
Poirot, Hercule (fictional character), xix, 154, 156–57
"Poor Richard" (Franklin), 159
Pound, Ezra, 292
POW: The Fight Continues after the Battle (U.S. Army), 273–74
President Fu Manchu (Rohmer), 271–72
Progressive Era, 148
Prohibition, 234
propaganda, 272–73, 274, 277
proverbs, 157, 158
Provincial Government (Hawaii), 38
Publishers Weekly, 132
Punahou School, 53, 59, 177
Punchbowl (Honolulu), 29, 153, 177, 292
Purdy, Jack, 33–34

queue (braid), 47
Quotations from Charlie Chan (Chertok and Torge), 285

racial burlesque, 280–82
racial fantasy, 274
racial parody:
  Asians as villains, 195, 201–2, 254–55, 269
  Birmingham Brown, xvi, 240, 263–65

and Charlie Chan character, xvi, xvii–xviii, 282–83
"Ching Chong Chinaman," 117, 119
depictions of Asian men, 135, 144, 279, 281, 287
Heathen Chinee, The (Harte), 20, *117*, 127–31, 132
"Hong Kong," 121–22, 134–35
John Chinaman in *The Land of Gold,* 134, 137, 147, 154
racialized characters, xvi, 147–48, 250, 287
"See Yup" (Harte), 64
Snowshoes in *Charlie Chan in Egypt* (film), 241–43
"The City That a Cow Kicked Over" (Matson), 55–56
The Heathen Chinee (Harte), 20, *117*, 127–31, 132
"Truthful James" (*Overland Monthly*), 128–30
see also Fu Manchu
racial ventriloquism, xvi, 138, 199–201, 287, 292
racism:
anti-Chinese, xvii–xviii, 17, 20, 38, 55–56, 117–35, 214–15, 219
anti-Japanese, 160, 192, 193, 194
Charlie Chan as racial stereotype, 277, 279–80, 282
"Chinese Problem," 126–27
eugenics, 215
in Hawaii, 38, 78–79, 216, 217, 231
motion picture industry, 240–43, 254, 264, 283, 284
nativism, 153, 215, 282
race wars, 221–22
racial hierarchy, 148, 151, 183
racial order and Chan films, 282–83
stereotypes in popular culture, xvi, xvii, 58, 147–48, 250–52, 272–77, 279–83, 287
see also exclusionism
radio broadcasts, 225, 272, 274
Red Lantern, The (film), 252
Red Scare, 274–75
Reed, David, 150
reincarnation, 46, 235
Republic of China, 58–60
Republic of Hawaii, 49, 51
Republic Pictures, 251
Return of Charlie Chan, The (Lynds), 285
Return of Dr. Fu-Manchu (film), 143, 201–2
Return of Dr. Fu-Manchu, The (Rohmer), 142
riots, 124–25
Roaring Twenties, 146–47
Robeson, Paul, 240
Robinson, Bill "Bojangles," 240
Robinson, David, 191–92
Rock Springs, Wyo., 124–25
Rogers, Will, 123
Rogin, Michael, 198–200
Rohmer, Sax:
creation of Fu Manchu, 138–41
Daughter of Fu Manchu, 254
death, 145
early life and career, 136–40
films blocked in China, 250
The Hand of Fu-Manchu, 142–43
The Insidious Dr. Fu-Manchu, 142
The Mystery of Dr. Fu-Manchu, 141–42
President Fu Manchu, 271–72

Rohmer, Sax (*continued*)
The Return of Dr. Fu-Manchu, 142
"The Zayat Kiss," 141
Roosevelt, Theodore, 148, 212–13
Rosicrucian Society, 138
Royal Hawaiian Band, 236
Royal Hawaiian Hotel, 9, 183, 184, 235
Rush Hour film series, 264

Sacco and Vanzetti case, 191
Sacred Hearts Academy, 167
San Francisco, 56, 123–24, 125
San Francisco Chronicle, 222, 236
sandalwood trade, 11–13, 32
Santayana, George, 96–97, 98, 99
sarsaparilla, xvii
Saturday Evening Post:
Charlie Chan serials, 112, 119, 172, 173, 179, 233
The Heathen Chinee (Harte), 130
history of magazine, 159
Korean War POW articles, 274
nativist articles, 148–49, 152
Saxton House (Canton, Ohio), *83,* 91
Scarlet Clue, The (film), 264
Schmitt, Robert C., 206
Schultz, Susan, 289–92
Scribners, Charles and Sons (publishers), 174
See Yup Man, *61,* 63–67, 185
Seinfeld, Jerry, 280, 283
Seven Keys to Baldpate (Biggers), 105–6, 234
Sewall, Harold M., 51
Shanghai, 248–49, 257, 269, 275
Shanghai Express (film), 251, 252, 254–55
Siamese Twins, 133–34, 135
Si-Fan society (in *President Fu Manchu*), 271
Signet Club, *96,* 98–99, 101
silent films, 142–43, 191, 195, 198, 200–202, 206–7
Simmons, William J., 149
Sinatra, Frank, 270, 274
Sklar, Robert, 190–91
Sky Dragon, The (film), 264, 265–66, 268
smugglers, 66–67
Snowshoes (fictional character), 240–43, 264
Sojin, Kamiyama, *187,* 191, 195, 255, 302
somnambulism, 137–38, 272
Spade, Sam (fictional character), xix, 258, 285
Speyers, Willoughby, 131–32
Stanford, Leland, 122, 125
Stannard, David, 214, 216, 221, 222, 224, 225, 226
Steadman, Alva, 216–17, 218
Stein, Gertrude, 100, 105, 296
stereotypes:
in American culture, xvi–xvii, 58, 147–48, 250–52, 272–77, 279–83, 287
Asians, xvi–xix, 144, 186, 250, 269, 277, 279–85
blackface, 199–200, 242, 283, 287
Charlie Chan as, 277, 279–80, 282
Chinatowns, 58, 269, 275–76
Jewface, 199, 200
minstrelsy, 134–35, 199
Negroes, 240–43
yellowface, 134, 197, 198–204, 242, 254, 258, 283–84
Stevens, John L., 49

Stevenson, Robert Louis, 40
Stirling, Yates, 214–16, 218–19, 220, 221
Stoddard, Lothrop, 149
Stone, John A., 121
stool pigeons, 163
Story-Teller, The, 141
Straus, Leon, 231–32
Strobridge, James Harvey, 122
sugarcane, 13–14
sugar industry, 11, 15–17, 18–19, 20, 216
Sun Mei, 58, 59
Sun Yat-sen, 22, 58–60
surfing, 179
Supreme Court, U.S., 151
Sutter, John, 17
SWEN (Chinese restaurant), 85
Sydney, Australia, Charlie Chan bar, *245*

tabloid journalism, 221–23, 226
Taiping Rebellion, 22, 23
Takaki, Ronald, 127
television, "The Great Chan Ban," 279
Thief of Bagdad, The (film), 255
Thind, Bhagat Singh, 151
Thurmond, Strom, 50*n*
Tiananmen Square student protest, 83–84
Time magazine, 211, 219
Toler, Sidney, xvi, 240, 258, *259*, 262–64, 296, 303
tongs, tong wars, 14, 60
Torge, Martha, 285
tourism, 8–9
transcontinental railroad, 122–24
transpacific trade, 10–13, 86
travelogues, 207
Trevor, John, 152
tricksters, 287
"Truthful James" (*Overland Monthly*), 128–30
Tucker, Chris, 264
Tung Meng Hui (Alliance Society), 59
Turner, Frederick Jackson, 49
Tuscaloosa, Ala., 84–85
Tuska, Jon, 262
Twain, Mark, 7, 19–20, 70, 124, 130, 179, 287
Twentieth Century-Fox Film Corporation, 131, 260, 261, 262, 263, 269, 291; *see also* Fox Film Corporation
Typhoon, The (film), 193

Uncle Tom, xvi, 147, 283
United States:
- Battle of Manila Bay, 50–51
- California gold rush, 17–18, 120–22
- Chinese immigration, 120–27, 131, 160
- foreign labor policy, 129–30
- Hawaiian annexation, 20, 48–53, 166, 178, 213, 218
- Hawaiian statehood, 178–79
- immigration policy, xvii–xviii, 62, 122, 125, 126–27
- Korean War, 269, 272–74
- Progressive Era, 148
- Roaring Twenties, 146–52
- transcontinental railroad, 122–24
- transpacific trade, 10–13, 86
- Vietnam War, 279
- *see also* exclusionism

Universal Studios, 192
unwritten law, 225–26
Ustinov, Peter, 286

Valentino, Rudolph, 183, 193
Van Ash, Cay, 138–39
Vance, Philo (fictional character), 174–75
Van Dine, S. S., 107, 173–74, 175
vaqueros, 34; *see also* cowboys
Variety, 262
Veblen, Thorstein, 98
Vietnam War, 279
vigilantism, 124–25, 215, 219–20
Vitaphone sound system, 199
Voice of America, 292

Waialae Avenue (Kaimuki), 166, 170, 212, 220
Waikiki, 8, 29, 75, 110, 165–66, 179, 213, 217
Wailuku, 16
Waimea, 16, 31, 35
Waipahu, Lehua, 207
Waipio, 7, 29
Wang, Wayne, 287–88
Warhol, Andy, 253
Warner Bros. Studios, 199
Warren, Ohio, 87–88, 92–95, 103
Weeber, Charles, *230*, 231
Welcome Danger (film), 251
Welles, Orson, 275
West Indies, 10
whaling industry, 17, 18, 34, 52
white power, and Asian stereotypes, 279–81
Whitman Publishing Company, 266
Wilder, Billy (film director), xx
Wilder, Elizabeth Kinau Judd, 38, 40, 42
Wilder, Helen Kinau, 35, 36, 37–43, 45, 53
Wilder, Samuel Gardner, 38–40, 42
Wilder family, 38–42
Wilkesboro, N.C., 133
Wilkinson, John, 16
Wilsonian idealism, 150
Winchester, Simon, 54
Winship, Jonathan and David, 12
Winters, Roland, xvi, 264, 303
Wit and Wisdom of Charlie Chan, The (Chertok and Torge), 285
Wo Fat (Chinese restaurant), 210, *210*
Wo Fat (fictional character), 137, 210*n*
Wong, Anna May, 196, *198*, 247, 252–56, 296
Wong, Tze-chun, 15–16
World War I, *see* Great War, the
wrestling, 69–70
Wurtzel, Sol, 262

xenophilia, 194
xenophobia, 141–42, 147, 148, 150, 156, 194, 269
"X" generation, 286
Xu, Guangping, 251
Xu Xinfu, 258
Xu Xinyuan, 258

yellowface, 134, 197, 198–204, 242, 254, 258, 283–84
Yellow Peril, 137, 140, 160
Yellow Uncle Tom, xvi, 147, 285
Youngstown, Ohio, 92
Yuba River, 121

Zanuck, Darryl F., 261
Zhang, Wei, 251, 252
Zukor, Adolph, 192

About the Author

Yunte Huang grew up in a small town in southeastern China, where at age eleven he began to learn English by secretly listening to Voice of America programs on a battered transistor radio. After receiving his B.A. in English from Peking University, Huang came to the United States in 1991, landing in Tuscaloosa, Alabama. As a struggling Chinese restaurateur in the Deep South, Huang continued to study American literature, reading William Faulkner and Ezra Pound on the greasy kitchen floor.

In 1994, Huang attended the Poetics Program in Buffalo, where, at an estate sale, he discovered the Charlie Chan novels. He was immediately hooked. After receiving his Ph.D. in 1999, Huang taught as an assistant professor of English at Harvard University, where he began researching the story of the Chinese detective—both real and fictional—and the life of Earl Derr Biggers, a Harvard graduate who had authored the Chan novels.

A poet, translator, and critic, Huang has published many books, including *Transpacific Imaginations* and *CRIBS*. He is currently a professor of English at the University of California, Santa Barbara.